T0354371

A ROSE FOR

My Mother

A MEMOIR

NANCY LEE CANFIELD

iUniverse, Inc.
New York Bloomington

A Rose for My Mother
A Memoir

iUniverse books may be ordered through booksellers or by contacting:

iUniverse
1663 Liberty Drive
Bloomington, IN 47403
www.iuniverse.com
1-800-Authors (1-800-288-4677)

Because of the dynamic nature of the Internet, any Web addresses or links contained in this book may have changed since publication and may no longer be valid. The views expressed in this work are solely those of the author and do not necessarily reflect the views of the publisher, and the publisher hereby disclaims any responsibility for them.

ISBN: 978-1-4502-3123-7 (sc)
ISBN: 978-1-4502-3125-1 (dj)
ISBN: 978-1-4502-3124-4 (ebook)

Library of Congress Control Number: 2010907554

Printed in the United States of America

iUniverse rev. date: 08/13/2010

In memory of my parents who, with their many struggles, loved their children and provided for them the best they could.
Ralph, 1915-1995
Lorraine, 1918-1976

And God spoke all these words, saying: "I am the Lord your God; honor your father and your mother…"
The Fifth Commandment
Exodus Chapter 20

Table of Contents

PREFACE

A Rose For My Mother is a unique tale of two worlds. The first is a tale of my survival in a world filled with crushing disappointments. The second is a tale of my evolution into the world of the paranormal. I suspect the first is what opened me to the second. I have had higher sensory perception (HSP) since I was a child and I often wondered why.

I had a very turbulent childhood, living with family members, a family friend, an orphanage and five foster homes—all before the age of thirteen. Ever searching for love, I found myself married at age seventeen and the mother of three by age of twenty. Needless to say that life brought me many challenges! Those challenges and my higher sensory perception have been interwoven throughout my life.

It has been claimed that psychic ability is a gift that some are born with. That may be so. However, I am a "sensitive" with the same abilities as a psychic and I believe that higher sensory perception may be developed by anyone. To assist you in that development, relaxation, cleansing and meditation exercises are included in the appendix.

As the founder of Psychical Research Awareness Association, I have visited many well-known places in New York State that were claimed to be haunted, such as the Opera house in Lancaster, Fort Niagara in Lewiston and Big Moose Lake in the Adirondack Mountains, which is the murder site of Grace Brown, described in *An American Tragedy,* by Theodore Dreiser.

I am also a member of the American Society of Psychic Research and a member of the Association of Research and Enlightenment. For many years, I have been a teacher in the development of higher sensory perception, as well as a meditation instructor and private consultant, whose main desire has always been to render information that was both informative and beneficial to my clients.

In my capacity as a sensitive, I have been asked to assist law enforcement agencies in the investigation of criminal cases. On numerous occasions I have been consulted in cases of demonic presence and deceptive practices of psychic readers.

It is my intent to show that there is a guiding energy presence beside us to help us, wherever we go and whatever we do. I know this is true because I have seen, heard, or felt a guiding energy presence many times throughout my life. Those experiences have convinced me that we are never truly alone. It is also my intent that my story will add to the belief that hopes and wishes can come true.

I start my story at the beginning of my life, the start of my identity formation. The paper memories of my early childhood are told in short vignettes as I remember them. I do not make excuses for the actions of myself, or others, because I believe reality is in the eye of the perceiver.

Perfect or imperfect as my life has been, I haven't omitted the embarrassing memories or selected only those that placed me in a good light. However, because my memoir is a true story, I've had to change some names and details to protect the identity of both the innocent and the guilty.

The mind naturally adds revision and exaggeration to the memory. Knowing this, I have kept a tight check on my memory by reviewing my files, tape recordings, court transcripts, diaries and photographs, keeping my story as close to the truth as I can. My life experiences have made me the person I am today and I like that person. I hope you will too.

Nancy Lee Canfield

It's true that beauty is in the eye of the beholder.
It's also true that reality is in the eye of the believer.

PART I
CHILDHOOD

CHAPTER ONE
Happy Days

Memories! Oh, how I love my memories of the earlier days, when my life was simple and I didn't know shame, envy or fear; the days when I shared adventures with my big brother, Tommy.

CAZENOVIA PARK IN BUFFALO, New York has always been a place where young people could gather and socialize. The park had a lake where on any warm Sunday afternoon you could see young men paddling their sweethearts around the clear, blue water in the rented canoes, while other couples sat along the shore, enjoying the cool breeze that came across the lake. It was there that Ralph first met Lorraine, the two young lovers who would become my parents.

Lorraine, a pretty seventeen-year-old brunette, with bright blue eyes, grew up in the town of West Seneca near the city line of South Buffalo. She lived a privileged life as an only child, in the lower flat of the two-family house her parents owned. They also owned a grocery store until the stock market crash of 1929. Her family was well connected in the upper levels of society.

Ralph, a dapper nineteen-year-old, grew up in South Buffalo in a rented flat, where his parents struggled to make a living. He was always clean-shaven and he kept his dark, wavy hair combed back with a little dab of Brill Cream. Although he was short in stature, his muscular body gave him the look of being much taller.

After a one-year courtship, Ralph and Lorraine married. The date was July 8, 1935. Seven months after the wedding, Lorraine gave birth to a baby boy. He had dark hair and dark eyes just like his father. They named him

Thomas Charles. The young couple had their financial struggles, trying to set up a home for their little son, stretching the dollar to make ends meet, as many newly married couples did.

They rented a lower flat on the south side of Buffalo. The neighborhood was made up of families with German and Scot-Irish backgrounds, with a few Hungarian and Polish families scattered about. This was true for most of the south side. The west side consisted mostly of Italian families; the east side had Polish and African-American families; people with Jewish heritage lived on the north side. Buffalo was the perfect place for a young couple struggling with the future. It was a blue-collar city of good neighbors with diverse backgrounds.

Although Ralph and Lorraine were very young, they were determined to make it on their own, making do with what they had, which was very little. Lorraine and Ralph were strong and healthy, and very much in love. They enjoyed marital bliss until one fateful day in August 1938, several weeks before my birth. That day was the beginning of what was to become a life of hardships and struggles for the two young lovers.

Buffalo was experiencing a heat wave, with the temperature still in the 90s as Ralph, Lorraine, and two-year-old Tommy, dressed in his little navy and white sailor suit, were heading home, after spending a pleasant afternoon dipping their feet in the lake at the park. It was a short walk from the park to the lower flat they rented on Bellwood Place, near the city line in the town of West Seneca.

Ralph carried little Tommy, who slumbered with his head resting on his father's shoulder. As they walked along Seneca Street, approaching Gil's candy store with its red-and-white-striped awning stretched across the length of the store, Lorraine said, "Go on ahead, Ralph, I want to stop in the store for a minute."

Ralph, dressed in a white, short-sleeve shirt and beige trousers, held up by a pair of brown suspenders, agreed to go on ahead. "I'll put Tommy down for a nap," he said, walking on. When he came to the corner, he turned onto Bellwood Place.

Tall oak and maple trees lined both sides of the street, their heavy branches casting shadows along the sidewalk, providing shade from the afternoon sun. In this quiet little neighborhood, every house had a front porch where people sat, hoping to catch a breeze and get some relief from the heat of the day. Ralph continued on until he reached the yellow house. He walked up the porch steps and into the house, where he lay Tommy down in his little bed.

Lorraine, being eight months pregnant, was wearing a light lavender pinafore over her lilac print sundress and on her feet she wore white, low

4

oxford shoes. She went into the store and bought a loaf of bread, a ten-cent package of cupcakes and a quart bottle of pop. She left the store carrying the glass pop bottle by the neck in her right hand and the bag with the bread and cupcakes cradled in her left arm. She turned the corner onto Bellwood Place, and was walking along the cracked concrete sidewalk when she caught her foot and stumbled to the ground.

The pop bottle broke, severing an artery in the palm of her right hand and cutting her fingers. The neighbors, who were sitting on their porch across the street from where she fell, saw what happened and came to her aid. One of the neighbors hurried down the street to tell Ralph, "Your wife fell and hurt herself! Her hand is bleeding really bad!"

Ralph picked up Tommy from his little bed and ran back to where Lorraine was lying on the broken concrete sidewalk. Someone had wrapped the front of her pinafore around her hand, trying to stop the bleeding. When Ralph got there he saw Lorraine's right hand, covered in a mass of blood-soaked material.

A neighbor took little Tommy away from the scene, trying to hush his crying. Ralph knelt on the sidewalk and talked reassuringly to Lorraine, which gave her little comfort. She was in pain and very upset. She worried that the fall may have injured her unborn baby. The police were called and they rushed Lorraine to Mercy Hospital on Abbott Road, where the palm of her right hand and her fingers were stitched and bandaged.

Her hand was slow in healing and caused her a great deal of discomfort; it was extremely sensitive to the touch. The Chief Surgeon at the Emergency Hospital in Buffalo re-examined Lorraine's hand and concluded, "She has a permanent twenty-five percent loss of function of the right hand, which might possibly be corrected by future operations to repair the adhesion of the tendons, which is causing the extreme tenderness in the palm of the hand."

Sometime later, Lorraine and Ralph sued the town for allowing the dangerous sidewalk conditions to continue to exist, despite repeated complaints from people living in the neighborhood.

Fortunately, the twelve-person jury awarded them the $2,000 medical costs and $1,000 legal fees. Unfortunately, the case was appealed and a panel of appellate judges overturned the jury's decision. Now, they were in debt for all medical, legal and court costs. This was a terrible blow to their already stretched income. Sadly, Lorraine would never have the operation. They couldn't afford it.

Lorraine was still concerned about the effects the fall might have on her unborn baby. One night, after tossing and turning, trying to get rid of the disturbing thoughts, she finally fell into a deep sleep. In the morning, she awoke with a sense of relief.

"Ralph, I had a dream last night," she said excitedly, turning in bed, reaching for Ralph's hand and putting it on her swollen belly. "I was sitting up in a hospital bed, and standing beside me was a nurse. Without a word, she handed me a baby. The baby was a perfectly healthy baby girl. Ralph, you know that sometimes I dream things before they happen. Now I know the baby will be all right."

Not long after the dream, during the late hours of September 30, Lorraine gave birth to a baby girl. I was that baby girl. I had auburn hair and hazel eyes. My father wanted to name me Bonny Lee, the name of the fictional daughter of Rhett Butler and Scarlett O'Hara.

"We're not going to tempt fate by giving her the name of the little girl who died in that book *Gone With the Wind*," my mother said. My parents compromised and I was named Nancy Lee.

And that's how my interesting and very unusual life began. Have I had paranormal experiences all through the years because I was born with them? Or, are paranormal experiences brought about by life's circumstances? Maybe my story will provide an answer to these questions.

Soon after I was born, my parents moved to a quiet, middle-class neighborhood in South Buffalo. The rented house on Duerstein Street was small, but big enough for our growing family. Like many of the other houses on the street, it had a big front porch. On warm, summer afternoons, my mother, wearing a cotton sundress and her hair secured in a snood, sat on the porch glider and talked to the neighbors as they walked past. In the back yard, hollyhocks stood tall and proud along the fence and there was a magnificent cherry tree, which in the springtime was full with pink blossoms.

Tommy, almost three years older than I, could climb the tree by standing on the wagon and swinging his legs up and around the low-hanging branch. Tommy and I had a lot of fun while we stayed in the back yard and played all summer and autumn.

Then, autumn turned into winter and on December 8, 1941, a few months after my third birthday, and the day after the attack on Pearl Harbor, the United States and Great Britain declared war on Japan. Following that, Italy and Germany declared war on the United States. It was becoming known all over the world that the Nazis were using gas chambers to murder millions of innocent men, women and children, just because they were Jews. The United States was now officially involved in World War II.

My father was twenty-six years old. He was a healthy, strong man who wanted to go overseas and fight, as his buddies were doing, but he was rejected because he had two young children at home and a pregnant wife, who had a partially disabled right hand. Instead, he served on the home front, working ten-hour shifts at the Buffalo Arms Corporation as a tool and die maker. Even though the money he earned working those long hours helped pay off their many bills, it wasn't enough to set some aside for a down payment on a house. Ownership of a house has always been part of the American Dream, but it wasn't to be for my parents.

That winter, dreadful childhood diseases were spreading throughout the city. Mumps, chicken pox, whooping cough and scarlet fever were just a few of the contagious and deadly diseases that floated in the air. My parents, like other parents, did everything they could to keep their children healthy, but sometimes it wasn't enough. Tommy and I became seriously ill with whooping cough. A quarantine notice was placed at the entrance of our front door.

It's strange that I can remember this, because I was not yet four years old in the summer of 1942. I can recall the time when my mother and father were asleep in their bedroom. It was a warm summer day and I wanted to go outside and ride my little, red tricycle. I was dressed in summer pajamas, standing at the front door in the living room. I reached up, turned the lock and pulled the door open. Outside, on the porch, was my little, red tricycle waiting for me to drag it down the stairs and take it for a ride in the fresh morning air.

My mother woke up and searched the house looking for me. "Nancy Lee, Nancy Lee, where are you?" Dressed in her cotton robe and bedroom slippers, she came out the front door and down the porch steps. "Nancy Lee, what are you doing out of the house? You can't go outside in your pajamas," she scolded.

The next day, I escaped the locked door again. This time, I did as I was told. I took my pajamas off before I went outside. As the legend goes, Lady Godiva rode naked on her horse through the streets of Coventry, to protest oppressive taxation. But, I rode naked on my tricycle on Duerstein Street because I thought my mother told me I should. My mother's words didn't convey her meaning. She had told me not to go outside in my pajamas—and, so I didn't. I soon discovered that words don't always convey the same meaning to everyone. That day was the beginning of a lifetime of trying to understand what people meant to say, but hadn't said.

Our family was growing fast. My brother, Billy, was born in June 1942; my brother, Bobby, was born fourteen months later, in August 1943. Now, my mother had two babies in diapers, and the diapers weren't the kind you would throw away. They were cloth diapers. They needed to be washed in the wringer washing machine and hung up on a clothesline to dry.

The two boys kept her busy, leaving Tommy and me to amuse ourselves, which gave us a lot of freedom. We didn't always stay in the back yard as we were told. Sometimes, we wandered about the neighborhood with Brownie, our German shepherd dog, trailing behind. Brownie always stayed close by when we were outside.

On a warm summer day, we discovered a shallow pond in the field at the end of the street. The water was clear and the surface sparkled in the sunlight. "Let's go in the water. It feels good," Tommy said, reaching down and splashing a handful at me. Without hesitation, I sat down, took off my shoes and socks, and waded in the shallow water. Brownie sat at the edge of the pond, watching us play and splash. We caught pollywogs by scooping them up in our cupped hands, holding them and watching them wiggle about, until all the water ran out from between our fingers. When we dropped them back into the pond, they swam away.

Tommy liked to chase after the dragonflies as they darted about over the water. While he did that, I walked around the pond to the far side, where I found some pussy willows. I liked the feeling of the velvet buds, as I brushed them against my cheek. Before heading home, we had more fun, tossing pebbles into the pond and watching the ripples spread out in the water. Tommy and I were a typical 1940's big brother and little sister. He was my hero!

Due to the war, the days of my childhood also had a serious tone. Congress had authorized the Office of Price Administration (OPA) to set price ceilings on most consumer goods. Rubber tires, gasoline, coffee, sugar and meat were in short supply. They had to be purchased with rationing coupons, issued by the federal government. Even if people had the money to buy more, they couldn't. They had to be satisfied with their limit.

Farm produce, including fruits, vegetables, dairy products and eggs hadn't come under the price controls, so the farmers drastically increased the price of these foods. Recipes for baked goods that didn't require eggs were not only necessary, but they were delicious. My mother often baked chocolate mayonnaise cake and tomato soup cake. They were my favorite desserts.

A lot of people in America planted a garden to grow some of their own vegetables, and so did we. My father planted our Victory Garden along the fence, separating our yard from Mrs. Albert's yard. Carrots, beets, lettuce and huge tomatoes grew in our garden. Being curious, as most children are, I decided to find out what was on the other side of the fence. I walked into our garden, carefully making sure I didn't step on the vegetable plants. Gathering my sundress at the hem, I tucked it between my legs and knelt down close to the fence, I reached my arm under one of the boards and searched around. I found something that felt like a celery stalk. I broke off one of the stalks and pulled it under the fence.

"Tommy, look what I got," I called to Tommy, who had climbed up the cherry tree and was sitting on a large branch. I was amazed that the stalk was red. I tasted it and it made my mouth water. It looked like celery, but it didn't taste like celery; it was tart. "Yuck, this tastes yucky," I mumbled to myself. I chewed on it for a little while and spit it out.

To my ghastly surprise, when I reached back for another stalk, a hand from the other side of the fence grabbed mine. It was Mrs. Albert's hand. I screamed, she let go, and I ran to the back door, leaving Tommy up in the cherry tree where he sat, fidgeting with the torn pocket of his corduroy knickers that had caught on a branch.

I scampered up the steps and into the kitchen with Brownie following behind. My mother turned from the sink, where she stood washing the dishes. In a low voice she said, "Shush, and stop running into the house, Nancy Lee. Your baby brothers are napping and you'll wake them if you're not quiet. What's the matter, now? What happened?"

With a frown, I told her, "Mrs. Albert grabbed my hand because I took her red celery."

"Don't ever do that again. That wasn't celery. It was rhubarb and the leaves are poison. You could get very sick doing that. And, you know you shouldn't be in Mrs. Albert's garden. Now, go back outside, Nancy Lee, and, if Mrs. Albert is still there, tell her you're sorry, and that you won't do it again. Now go!"

Tommy and I found the necessary actions to protect our country exciting. The realities of the war didn't register on our young minds. To us, everything was an adventure. I remember the air-raid alarms, signaling the people to pull down their black, window shades. Every house had to have them. The streetlights were turned off and the neighborhood was in total darkness. Not even the red glow of a cigarette was allowed once the sirens sounded. If any light from inside the house showed through the outer edges of the shades, the neighborhood air-raid warden knocked on the door and issued a warning. Repeated warnings brought serious consequences.

On some nights, when the sirens blared, my mother let Tommy and me get out of bed to sit on the steps of the front porch with our dog, Brownie. We watched the broad bands of light moving through the dark night sky, searching for the enemy planes. It was all so very exciting. The front door was left open, and we could hear the songs playing on the radio in the living room. *"Don't Sit Under the Apple Tree,"* sung by the Andrew sisters was one of my favorites. My mother liked to listen to the music on the radio. At night, while my father was working late, she turned on the radio and danced alone with her eyes closed and her arms out, pretending she was dancing with someone.

Tommy kept his toy rifle across his lap, ready to shoot down the enemy planes, when and if they appeared in the sky—but none ever did, of course. It was thrilling to see the many bright, twinkling stars scattered about in the blackness high above, and the bright searchlights beaming into the dark sky.

When the searchlights abruptly disappeared, the all-clear sirens sounded. The streetlights came back on and the houses returned to their warm glow.

"Come into the house, Nancy Lee and Tommy, and bring Brownie; it's past your bedtime," my mother called, as she turned on the lights and rolled up the dark shades. The excitement of the night was over. Tommy was only seven in the summer of 1943, but I felt safe sitting in the dark on the porch steps because he was there, my big brother, my hero!

A few days before I started kindergarten, a terrible thing happened. Duerstein Street was only several blocks long. It didn't have a lot of traffic. When cars came by, they drove slowly. Tommy and I were in the back yard, playing in the tent my father had put up for us. In front of the house, a car screeched, followed by a lot of commotion. I ran to see what was happening.

Our dog, Brownie, was crawling his way toward the field of tall grass on the other side of our house. The black car parked in the middle of the street had hit him! I ran into the tall grass and sat down beside him, putting his head in my lap. "Nancy Lee, get away from Brownie! Get back here! He'll bite you!" my mother called.

Brownie protected Tommy and me. I knew he wouldn't bite me. I turned my head to see if my mother was coming after me. Tommy stood beside her on the sidewalk and Bobby was in her arms. She was wearing a cotton housedress and silk stockings. She wouldn't come into the tall grass after me. She was fussy about keeping herself clean and her hair combed in a pretty fashion.

I stayed with Brownie until his eyes closed and never opened again. I cried because I loved Brownie. A policeman came into the field, reached for my hand, pulled me up and led me out of the field to the sidewalk. "Tommy, take Nancy Lee into the back yard!"

The only time I had seen Brownie growl was at Uncle Hank, when he, Aunt Molly, and my cousins came to visit. Brownie and I both sensed that despite Uncle Hank's silly smile, he could be very mean. Later, I would find out just how mean Uncle Hank could be.

That night, before falling to sleep, I said my prayers the way my father taught me. "Now, I lay me down to sleep. I pray the Lord, my soul to keep. If I should die before I wake"—What! My eyes flew open, when I realized what I was saying. I don't want to die before I wake. I don't want to die, ever! I quickly ended the prayer with, "Amen" and closed my eyes again, trying to fall asleep.

I dozed off, imagining what it must be like in heaven and wondering if Brownie was happy there. I had a strange dream. I was standing alone. A soft white, nimbus floated all around me. It was very quiet, except for the sounds of bells chiming in the distance. In my dream, I saw a man coming toward me. He looked at me with a loving smile. I didn't know him. I felt that I shouldn't be there. I awoke, with a feeling of being loved.

Sometimes, dreams are more than a jumbled rehash of the events in our life; they may also be a means for spiritual contact and spiritual guidance. Many years later, I learned that was my first dream of a spiritual nature. I also learned that my mother had dreams of a spiritual nature.

Another paranormal experience followed soon after, during a funeral service. Uncle Harold was driving his car with my father sitting next to him. They were talking about the town of Ebenezer and the last time they had been there for a visit. I sat between my grandparents in the back seat of the car, wishing I had a seat by the window, where I could raise my chin and look out. Tommy didn't come with us. He always stayed home with my mother whenever my father and I went places with my grandparents. It wasn't a long ride. I was glad for that because my grandparents looked sad. Even my father didn't have his usual smile when I looked up and saw his face in the rear-view mirror.

When Uncle Harold pulled up in front of the long line of parked cars, he stopped and we got out. My grandparents led the way with my father and me following. Uncle Harold drove off to park the car. We walked up the steps and past the men standing near the door. They tipped their black hats in greeting and opened the door for us to go inside. The room wasn't much warmer than the air outside, where cold winds blew the fallen leaves from the tall trees now standing with their branches bare.

I noticed right away how cold and plain the room seemed. Wooden benches, filled with people dressed all in black, lined both sides of the aisle. Even the women's bonnets were black, just like the one my grandmother was wearing. At the end of the aisle, a tall man with a beard stood next to a long, wooden box that lay on top of a long table.

"Now, remember, Nancy Lee, you can't talk, not even a whisper," my father said, in a hushed tone when we took our seat on the bench beside my grandparents, saving room for Uncle Harold to join us. It was hard to sit still for so long, while we waited and waited. I didn't know what we were waiting for. I sat there with my vision blocked by the people sitting on the bench in front of me. Finally, the tall man with the long beard began to talk. He said things about dust, his father's house and heaven.

My mind began to wander and his voice drifted. Then, I heard a lady's voice say, *"Hello, Nancy Lee ~ You're a pretty little girl ~ My name is Nancy, too."*

Where was the voice coming from? Who was speaking to me? I squirmed about, trying to see where she was.

"Nancy ~ Nancy ~- Nancy," I heard her say again and again. Then, I knew without a doubt that it was the lady who was lying in the wooden box up front, next to the tall man with the long beard.

"Daddy, Daddy," I said excitedly, tugging on his arm and blurting out loud. "The lady in the box talked to me. She said her name is Nancy, too." The tall man stopped talking and the people turned around and looked at me, with gasps and frowns wrinkling their brows.

My father yanked me by the hand, pulling me outside, where I got a hard slap on my bottom, making tears roll down my innocent cheeks. "What did I tell you? I don't want to hear you talk like that," he said, taking his handkerchief from his pocket to wipe my tears.

"But Daddy, the lady did talk to me," I whimpered, as he brought me back inside. With my head hung low, we quietly returned to our seats. Slowly, I lifted my head and looked at my grandfather. He was looking straight ahead. I looked at my grandmother. She gave me a look that told me she was angry about the commotion that I made.

That was the first time that I was wide-awake and heard a spirit voice, but it wouldn't be the last. When I was a child, I thought the voice was that of a living person. Today, I realize that it was the voice of a spirit. Hearing the spirit voice didn't frighten me, but it did confuse me. I had no one to turn to who could explain what I had experienced. An explanation of that experience wouldn't come until later in my life.

Following my father's misunderstanding of my behavior at the Ebenezer funeral, I experienced another heartbreaking incident. PS No. 70, where

Tommy and I went to school, didn't have a cafeteria. Tommy came home for lunch. After lunch, I walked back with him for my afternoon session at kindergarten. One day, I wanted to ride my little red tricycle to school. My mother, of course, wouldn't allow that. Tommy and I began our walk. After the first block, I turned back to get my tricycle. I rode it as fast as I could, so I wouldn't be late for school. I got off and left it by the side door.

Miss Wadge, my kindergarten teacher, was very young and very pretty. She had long, blonde hair, which she pulled back in a bun. I liked her, because she always smiled. After we finished coloring our pictures, I sorted all the broken crayons from the good ones. As a reward for doing that, Miss Wadge let me take home the broken crayons. The red crayon was my favorite. If there weren't any broken red crayons, I broke one, when I thought Miss Wadge couldn't see me. "Miss Wadge, I have all the broken crayons, may I take them home?" I asked in an innocent, charming voice.

The kindergarten session ended. It was time to go home. I walked out the side door to get my tricycle—and, it wasn't there! Tears welled up in my eyes as I looked for it in every driveway of every house, on the walk home. But, I couldn't find it. "Mama, Mama, someone stole my tricycle," I cried, as I ran up the back steps and into the kitchen.

My mother wasn't sympathetic at all. "Let this be a lesson to you, Nancy Lee. Maybe you will listen to me the next time I tell you not to do something." When my tricycle was stolen, my parents didn't replace it—and I never found out who took it.

After that day, I continued to walk to school with Tommy. Sometimes we walked backward to make the walk more interesting. That was something a lot of kids did, especially in the winter. Walking backward was also a necessity because of the bitter cold of the Buffalo winter. We tried to keep the wind to our back, so the wet snow and the blustery blasts wouldn't sting our faces. Walking backward gave us some relief from the blowing snow, but my cheeks were still rosy and wet by the time I reached my destination. My legs were always frozen because I didn't like wearing leggings to school.

Our house was heated by a huge coal furnace, which stood in the middle of the basement. At night my father shoveled chunks of coal into the furnace. That heated the water, which ran into and through the gray, cast-iron radiators that were in every room. The furnace had two heavy metal doors. The black coal was shoveled into the upper door and the lower door opened for the gray ashes to be scooped out.

Sometimes, on Sundays, after my father and I came back from church, I stood in the cold basement, clutching my jacket closed across my chest, watching him shovel the ashes into a black metal pail. Then I followed him up the basement stairs and into the back yard. He scattered the ashes over the area where the Victory Garden would be planted in the spring. "Daddy, why do you throw the ashes on the garden?"

"Ashes make good fertilizer," he answered, as he sprinkled them from the pail onto the light dusting of freshly fallen snow. I didn't know what fertilizer was, but I knew it must be good, because my father said so. I was definitely Daddy's little girl. Wherever he went, I wanted to go with him. Whatever he did, I wanted to watch. Whatever he said, I believed.

The coal truck brought the coal to our house and dumped it in the driveway. When my father had time, he shoveled it through the open basement window into the bin that was built below the window to hold the coal. "Daddy, why did the man dump the coal out in the driveway? Why didn't he put his slide through the window and let the coal go into the basement like he did at Jeanie's house?" I asked with the inquisitive five-year-olds' desire to know everything.

"Because, that costs extra money. The coal man doesn't do that for free," was his answer. My father wouldn't spend the money on such a luxury. Several times, in the bleakness of a winter day, as my cheeks burned from the cold air and my eyes blurred with tears caused by the blowing wind, I stood outside and watched my father shovel the tons of black coal through the open window, one shovel at a time. My father wasn't as tall as my girlfriend Jeanie's father, but he was stronger. He had a lot of big muscles, too. He used to play football and baseball when he was younger, and he still practiced boxing with his brothers. My father could shovel tons of coal easily!

Throughout the winter, my father continued to work for the Buffalo Arms Corporation. Then, on April 12, 1945, President, Franklin D. Roosevelt died, so Vice President Harry S. Truman finished out his term. On May 8, Germany surrendered (V-E Day). At the end of June, my father stopped working for the Buffalo Arms Corporation, and began working for the Curtiss-Wright Corporation. It was another war plant in the town of Cheektowaga.

The Tiorunda housing project was built near the war plant for the families of the plant workers as part of the war effort to reduce travel time, thus reducing the consumption of gasoline and wear on the rubber tires. It also had affordable rent. My parents made the necessary preparations for our family to move into one of the units.

The community was very different from the neighborhood of single-family homes on Duerstein Street. The housing project didn't have a private backyard or a paved driveway on the side on the house. It had a crushed

14

stone parking space at the door that opened into the kitchen. The front door opened to a grassy area that we shared with the four-unit row house across the way.

There wasn't a basement. The coal furnace, hot water tank, laundry tub and my mother's wringer washing machine were all in the utility room off the kitchen. A clothesline was strung there for my mother to hang the laundry when the weather was bad. At the bottom of the outside wall of the utility room was a chute that opened into a coal bin, which was attached to the outer wall of the house. At this house, the coal would be dumped from the truck directly into the bin. In the corner near the furnace stood a shovel and a broom.

The kitchen was small but it was efficient. The white, ceramic sink, with drain board attached, was between the white stove and refrigerator that came with the units. Our kitchen table, covered with a red-and-white-checked oilcloth, and four chairs were across from that wall. In the corner of the kitchen sat a baby's wooden highchair. The lamp with a picture of a rooster on the shade hung on the wall above the kitchen table. The utility room, kitchen and living room were all downstairs.

In the living room was a maroon-and-blue couch, where my mother would sit reading her magazines, while Tommy and I would lie on the gray wool rug on the floor and play checkers or listen to our favorite radio shows before bedtime. Tommy liked the mystery stories, especially *Sherlock Holmes* and *The Shadow*. The floor-model Zenith radio was placed against the wall opposite the staircase leading up to the bedrooms. On that side of the living room near the radio was my father's chair that matched the couch. A brass floor lamp sat next to the chair, and a small mahogany table was in front of the lamp. My father would sit there at night, reading the newspaper, smoking a cigarette, and listening to the radio news broadcasts about the progress of the war.

Three small bedrooms and a bathroom were upstairs. The walls in all of the rooms were painted white. In the bathroom were a toilet, a sink attached to the wall, a bathtub and a small medicine cabinet above the sink. My mother and father shared one bedroom and my brothers, Billy and Bobby, ages three and two, shared a second bedroom. Tommy and I, ages nine and six, shared the third.

When we first moved into the new housing project, the coal bin was empty. Tommy, who was always looking for an adventure, wanted to know if I could fit through the opening of the chute that led into the house. I didn't want to try to do it, but Tommy called me a "Scaredy-Cat." He kept calling me "Scaredy-Cat, Scaredy-Cat!"

Well, that did it! I was going to show him that I wasn't a scaredy-cat. He boosted me up and I climbed in. "Tommy, there are spider webs in here, I want to get out!"

"No, get through the chute, if you want to get out." He closed the lid, and I was in total darkness. "Spiders are crawling all around you, he teased. You better get through the chute, or the spiders will bite you." I was frightened and became hysterical, screaming and screaming! The lid flew open and there was my mother. She lifted me out, brought me into the house, and scolded me saying, "Why do you always listen to everything your brother tells you? When will you learn?" My mother didn't scold Tommy, as I thought she should—probably, because she couldn't find him. He ran off when I started screaming.

When my father came home from work, I told him what Tommy did. "You shouldn't be afraid of spiders. They can't hurt you. You were afraid because you let yourself be. Nothing can hurt you if you're not afraid of it. And, don't climb in the coal bin again."

My father didn't scold Tommy, either. What my father said didn't make sense to me, but I said, "Ok, Daddy, when I get afraid, I'll just think that I'm not, then I won't be." Throughout my life, I would use this mental technique many times, especially when I walked into situations that I shouldn't have—places where angels feared to tread. Franklin D. Roosevelt was right when he said, "The only thing you have to fear is fear itself."

On July 16, 1945 the Manhattan Project tested the first atomic bomb in New Mexico. On August 6, the atomic bomb was dropped on Hiroshima. Three days later, on August 9, a second bomb was dropped on Nagasaki. On August 14, Emperor Hirohito ordered the Japanese to cease fighting. On September 2, Japan surrendered.

We had just settled into our housing unit when the news that my father and all of America had been waiting for came over the radio: "World War II is over!" There were celebrations everywhere in America, including Buffalo. The soldiers would be coming home. Some would be marrying their sweethearts and looking for apartments. That was the good news.

The bad news was that the war plants would be closing. When the war ended, the fight for job security began. All of the soldiers who were heading home would be looking for work. Over the next year, all of the women known as "Rosie the Riveter" and thousands of male war plant workers would be laid off and looking for new jobs. My father was one of them.

Tommy and I, unaware of those circumstances, continued with our adventures. The housing project wasn't far from a wooded area where the trees were tall and thick. The leaf-covered branches spread out overhead, reaching across, touching the branches of other trees, blocking most of the sunlight from reaching the ground. Big rocks and fallen tree trunks covered with velvety moss lay about the earth. Tommy and I often went into the woods exploring. To our delight, we discovered a stream of water that trickled into a shallow pond, which was a little bigger than the one that we used to play in at the end of Duerstein Street. "I've got an idea, let's go fishing tomorrow," Tommy said with excitement.

"We don't have fishing poles," I reminded him.

"We'll find some." On the way out of the woods, we found two long sticks that we could use for fishing poles. When we got home, Tommy tied a string to one end of the poles and fastened an open safety pin for the fishhook on the end of the string. Tommy was so clever. To get our bait, we waited for night to come.

"Mama, Mama, can we go outside to catch worms?"

"Only in front of our house. Don't go wandering off—and stay quiet, you two. People may be trying to sleep," my mother said, as she headed up the stairs to tend to Billy and Bobby, who wouldn't go to sleep.

With an empty coffee can half filled with dirt and a flashlight in hand, Tommy searched for earthworms in the grass area in front of our unit. When we spotted one wiggling to get out of the beam of light, Tommy told me, "Grab it quick and put it in the can."

The dark of the night also brought out the frogs. "Ribbit-ribbit, ribbit-ribbit," they sang to each other. Laughing and frolicking, we tried to catch them as they hopped across the lawn, but they were too fast. "You two stop the noise out there! Hurry up and get the worms, it's past your bedtime!" my mother called to us. We continued hunting for the worms until we had more than a dozen big, fat ones. That night I went to sleep with thoughts about catching a whole bunch of fish. I especially wanted to catch a goldfish. My girlfriend, Jeanie, had two goldfish in a bowl at her house, so I wished I had some goldfish, too.

The next morning, when my mother woke us, we quickly hopped out of bed and got dressed. Tommy put on his corduroy knickers and a short-sleeve shirt. I put on my dress with the Peter Pan collar, and tied the bow in the back. My mother was still in the boys' bedroom, helping Billy and Bobby put on their clothes. We looked forward to our new adventure, as we stood at the bathroom sink brushing our teeth and excitedly chatting.

"Tommy, do you think we'll catch a goldfish?"

"You don't catch goldfish, you buy them."

We hurried downstairs to the kitchen. I poured the corn flakes into the bowls and Tommy poured the milk. We gulped our breakfast down as fast as we could. When we finished, we grabbed our fishing gear from the utility room. "Don't you two stay in the woods all day, and keep out of mischief," my mother called down to us as we headed out the door. Tommy carried the fishing poles and I carried the can with the worms. Outside it was warm and the blue-sky morning made it a perfect day for fishing.

Into the woods we ran, stepping over the fallen tree trunks and around the mossy-covered rocks. We followed the little stream through the woods and watched the frogs as they hopped along ahead of us. Immense mushrooms seemed to have sprung up overnight. We came to the clearing and the pond, where brown cattails swayed in the breeze at the water's edge. It wasn't a very big pond, but it was wide, and the bottom was sandy. I sat down and started to take off my shoes and socks to wade in the water.

Tommy stopped me, "You can't go in the pond. You'll scare away the fish." I put my socks and shoes back on and got ready for fishing. Tommy held the poles steady, while he instructed me how to put the pin through the worm so the worm wouldn't fall off in the water. After several tries, I was able to get it right. I was happy when Tommy said, "Good job."

We saw some minnows and turtles, but we didn't see any fish. Finally giving up, we left the pond and followed the stream back through the woods. On our way home, I tripped, spilling the contents of the coffee can. The worms crawled all over the damp ground. "Pick them up! Pick them up!" Tommy shouted in panic. I couldn't believe it. I looked at him and saw he was afraid to touch the worms. Tommy, my hero—he was a Scaredy Cat!

When Tommy wouldn't play with me, I went into the woods alone. I loved the smell of the damp leaves as I dragged my feet along the earth to stir up the scent and I loved the shafts of sunlight squeezing through the branches. I made a small play area in the woods by rolling some of the smaller, fallen tree trunks, gathering some branches and moving some rocks to make the woodland furniture. I loved playing in the woods.

One day, walking toward my play area, I saw a frog sitting near the little stream. I tried to catch it, but it spotted me. Splash! It went into the water and slipped away. Then, I saw something very strange ahead of me. For a moment, I thought maybe it was the wind blowing some low branches, but there wasn't even a light breeze on that summer afternoon. When I got closer, I saw two people, but they weren't solid, like regular people. I had the feeling that one was a man and one was a woman. They were very old people and they wore funny clothes. They looked at me and then at each other. Poof! They disappeared. I quickened my steps. When I got to my play area, I looked around, but I couldn't see where or how the two old people could disappear so fast.

I had never seen anything like them before, and I wasn't sure if I ever wanted to see people like that again. I wasn't afraid of them, but they did startle me, and left me very confused. To this day, I am not really sure what I saw in the woods that day. Were they spirits or just a young girl's imagination?

On another day, Tommy and I were exploring the neighborhood when dark clouds appeared in the sky; in the distance we heard the rumbling of a thunderstorm about to appear. When the autumn storms roared across the sky, we would stay outside if we could, but my mother said that lightning was dangerous. So, with the first flash of lightning I ran toward home. "I'll race you," I called back to Tommy, running as fast as I could, racing against the heavy raindrops. "One Mississippi, two Mississippi, three Mississippi," I counted the seconds between the flash and the clash of thunder. My father had explained to us that the total number of seconds is the total number of miles from where the lightning strikes.

Safely inside the kitchen, I went to the window and looked for Tommy who had been running close behind me. He was having a grand time splashing in the puddles near our house. "Tommy, come in the house. Mama said that we have to come in when it storms." He didn't pay any attention to me.

I started back outside to play in the puddles, too. My mother came into the kitchen and put a halt to that. "Tommy, get out of those puddles and get in here!" she yelled out the kitchen door. After a few minutes, the heavy downpour stopped, leaving a beautiful rainbow in the sky. My grandmother had told me that rainbows are a reminder of God's promise not to flood the whole world again. I loved rainbows!

"Stay around the house and don't go far, you two," my mother often yelled after us as we headed out the door. We didn't always obey. Tommy wandered near and far and I followed after him. Wherever Tommy went, I went.

The housing project was located near Genesee Street. We knew that my mother's parents, Nanny and Grandpa Meyer, lived on Goodyear Avenue off Genesee Street, because our father had driven us to their house on several occasions.

On a Saturday in September, Tommy said, "Hey, I've got an idea, let's go to Nanny's house to surprise her."

"No, I don't want to—it's too far."

"Don't be a baby, it isn't far."

I didn't like him calling me a baby, so I agreed to tag along with him. Whenever Tommy wanted me to do something, and I didn't want to, he said I was a baby. Walking to Nanny's house would be the farthest we had ever strayed from home, so I was a little afraid. But I wouldn't let him know that.

Tommy, dressed in shorts and a short-sleeve shirt, and I, dressed in a sundress, with my hair bobbing loosely about my shoulders, wandered through the narrow streets of the project until we reached Genesee Street. Then, we turned toward the right, the direction our father took when our family went to Nanny's house. By car, it didn't seem too far away, but it would be a long walk down the busy city street.

We traveled quite a ways, passing the many shops, restaurants, various places of business and a cemetery. "Hey, do you know how many people are dead in that cemetery?" Tommy asked, pretending that he knew the answer.

"No, and you don't either," I answered."

"All of them," Tommy said, laughing at his joke. Tommy knew a lot of trick questions, and I always fell for them.

I was getting tired and told Tommy, "I want to go back home. I'm tired and I'm hungry."

Tommy looked at me and said, "Don't worry, I'll get us something to eat, we're not going back home."

"How are we going to get something to eat? We don't have any money to buy anything."

"We'll go into a tavern and pretend we're looking for Dad." Tommy said it was pretending, but I knew it was lying. Our father was at work at his new job in South Buffalo and we both knew it.

Tommy opened the heavy door of the first tavern we came to and we went in. I had never been in a tavern before. Not knowing what it was going to be like inside, I stayed close behind Tommy, hanging onto his shirt. Inside the tavern, it was refreshingly cool and dark. It had a stinky smell and a cloud of cigarette smoke hung heavy in the air. There were mirrors with names of different beers hanging on the wall on the other side of the long bar.

Several men were sitting on wooden stools at the bar drinking mugs of frothy beer. Tommy walked up to one of the men and I followed behind. He was a big, burly man, with bright, red cheeks and a bubble-nose, streaked with purple veins.

"Did you see our father? He didn't come home from work, and we're trying to find him."

The man asked Tommy what our father's name was, so Tommy gave him a name that he made up "His name is Ralph Rusert."

"Nope, don't know 'im, and haven't seen 'im. Ya kids want some ginger ale to cool ya off?" he asked, wiping the back of his hand across his mouth.

"Sure," Tommy said, looking at me with an "I-told-you-so" grin.

We hopped up on the bar stools and sat next to the man. He called to the bartender, "What do ya say? Give these kids some ginger ale and chips, will ya?"

As we sat on the bar stools enjoying the treats, another man came over to Tommy and me and said, "Well there, lad, where does your father work?"

After Tommy told him, the man said, "Maybe he's working overtime. You kids go home. Here, take this nickel and get going."

"Thank you, mister," Tommy took the nickel, put it in his pocket and hurried out the door. Continuing our journey down Genesee Street, we stopped in a store and bought Necco candy wafers. Tommy divided them, giving me all the black ones because he didn't like licorice. They were my favorite.

I don't know how long it took us to reach Nanny's house, but it was late in the day and the sun was low in the sky. Eventually, we made our way to the light-blue house with the white trim. We walked up the steps to the porch. Tommy opened the door and we walked into the hall. The scent of lemon oil greeted our nostrils, as we walked up the stairs to the second floor flat. Tommy knocked on the door, saying, "They'll be surprised to see us."

Nanny was a small lady with bright blue eyes and hair just starting to turn gray. She kept it curled and neatly combed. She wore pink lipstick and always smelled like a bouquet of flowers. Grandpa was tall with broad shoulders, a broad jaw and a big nose. He was rather good looking and wore wire-rimmed eyeglasses; his hair was just beginning to turn gray, too. He also smelled good because he splashed his face with aftershave.

When the door opened, Nanny and Grandpa were both standing there. Nanny was dressed in a cotton sundress. Grandpa wore trousers and a short-sleeve shirt. "Surprise!!" we shouted in unison, with big smiles on our faces.

They were surprised all right, but not happy. "Where have you two been? Your mother is worried sick! The police are looking for you!" Nanny and Grandpa scolded. We didn't even get to stay for a visit. Without another word, Tommy and I were immediately put into Grandpa's car and driven back home.

All that summer, I wore my hair loose; it just bobbed around my shoulders. "Nancy Lee, we have to cut your hair; it's too long," my mother complained, as she brushed out the snarls in the morning, helping me get ready for school.

"No Mama, please. I don't like short hair."

"If you learn how to braid it yourself, I'll let you keep it long," she promised. It was difficult for my mother to braid my hair because of the long scar on the palm of her right hand. I asked about the scar, she told me she had fallen and hurt it long ago. So, at night, before I went to bed, my father braided my hair, teaching me how to do it for myself. In no time at all, every morning before school, I braided my hair, securing the ends with the rubber bands. It wasn't as nice as my father did it, but it was good enough.

On an October day, after we came home from school, my mother said, "Nancy Lee, you and Tommy can go around the neighborhood and trick-or-treat this Halloween." I was so excited. In the past, Tommy and I were only allowed to dress up and hand out the candy. We weren't allowed to leave the house.

On the following Saturday, when Tommy and I went outside to play, we found a pile of junk that someone had put out for the trash. We searched through it looking for treasures and things to play with. Tommy found a funny umbrella and a suitcase with a broken handle. I found an old, dark-green velvet dress. "This will be my Halloween costume," I said, hurrying away to our front yard, where I put the dress on over my clothes.

Almost immediately, everything around me changed. I became very sad. I didn't understand what was happening to me or why. In my mind, I saw a very little, old woman, wearing the green, velvet dress. She had gray hair and was sitting in a rocking chair. She had a string of black beads in her hands. I knew she was going to die soon. Then, the picture in my mind changed. She wasn't in the chair anymore. She was dressed in a long, pink dress with long sleeves and a high collar. Her hands were resting together with the string of black beads. The beads had a silver cross on the end. I knew she was dead and I started to cry.

Tommy turned to me and asked, "What happened? Does the dress itch? Did something bite you?" Helping me, he pulled the dress over my head. I wanted to answer him, but I didn't know what to say. I stood there, looking at the dress that lay on the ground. The sadness slowly left my body and I stopped crying.

I wanted to get away from the dress, so I ran into the house. I didn't tell my mother what happened, because she would be angry with us for going through the trash. That night, I told Tommy what happened to me when I put on the dress. "First, you tell me that you hear people talking when I can't hear them, and now you tell me you see dead people. You're spooky!"

I tried to understand what I had experienced. Who was the woman and why did I see her lying in a coffin? Even today, I can still smell the old, dark-green velvet dress and recall that feeling of sadness. Many years would pass before I had the answer to the mystery of the green velvet dress.

Soon after Thanksgiving, the days turned bitter cold and darkness came early. Tommy and I didn't play outside after dinner, as before. Instead, we took a warm bath and settled in for the night, playing checkers and listening to the radio. The cold winds outside may have been the reason my mother got an ear infection and had to go to the hospital for a mastoid operation. She would have to stay in the hospital for more than just a few days.

Miss Thom—my mother's friend, a pretty brunette—stayed at our house to take care of us. She was always smiling at my father. She and my father liked each other, but more than they should have. While my mother was away, Miss Thom slept in the bed with me. Tommy slept in my parents' bedroom with my father.

One night when I was in bed sleeping with Miss Thom next to me, I awoke to the sounds of her giggling and playfully objecting to something my father was doing. "Ralph, what are you doing? Your daughter is right next to me. Stop it!"

"Shush, You'll wake her up," my father whispered.

I knew my father didn't want me to be awake, so I kept my eyes closed and pretended to be asleep. But, I could tell that he was sitting on the side of the bed next to Miss Thom, leaning over her, as she laid on her back. My father's hand was moving around between her legs. I knew that because her leg bumped against me when she spread them farther apart.

I didn't like what they were doing. I let them know I was awake. "Daddy, why are you here? What are you doing?"

My father stopped and straightened up, saying, "I just came in here to tell Miss Thom a bedtime story." Then, he began telling the story of *Little Red Riding Hood,* in a low, slow voice. As he told the story, I drifted back to sleep.

My mother came home from the hospital. The surgery went well and she made a full recovery. "Was Miss Thom nice to you, and were you good for her while I was gone?"

"Yes Mama, I was good, but Tommy sassed her and wouldn't listen sometimes," I tattle-tailed on my brother.

"No, Lorraine, the children were good and they weren't any trouble,"

Miss Thom said with a smile and a wink at me. I never told my mother about what my father and Miss Thom did. I knew it was wrong and my mother would be angry with both of them.

Soon after, following the Christmas holidays, Miss Thom was back. She came to take care of us when my mother went to the hospital again, where she gave birth to my sister, Carol Jean, who was born in January 1946. She was a beautiful baby and in perfect health despite my mother's recent mastoid operation. My mother stayed in the hospital for a week, as was the custom in those days.

This time when Miss Thom stayed at our house, I awoke one night and Miss Thom wasn't in bed beside me. Music was playing on the radio in the living room. Quietly, I walked down a few steps of the staircase. Miss Thom and my father were on the couch doing what they shouldn't be doing.

Once again, I didn't say anything to my mother. However, when I was older, I learned that my mother had found out about it and was consumed with anger to the point of refusing my father's sexual advances and wanting a divorce. His brief adultery—with my mother's girlfriend—was the first step toward my parents' marital destruction.

For the past year, my father had been working at Socony-Vacuum Company, a division of Standard Oil. His job was in South Buffalo on the other side of town where we used to live. It was far from the housing project. Sometimes when he came home he smelled like the beer he had been drinking. That made my mother even angrier. When I was in bed, I heard them arguing. "Ralph, I'm not changing my mind and you'll just have to live with it!"

Finally, the winter snows melted and sunlight shined through the breaks in the clouds. It was unusually warm for April and our Sunday dinner of chicken roasting in the oven filled the air with a delicious aroma and added to the warmth inside the house. "Daddy, can I go outside and watch Susan's father put up her new swing?" I asked my father who was sitting in his chair reading the newspaper, as he did every Sunday before dinner.

"Stay out of Mr. Johnson's way and don't go off the stoop. We're going to eat soon." Susan and her family had just moved in next door. Sitting on the porch stoop, I watched Susan's father put the swing together. He set it up on the grass area in front of their unit.

My view of the world was colored by the innocence of childhood. I believed in the magic of Tinker Bell, the dainty fairy, with the shimmering dress and wings, lucky four-leaf clovers, and wishes coming true. I believed in all these things. I crossed my fingers, closed my eyes tight, and mumbled silently to myself, "I wish I may, I wish I might, have a swing, shiny and bright."

From that day on, whenever I saw curly-haired Susan outside on her swing, I went over to play with her. I don't think Susan's mother liked me using the swing. "Nancy Lee, get off the swing. Susan has to come in for dinner!" I hopped off and stood by our door until Susan went into her house. Then, I went back and sat on the swing until my mother called me for dinner.

One Saturday, after dinner, Tommy and I were sitting at the kitchen table playing checkers. I heard my father's car pull into the parking area outside the kitchen door. "Daddy's home," I called to my mother, who was upstairs bathing the younger children, getting them ready for bed. My father didn't come into the house right away. So, I went to the door to see what was keeping him. He was standing in front of his car, arguing with Susan's father. Tommy and I went outside and stood on the stoop, near the door.

"Daddy, come into the house! Daddy, come into the house!" I pleaded with dread in my voice, because I saw he was getting ready for a fight with Susan's father. He took off his glasses, tossed them onto the hood of his car, and rolled up the sleeves of his blue work shirt. With a quick swing of his powerful fist, he landed a punch right square in the face of Susan's father, who reached his hand to his nose and saw it was bleeding.

The fistfight began with punches to each other's face and blood droplets splattering everywhere. They wrestled to the ground, and continued with body punches. My father grabbed Susan's father by the hair, smashing his face into the bumper of our car. Susan's father fell to the ground. "Son of a bitch! Take care of your family and I'll take care of mine!" my father blurted loudly, looking down at Susan's father. My father wasn't a violent person, although lately he got angry easily. That fight was the first time I saw him hit anyone. I was horror-stricken!

The commotion brought a lot of people out of their units. A police car came down the road and stopped in front of our house. My mother rushed outside saying, "Nancy Lee, Tommy, get into the house, you two!" I ran into the house and stood by the kitchen window and cried, because my father was hurt. He had blood running down his nose; the front of his shirt was torn and bloody. The policeman helped Susan's father up, and took him into his house. The crowd of people went back to their units. My mother brought my father into our house where he sat at the kitchen table. She washed the blood off his face with a wet cloth. "Get upstairs, wash up, and get into bed, you two!" she yelled at Tommy and me.

A few days later, after Susan went into the house for dinner, I was back on her swing, happily swinging and enjoying the last warmth of the setting sun. I didn't know my father was home, but there he was standing at the door. "Nancy Lee, get into the house!" He was very angry. "Didn't I tell you not to play with that girl, anymore?" He held my arm, swung me around and landed a few hard slaps on my bottom with his other hand.

"But, Daddy," I cried, with tears wetting my cheeks, "I wasn't playing with Susan. I was swinging by myself." Then, I realized the fistfight was because I used Susan's swing.

The cool winds of autumn became freezing winds of winter. "Look Tommy, it's snowing! Look out the kitchen window," I said, watching the fluffy flakes beginning to fall. They brought with them a sense of quiet and the promise that Christmas was not far away. I could almost hear sleigh bells off in the distance, as I watched the fluffy, white snowflakes falling softly to the ground. I liked the first snow of winter, when the white snowflakes swirled down in little swoops and spins. I liked to catch them on my tongue and pretend I was eating the sky. I tried to imagine what it was like at the North Pole where Santa lived. But, Santa had put up a magic shield, so children like me couldn't peek. All I could see was white nothing.

That winter, I noticed my father was becoming angry with my mother for things she did or didn't do, and he wasn't home to eat supper with us every night. My mother was changing too. She wasn't taking care of herself and she spent a lot of time reading romance magazines.

In the spring, I was eight years old and in third grade, when a horrible tragedy happened. I will never forget that day. On a crisp, spring morning in 1947, Tommy and I were sitting at the kitchen table, eating our corn flakes and reading the print on the cereal box, before leaving for school. Four-year-old Billy, and three-year-old Bobby were upstairs, still in their pajamas. My mother was in the living room with baby Carol Jean, trying to change her diaper, as she was lying and squirming on the couch. Suddenly, we heard Billy and Bobby yelling loudly about something!

"Run upstairs and see what's wrong with your brothers!" my mother shouted to us. I jumped from the chair and ran up the stairs. Billy was engulfed in flames from the bottom of his pajamas up to his neck. He was all in flames, like a torch! My first instinct was to get water.

"Mama, Mama, Billy's on fire, Billy's on fire!" I screamed, as I ran into the bathroom. I quickly filled a glass with water, hurried back to Billy and threw the water in his face. The water stopped the flames that were shooting up from the collar of his pajamas. My mother was up the stairs in an instant. She grabbed Billy and carried him into the bathroom, put him into the bathtub and turned on the cool water. "Go to Mrs. Stone! Tell her to call an ambulance!"

I ran as fast as I could to her house at the end of the unit. "Mrs. Stone, Mrs. Stone," I hollered, as I banged on her door, "Billy is burned! Mama said to call an ambulance!"

Mrs. Stone, a short, stocky woman with intense eyes and black hair streaked with gray, was wearing a pink chenille robe when she answered the door. "Where's your mother?" was her irritated response as she stood, looking at me through squinted eyes.

"She's upstairs, in the bathroom with Billy. Please hurry and call an ambulance," I sputtered, with my heart beating hard and fast.

Mrs. Stone grabbed my hand and walked me back to my house. I broke free when we got to the door and ran up the stairs to the bathroom. Mrs. Stone followed behind. My mother was on her knees at the side of the bathtub, splashing Billy with cool water and trying to comfort him, as he cried out in pain.

"Did you call the ambulance?"

"No, I didn't think it was serious."

"Damn you! Call the ambulance!"

When the ambulance came, the men from the ambulance lifted Billy from the bathtub and carried him into my parents' bedroom, where they gently placed him on a white sheet that they had put on top of the bed. I stood in the doorway watching and crying, as the ambulance attendants carefully removed the pajamas that were charred and stuck to Billy's skin.

"Go downstairs!" my mother yelled when she saw me out the corner of her eye. I hurried down the stairs and sat on the couch with Tommy and Bobby. Mrs. Stone had put Carol Jean in the highchair and sat in the kitchen with her.

"Can't you give him something? Can't you give him something for the pain?" My mother kept pleading with the ambulance attendants while they continued their work of removing Billy's charred pajamas and covering his burned body with moist gauze to prepare him for the trip to the hospital.

The whole ordeal was excruciatingly painful. Billy never stopped crying out in pain. At last, the attendants brought the stretcher down the stairs. Billy was bandaged up to his face and covered with a white blanket. My mother pulled a hanky from her apron pocket and wiped her tears. As she walked past us, following the stretcher out the door, she said, "Stay here with Mrs. Stone."

When the ambulance left, Mrs. Stone said, "Tommy, I want to call your grandparents to watch you kids. What's their name, the ones that come here all the time?"

"Rosa and Joseph Meyer," Tommy answered.

Mrs. Stone went to her house to make the phone call. When she came back she said, "Tommy, you and your sister go to school, now." Upset as we were, we did as we were told.

That was an era when children's pajamas weren't required to be flame-retardant. Because Billy was in my parents' bedroom when I saw him in flames, it was assumed that he was playing with matches that were left on the night table near the ashtray. It was assumed that he lit a match, dropped it and the flames ignited his pajamas.

Billy suffered second and third degree burns over most of his body, from his neck down to his knees. Skin from the places on his body that weren't burned would be used to cover the raw wounds. He would have to undergo a series of twelve skin grafts that would take more than a year to complete. It seemed like everyone in the city of Buffalo came together to help in Billy's recovery. The chief surgeon waived his fees. The Shriners organization helped with the hospital expenses and the employees at Socony-Vacuum Company gave over sixty-four pints of blood that Billy would need.

Not long after the fire, I finished the third grade and school was over for the summer. I didn't see much of my father during that time because he worked weekdays and visited Billy in the hospital on weekends. Once a week, Nanny and Auntie Alice came to our house. Nanny stayed with us children while Auntie Alice drove my mother to the hospital to visit Billy.

Nanny and Auntie Alice were good friends and both had ties to some of the Meyer relatives. Out of respect, we called her "Auntie Alice." She was short like Nanny and wore her dyed brown hair short and curly, in the same fashion as Nanny wore her hair. They both were always impeccably dressed. The main difference between them was that Auntie Alice had a lot more money. She drove a black car with a fancy, chrome ornament on the point of the hood. Auntie Alice was married to Uncle Will, and I had heard something about the Pierce Arrow Automobile Company and him in the same conversation. I think he was connected to the company somehow.

Nanny let Tommy and me wander about outside, as long as we were quiet and didn't wander far. After our lunch, Nanny said, "Tommy, you and Nancy Lee go outside and play, but don't do a lot of hollering. I'm going to put your sister down for a nap."

Tommy thought it would be a good adventure to explore Genesee Street, this time in the opposite direction from where Nanny and Grandpa lived. We took a shortcut through the housing project and when we got to the corner, we turned left.

A short time into our walk, we came to a white shack. The sign over the top of the shack had the words "ICE CREAM" painted in bold, black letters. The front of the stand had a big, drop-down board, hinged at the center top. When it was dropped down, it became the opening for serving the customers. But, today, it wasn't dropped down. The ice cream stand was closed.

Tommy went to the door on the side of the shack; it was closed, too. He turned the doorknob, and the door opened. "Hey, look! There's an ice cream freezer here," he said, as he walked inside. Tommy opened the lids, one at a time, and peered down into the long rectangular freezer box that sat near the back of the shack.

"Tommy, let's get out of here. We're going to get into trouble," I warned as I waited near the door.

"Don't be a baby. What kind do you want?" he asked, with the ice cream scoop in his hand and all four of the freezer flaps open.

"I don't want any Tommy—let's go!" I warned again. In my mind, I had an image of an old man coming out of the house and running down the driveway, toward us. I told Tommy, "A man is going to come out of the house and catch us. Tommy, quick, get out of there," I yelled to him, as I left the shack. I hurried away, not quite running with my heart beating hard. Turning, I looked back over my shoulder and saw an old man coming out of the house. I stopped in my tracks and yelled, "Tommy—Hurry! Hurry!"

As Tommy walked out the door with his ice cream cone, the old man neared the shack. Reaching out, he caught Tommy by the back of his shirt. Tommy dropped the ice cream cone and broke free from the old man's grip. Tommy could run fast and he did, leaving the old man standing there, waving his fist at us. Tommy caught up with me, looked back and yelled to the old man, "Run, run, as fast as you can! You can't catch me! I'm the Gingerbread Man!"

My imagination was beginning to envision things before they occurred—not a long time before but shortly before they occurred. I'm not sure if my visions would be considered psychic predictions or telepathy. Tommy thought of my paranormal experiences as "spooky". I didn't think much about them. I just accepted the fact that strange things happened to me and I wouldn't have an answer for the mysterious events of my life until I took an interest in the study of parapsychology.

I may have been able to read minds, but Tommy was able to get money for candy. On a summer day that was already scorching hot, Tommy and I finished our cereal and milk and went outside to play. We took our wagon and went from door to door, collecting empty pop bottles, so we could return them for the two-cent deposit. We often did that when we wanted to get money for candy.

I knocked on the door and Tommy did the talking. "Good morning, Mum, do you have any empty bottles we could take off your hands?" Tommy asked, faking a proper English accent. It wasn't very convincing, but it did make the people smile. When we finished collecting bottles, we headed for the grocery store.

As we approached the grocery store, we saw some men working on the flat roof of the store. They were spreading hot, black tar. We stood watching them for a few minutes. One of the workmen on the ground was trying to get water out of the yellow jug on the back of a truck. "What the hell happened to all the water? Didn't you fill it this morning?" he yelled up to someone on the roof.

"Hey, I have an idea—instead of taking the empty bottles back now, let's fill them with water and sell the water to the men," Tommy said, turning the wagon around and heading back home. I hurried after him.

"Tommy, Mama won't let us do that. She said that we should stay outside and play." Tommy didn't pay any attention to me. He just hurried along.

"Mama doesn't have to know. We'll fill them from the water spigot outside the house."

That's just what we did. We sold the bottles of water for two cents, taking back the bottles after the men drank the water. Then, we returned the bottles to the grocery store for another two cents. Tommy was so smart!

That night, my mother and father were downstairs in the living room and I was upstairs in bed, listening to them argue about something. "Ralph it's too late, I'm not changing my mind!" my mother said in a determined voice.

"This isn't only about us, Lorraine, we've got to think about the kids, too." They went on talking, but I couldn't hear everything. I dozed off, trying to figure out what it was they were talking about.

I was only eight years old when our family moved from the four-unit house in the housing project. The unit had been sold to Mrs. Stone, the neighbor at the end of our unit. She didn't like our family and she didn't like when Tommy and I played on her grass.

"Where are we going to live, Mama?" I asked the next day, when my mother began packing things into boxes. She didn't look at me. She just went on packing.

"I don't know. Ask your father." Her answer was more of a criticism than a reply. I didn't ask anymore.

Over the next few weeks, my mother went through the cupboards and closets, throwing some things into the trash and packing the rest. The time passed with very little talking between my parents. I could tell my mother didn't like that we had to move because she got angry at the littlest things that Tommy and I did. Sometimes tears ran down her cheeks for no reason.

Sunday morning came and I awoke to a warm summer breeze blowing through the bedroom window that had no curtains. The curtains were taken down, washed and packed in a box to be put up in the next house we were moving into. It was a great day for a new adventure. Tommy was already out of bed, putting on the shirt and shorts he wore the day before. I jumped out of bed, grabbed my dress from the top of the packed boxes and put it on over my head, tying the belt in the back.

"Hurry and get down here, you two, if you want something to eat," my mother called up to us from the living room, where she sat on the couch with baby Carol Jean on her lap. Little Bobby sat by her side, holding his stuffed bear. Tommy and I raced down the stairs and hurried to the kitchen table. My father was sitting at the table smoking a cigarette and finishing his cup of coffee. Tommy poured the milk into the bowls of corn flakes and we hurried through our breakfast. We were so excited! This was the day our family was going to move into our new house.

My father got up from the table, put the pack of cigarettes in his shirt pocket and headed toward the kitchen door.

"Daddy, where are you going?"

"It's okay, I'll be back in a little while." Something was wrong. I felt a profound sadness as I watched my father get into his car. I was speechless and just stared off into space.

"Hey, what's the matter with you? There you go again, being spooky. Mama, Nancy Lee is spooking me again. Make her stop," Tommy called to my mother. I left the table, ran upstairs to the bathroom and splashed cold water on my face, so I wouldn't cry. I couldn't understand why I felt so sad. This was supposed to be a happy day. A new adventure awaited us. What was wrong?

When I came back down stairs and went outside, I couldn't find Tommy. He had wandered off to say goodbye to his friends. Nanny and Grandpa Meyer pulled up and parked in our driveway. Grandpa loaded his car with the baby crib and some packed boxes.

My mother walked about with Carol Jean slung on one hip and little Bobby tagged along by her side. "Take Anna Belle's box, too," she told

Grandpa, handing him a cardboard box. Who was Anna Belle and what was in Anna Belle's box? Nanny and Grandpa looked serious. They didn't say anything to us children; they just hurried about doing what needed to be done.

When their car was fully packed, they got in and drove away. Nanny didn't say goodbye this time. She even tried to avoid looking at me. That was strange! Shortly after Nanny and Grandpa drove off, a white truck backed up to our kitchen door and parked. The words "Sampson's Moving and Storage" were painted in black letters on the side. Tommy and I stood outside and watched the men as they carried our furniture outside and put it into the back of the truck.

While the men were still loading the truck, my father returned and went into the house. The men finished loading a few more boxes. My father went back outside where one of the men gave him a slip of paper. He studied it for a minute, folded it and put it into his wallet. The white truck drove away. I scampered past my father, running into the house for a last look. The house was completely empty except for the stove and refrigerator that came with the units. In the early afternoon, on Sunday, August 31, 1947 we moved out of the housing project.

Nancy Lee, eight years old. Before I went to bed, my father braided my hair, teaching me how to do it for myself. In no time at all, every morning before school, I braided my hair, securing the ends with tight rubber bands.

CHAPTER TWO
A Family Divided

Being born in the United States of America to a young married couple and living in a postwar society does not guarantee a happy childhood.

MY MOTHER, WHO USUALLY had a gentle smile, was now stone-faced as she got into the car and sat on the front seat next to my father, with Carol Jean on her lap. My parents' mood was somber on this beautiful day and I couldn't understand why. Even Tommy, who usually teased me, was quiet. Why was everyone so serious?

Tommy and I had the window seats in the back, where four-year-old Bobby sat between us. Billy was still in the hospital. As we rode, I sat silently, looking out the window. After awhile, the sights became familiar to me as my father drove down Seneca Street. I recognized the gray, two-family house where my father's parents lived. It was across the street from Cazenovia Park, the pride of South Buffalo. My father turned into the driveway, going all the way into the back yard, where he parked the car.

"Why are we going to visit Grandmother and Grandfather before we go to our new home?" Neither my mother nor my father answered me. They got out of the car. Tommy, Bobby and I followed. My father took Carol Jean from my mother, holding her in his left arm. He reached out to Bobby with his right hand and walked toward the side door of my grandparents' house.

"Come with me, Nancy Lee, we're going in the house to see your grandmother." I started to follow after my father, but when I took a quick glance behind me, I noticed that Tommy and my mother weren't coming.

34

They stayed by the side of the car. My mother's hands rested on Tommy's shoulders, as he stood in front of her.

"No, I don't want to. I want to stay here with Mama and Tommy!" I answered back defiantly, with a stomp of my foot.

Just as my father went into the side door, Grandpa Meyer's car pulled into the driveway. He was the only one in his car; Nanny wasn't with him. The thought flashed through my mind that he must have taken her along with the baby crib and boxes to our new house. But, why did he come here?

Grandpa didn't get out of the car, or even turn off the engine. I smiled at him when our eyes met, but he didn't smile back. He turned his eyes away. Didn't he like me anymore? Why didn't he like me anymore? My mother hurried to the car with Tommy following and they got in. There were tears in my mother's eyes. I was scared!

"Where are you going, Mama? Don't go, Mama! Why aren't you staying with us?" I ran to the car, pulled at the handle, trying to open it to stop my mother and Tommy from leaving, but the door wouldn't open.

"Mama, Mama, take me too! I want to go, too!"

"No, I can only take Tommy."

"Come back, Mama! Come back, Tommy!" I cried as the car pulled out of the driveway. I stood there feeling abandoned. Why did my mother take my brother Tommy with her? Why didn't she take Bobby, Carol Jean or me wherever she was going? What would I do without Tommy, my big brother, my hero? I was broken-hearted and burst into wailing sobs, letting the hot tears roll down my cheeks. I didn't even get a chance to say goodbye.

A firm hand on my shoulder brought me out of my shock of being abandoned by my mother and back to the moment. My father was standing behind me. He came back outside, but not in time to see my mother and Tommy ride away with Grandpa Meyer.

"Let's go in and see your grandmother. Here, blow," he said, holding his handkerchief to my nose.

"Daddy, why is Mama going to Nanny's house with Tommy? When are they coming back? Aren't we going to our new house today?" I sobbed, looking up at him. He just looked sad, as he took my hand and walked me into the house. We walked up the steps of the back hall and he opened the door to the kitchen. My grandfather was sitting at the kitchen table, holding Carol Jean. She was usually a good little girl, but now she was being a real handful. "I think she needs a diaper change, Ralph," my grandfather said, as he bounced her on his knee, trying to get her to stop crying.

My father went outside and brought in a diaper from one of the brown paper bags that he had put into the trunk of his car that morning. When

Carol Jean saw my father, she reached out for him to take her. He did and her tears stopped. My father laid her down on the kitchen floor and changed her cloth diaper with a clean one.

I was familiar with my grandparents' flat, because years ago when we lived around the corner on Duerstein Street, my father and I walked to their house many times. Their first-floor flat had a kitchen, dining room, living room, three bedrooms and one bathroom. It also had a sunroom in the front of the house that my grandmother used as her sewing room.

My grandmother was a skilled dressmaker, doing alterations for three local dress shops. Even when she was behind in her sewing, she wouldn't pick up a needle to work on Sunday. Her life revolved around her religion and the church. It was probably because her father was the Elder Jacob Swartz that she referred to Sunday as the "Lord's Day." Although, now a Baptist, she kept her Mennonite ways, dressing in plain dresses and not wearing make-up; soap and hand lotion were her only beauty products. She was short and slender, just like my grandfather and she kept her dark hair with strands of gray, cut short. When she was a young girl, she was afflicted with polio, so now she had to wear a metal brace strapped to her right leg so she could walk.

When my grandfather was younger, he lived in Beech Creek, Pennsylvania where he worked in a lumberyard. After he and my grandmother married, they moved to the town of Ebenezer, outside of Buffalo. On an early 1900s census form, my grandfather was listed as a shopkeeper, but I never saw him work outside the home. Grandfather had a big smile, big ears, and a big heart. He had the red hair of the Irish. He got that from his mother, who was the daughter of the famous evangelist, William Alonzo Ridge.

My father's bachelor-brother, Uncle Harold, lived with my grandparents. He was a few years older than my father. He wasn't as muscular as my father, but he was the same height and had the same dark, wavy hair and handsome looks. Uncle Clarence was my father's oldest brother, but he was scalded to death in an accident at work. I never met him. The youngest of my father's brothers was Uncle Saul. He had dark, wavy hair and was also handsome, but much taller than my father. Uncle Saul was married to Aunt Mary Ann and they lived off Seneca Street, several miles away. My grandmother instilled a strong sense of duty in her sons, telling them, "Hard work, charity to others, and honesty would make them men of good character." But my mother didn't see it that way. She called my grandmother's sons, "Mama's boys."

Standing in the kitchen doorway, while looking into the living room,

I saw Bobby by the birdcage, watching the yellow canary. "Sing birdie, tweet-tweet; sing birdie, tweet-tweet," Bobby repeated over and over again in his little-boy voice.

My grandmother, dressed in one of her plain dresses, was sitting on the brown couch in the living room, watching Bobby. When she saw me, she said, "There you are, Nancy Lee." Then, she stood up, locked the metal brace on her leg and walked toward the kitchen. "Ralph, sit the children down and we'll have something to eat," she told my father as she walked past me.

Bobby followed my grandmother into the kitchen, climbed up and sat on a chair. His chin reached only a little above the top of the table. I sat down next to my father, who was holding Carol Jean on his lap. My grandfather cut slices from a loaf of bread, while my grandmother brought out a block of cheese and a round of baloney from the wooden icebox, setting them on the table. The blessing was said and we ate in silence.

After the meal, my father said, "Stay here and be a good girl until I get back." He took Carol Jean and Bobby and went out the door. I ran to the kitchen window, looked out and watched as my father's car left the driveway.

I was confused. I went into the living room and sat on the couch next to my grandmother, where she sat reading the Bible. "Grandmother, why aren't we going to our new house?"

She didn't give me an answer; instead she said, "Nancy Lee, this is what Jesus said to the people. Listen carefully: 'Suffer little children to come unto me, and forbid them not; for of such is the kingdom of God. Verily I say unto you, whosoever shall not receive the kingdom of God as a little child shall in no way enter therein,' St. Matthew 19:14." I loved God and I knew God loved me. I didn't want my grandmother to preach to me. I wanted her to answer me.

My grandfather finished cleaning up the kitchen and he came into the living room to join us. "Here, my little Dutch Girl, take a piece of candy," he said, as he held out the candy dish filled with maple-flavored candy. Little Dutch girl was what he usually called me.

"Thank you Grandfather, but I don't want any," I said, in a low, sad voice. He put the candy dish on the table, sat down in the brown chair next to the brown couch and dozed off. I wondered what Tommy was doing now at Nanny's house. I was sure that he didn't have to sit still and listen to a Bible reading. He was probably outside in Nanny's backyard trying to catch the crickets as they sang their songs and hopped about the grass.

"Grandmother may I go into the back yard and play?" I asked, holding back the tears that stuck in my throat.

"No, sit right here, next to me, while I read some more to you. Your father will be back soon." I scooted to the corner of the couch, sat back, and listened as my grandmother continued to read to me from the Bible. Soon her words were muted with the sounds of my grandfather's light snoring and the ticking of the old clock that sat on the buffet.

The kitchen door opened and my father walked into the living room. "Daddy, where are Bobby and Carol Jean?"

"Carol Jean is going to stay with Aunt Molly for a little while and Bobby is going to stay with my friends. They're all right, so don't worry," he said, trying to assure me they were okay. Aunt Molly was my father's only sister. She was married to Uncle Hank. Just then, Uncle Harold came into the house. He and my father walked down the back hallway toward the bedrooms. They stayed there for a while, talking.

When it was time for supper, I followed my grandmother into the kitchen and sat at the table. She took some food out of the icebox and put it on the table. We ate a meal of cold, sliced, roast beef, red cabbage and potato salad. I didn't like the potato salad. It wasn't the kind made with mayonnaise. My grandmother made her potato salad with onions and vinegar. She said it was "German" potato salad. For dessert, we had applesauce cake with white frosting. I liked that. After supper, I sat next to my father on the couch, while he read the Sunday paper. Soon, I was tired and it was time to get into the bed, which was made up on the little, velvet settee in the dining room.

"Goodnight, Daddy," I said, snuggling under the coverlet.

"Goodnight, Nancy Lee," he answered, as he walked away.

As tired as I was, I couldn't go to sleep right away. I kept thinking about our house on Duerstein Street, where I used to live when I was very young. I drifted off to a fitful sleep, dreaming of those happier days.

The sweet dreams of my yesterdays faded from my mind as I awoke to find myself on the little, velvet settee in my grandparents' house. Why wasn't I waking up in our new house? I rubbed my eyes, stretched my arms overhead and became fully awake. Throwing the coverlet off, I got up and went into the kitchen where my grandfather and father sat at the table, talking.

"Well, I don't know what to tell you, Ralph—it looks like there's not much you can do. You'll just have to wait and see what Lorraine is going to do." I didn't have any idea what they were talking about, but whatever it was, it made my father sad.

"Look who's here; it's my little Dutch girl," my grandfather said, when he saw me at the kitchen doorway. I walked over to the table and sat on the chair next to my father.

"Your clothes and tooth brush are in the bag next to the buffet. I have to leave for work now, so you stay here and be a good girl," my father said, as he got up from his chair and walked out.

My grandfather put a bowl in front of me saying, "Here's something that'll make your hair curly." It was a bowl of hot Cream of Wheat, with brown sugar on top.

"Thank you, Grandfather, this is my favorite breakfast." After I finished eating, I took my clothes and toothbrush into the bathroom where I washed up, brushed my teeth and dressed. I didn't have a comb, so I used the comb that was in the bathroom to comb and braid my hair, hoping that my grandmother wouldn't mind.

My grandmother was a serious woman; she didn't smile much like Nanny. She was already busy at work in her sewing room when I asked, "Grandmother, may I go out and play?"

"No, you sit here, where I can keep an eye on you." Looking up from her sewing, she handed me a jar of buttons adding, "Here, you can sort out these buttons." I tried to amuse myself, but it didn't work. I was still bored, just sitting there on the floor, while she worked at her sewing machine.

"What's the matter with you? Why the sour face?"

"When will Daddy be back? I want to go outside."

"Enough of that talk, I'll get you something to keep you busy." My grandmother got up, locked the metal brace on her right leg, and opened the drawer of the gray dresser, where she kept remnants of cloth, threads and patterns. "Here, you can embroider a dresser scarf." She handed me two wooden, embroidery hoops and a piece of cloth with a stamped pattern of a basket of flowers printed at each end. She sat back down at her sewing machine and gave me instructions on how to put the cloth between the two hoops and press them together to pull the cloth taut. Then, she handed me a little box of colored threads. I kept busy embroidering the dresser scarf, until it was finished.

"Now, what can I do, Grandmother? May I go down Duerstein Street and see if Jeanie Hart still lives there? Please, please," I pleaded, with my hands held together, like I was praying.

"You walk down there and come right back. I don't want you staying down there. If she can play, she has to come here, where I can keep an eye on you. Do you hear?"

I ran out the door to the corner and down the street. I was happy to be outside in the sunshine, going to see Jeanie again. She was the little red-haired girl who lived across the street from us when we lived on Duerstein

Street. I hadn't seen her since we moved away, two years ago. I hoped she would remember me. Back then Jeanie's mother walked her across the street with her tricycle. We rode up and down the sidewalk together. When we got tired of riding our tricycles, we went into my backyard to play and do somersaults both forward and backward.

I reached the little white house where Jeanie lived and walked up the back porch steps. The kitchen door was open. I put my face up to the screen door. "Oh, Jeanie," I called real loud. Mrs. Hart came to the door. She was just as I remembered her, a heavy-set woman with red hair and blue eyes, like Jeanie.

"Well, if it isn't little Nancy Lee. Come in."

"I'm glad Jeanie is still living here," I said.

"We own this house, Nancy Lee. Jeanie will probably live here for a long time. What are you doing back here?"

"My father and I are staying with my grandparents today, and my grandmother said that Jeanie could come to her house to play. My grandmother lives at the corner, on Seneca Street."

"Your grandmother makes dresses for me; I know where she lives. She lives across from our church," Mrs. Hart said, walking to the sink to get a glass of water.

Hurrying into the kitchen from the living room, Jeanie, dressed in shorts and a striped T-shirt was bursting with excitement. "Hi, Nancy Lee, when did you move back here? Are you going to live back here now? Your hair got longer. What grade are you in now?" The questions flowed one after the other. She didn't even give me a chance to answer. Jeanie's excitement at seeing me again made me feel good. "Can I, Mom? Can I go with Nancy Lee, to her grandmother's house and play?"

"All right, go ahead, but walk straight there and don't cross Seneca Street or go into the park. Stay at her grandmother's house." Jeanie and I headed out the door. We held hands and swung our arms, like the pendulum of a clock, as we walked down the steps.

"I got a new two-wheel bicycle from Santa last Christmas. Wait till you see it," Jeanie said, as she headed toward the garage. There was no door on her garage. I could see the bicycle standing inside near the sidewall. It was shiny blue with chrome fenders. It had a basket on the front and a bell on the handlebars. Jeanie was so lucky; I wished I had a bicycle. Before we headed back to my grandmother's house, Jeanie showed me how she could ride it.

"May I take a turn, Jeanie?"

"Do you know how to ride a two-wheeler?"

"Sure, where we used to live, Tommy's friend and his sister had bicycles.

Sometimes they let us ride them." I gripped tight onto the handlebars, and my feet peddled a round slowly on the pedals. I rode down her driveway without falling off, to Jeanie's surprise. Then, I got off, remembering that my grandmother was waiting for us. "We have to go, Jeanie, Grandmother will be worried."

Jeanie put her bicycle back in the garage, ran into her house and brought out a deck of Old Maid playing cards. We skipped, hopped and jumped all the way down the street, happy to be together again.

Until her mother mentioned it, I didn't know that Jeanie and her family were Catholic and went to St. John the Baptist Church. That didn't matter to me, but it would sure matter to my grandmother. "Jeanie, don't tell my grandmother that you go to St. John's Church. She doesn't like Catholics. She only likes Protestants."

Jeanie had never been to my grandparents' house before. We walked into the driveway and used the side door that led up the steps and to the back door of their flat. I knocked on the kitchen door and my grandfather let us in. "Hello, little redhead, you must be the Jeanie that I heard about. And, I know, you live in a magic bottle. Am I right?"

"Oh, Grandfather you're so silly. You know Jeanie lives on Duerstein Street."

"Nancy Lee, come in here with your friend," my grandmother called out when she heard my voice. We went into her sewing room. My grandmother said "Hello" to Jeanie. Jeanie said "Hello" to my grandmother. To my relief, nothing was said about a church.

I tucked my dress around my legs and sat on the floor across from Jeanie. We had fun laughing and chattering while we played with the cards. "Don't be so loud girls, you'll wake the dead," my grandmother scolded. Jeanie and I hushed to a whisper, trying to be quiet and not giggle. It was hard trying not to giggle when Jeanie and I made frowning faces in my grandmother's direction. All too soon, it was time for Jeanie to leave.

"Your friend will have to go home now; it's almost time for dinner," my grandmother said, as she finished sewing on the sleeve of the dress she had been working on. She got up from her chair, locked her leg brace, and stood waiting for us to pick up the cards.

"May I walk Jeanie to the corner, Grandmother?"

"Yes, but come right back, don't dilly-dally, you hear me?" We hurried down the back stairs, out the door and to the corner.

Before heading down Duerstein Street, Jeanie paused, "Your grandmother isn't very nice."

"My grandmother is nice. She just doesn't like us playing cards. I think it's against her religion. Christians can be very fussy you know. Tomorrow,

I'm going to ask my grandmother if I can go to your house to play. Do you think it will be okay with your mother?"

"My mother is a Christian too, and she isn't fussy. I'm sure we can play at my house."

When I got back, my grandmother told me, "I don't like that girl. She wipes her nose on her arm. Doesn't she have a hanky?" I didn't know what to say. I hadn't seen Jeanie wipe her nose on her arm. How did my grandmother see her do that? She was busy and didn't look our way very often. Well, Jeanie didn't like her either, but I would never tell my grandmother that.

I went into the kitchen and stayed with my grandfather, while he busied himself with preparing dinner. "How about you setting the table for me, while I empty this drip pan?" he said, handing me five dinner plates. I knew that he wasn't asking because he really needed my help. He just wanted to give me something to do.

The kitchen had a wooden icebox. It had three doors. On the right was a full-length door, where food was kept. On the left were two smaller doors, one on top of the other. Behind the top door was a big block of ice and behind the lower door was a drip pan. My grandfather opened the bottom door, took out the drip pan, carried it to the sink where he dumped the water from the melted ice.

"Grandfather, why don't you have a refrigerator like Nanny has, and like we had where we used to live?"

"This is what came with the house when we rented it. That's how it usually works. People who rent have to be satisfied with the stove and icebox that are already in the house. Beggars can't be choosers."

"Grandfather, we're not beggars," I told him in a huff, not liking what he said.

"No, my little Dutch girl, you're right; we're not beggars. We're just not rich, that's all."

The next day, I asked, "Grandmother, may I go to Jeanie's house to play?"

"No, you don't want to make a pest of yourself, do you? Your grandfather is going to take you to the park today, after he finishes the laundry." The morning passed too slowly for me. I was anxious to get out of the house. I wished my grandfather would hurry up. He seemed to take forever, hanging the wet clothes on the clothesline in the basement. Finally, he finished.

When he came up from the basement, he made grilled cheese sandwiches for us in a big, black frying pan. After we finished our lunch, my grandfather and I walked across the street. We walked to an area in the park where there were swings with smooth, black rubber seats. "Push me higher, Grandfather, higher," I yelled out with each push he gave me.

"Pump your feet back and forth and you'll make yourself go higher," he said, as he pushed me one last time. I wanted to stay longer, but I knew my grandfather wanted to go back, so I didn't fuss when he said, "Ok, my little Dutch girl, it's time to leave."

On our way back to the house, my grandfather picked a dandelion that had blossomed into a white fluff. He held it to my lips saying, "Blow and watch all the tiny parachutes fly about and land." I did, and then he said, "The leaves of the dandelion plant are good to eat. But, they have to be picked in the spring before the yellow flowers grow, or the leaves won't taste good."

"I thought leaves were poison," I said, remembering what my mother had told me about the rhubarb leaves.

"Not these leaves, they're like spinach leaves and good to eat when they're cooked with bacon and onions. With vinegar and honey dressing, they're delicious."

I only stayed at my grandparents' house for that week. My father knew my grandmother wouldn't let me go outside to play and she didn't like Jeanie coming to her house. The following Saturday, my father took me to Aunt Molly's house where my baby sister, Carol Jean, was staying.

Aunt Molly was as round as she was tall. She had dark, short-cropped hair just like my grandmother's hair. Uncle Hank was of medium height, with red hair. He always had a silly grin on his face. They lived in a village of row houses. Their house was the last unit. It had three bedrooms, a living room, a kitchen and bathroom, all on the first floor.

My four cousins, Ruth, Al, Rich and Harry slept in twin-size beds, two in each bedroom. Aunt Molly and Uncle Hank slept in another bedroom, where they had a crib set up for Carol Jean. There was no bed for me. I slept in one of the twin-size beds with my cousin, Ruth. Her head was at the top of the bed and my head was at the foot of the bed. Ruth resented that she had to share her bed. She kicked me hard with the heels of her feet. I kicked her back.

"Nancy Lee's kicking me—get her out of my bed!"

"Nancy Lee, you stop that, or you'll get a whipping," Aunt Molly called out from the bedroom across the hall. I couldn't kick Ruth back. I had to take it. There was nothing I could do about it.

Ruth was a few months younger and she was shorter and chubbier than I. She had beautiful, long, blonde ringlets that hung past her shoulders. I envied her for that. I wanted to be friends with her, but she wouldn't play with me. She didn't want me at her house and I knew it. Sometimes, when I tried to talk to her, she wouldn't even answer me. "My Daddy bought me Pick-Up Sticks. Do you want to play with me?" I asked, one more time. She just gave me a smirk and a grunt and walked away.

Her three older brothers were nice. They always let me play softball with them in the open field next to their house. Harry was the oldest, but Rich made most of the decisions about who played which position on the field because Harry wasn't as smart as Rich. The youngest brother, Al, played catcher, at the home base, and I played in the outfield. Harry and Rich took turns pitching and batting. I wished I didn't have to keep running after the ball.

"Rich, may I have a turn to bat?"

"No, you're too little. You have to be an outfielder."

I only played softball with them one Saturday and a few times after school. I was registered in the fourth grade and rode a school bus to school. I thought it was fun sitting in the back of the bus with Al, Rich and Harry, listening to the kids making a lot of noise, laughing and teasing each other.

"Look at the new girl. What's your name?" asked the girl who was sitting in front of me.

"Nancy Lee," I answered quietly.

"Don't talk to her!" Ruth ordered in a loud voice from where she sat in the front of the bus. The girl turned around. After that day, she never said anything to me again.

The school playground, which we used at recess, had swings and slides, just like the park. Whenever I got a turn to swing, I made it go high by pulling back on the chains that held the seat and pumping my legs, back and forth, the way my grandfather taught me. I liked the way it made my belly tickle and the feel of the breeze as it swished the cool air against my face.

Saturday was the day Aunt Molly and Uncle Hank went grocery shopping. It was also the day I found out how mean Uncle Hank could be! The boys and I were outside playing softball. Ruth stayed in the house. She didn't like to play softball with us. Aunt Molly came out of the house carrying Carol Jean and sat her down in the sandbox. "Nancy Lee, watch your sister until we get back. And, don't go in the house. Ruth isn't feeling good." Then, she walked away with Uncle Hank pulling the red wagon behind him.

After the softball game ended, I checked on Carol Jean and discovered that she had peed her diaper. It was sandy and dirty. I wanted to change the diaper, because I didn't want to get into trouble with Aunt Molly for not taking care of her as she told me to. "May I go in the house and get a diaper?" I asked Rich.

He said I could. I went in the house, passing Ruth who was lying on the couch listening to the radio. "Get out! You're not supposed to come in here!" Ruth screamed at me.

"Your brother said I could," I answered back, quickly grabbing a diaper from the top of Aunt Molly's dresser and running out the door. I changed Carol Jean's diaper just in time. Aunt Molly and Uncle Hank were coming back with the wagon full of groceries.

Although it was September, it was a warm day. They were both hot and sweaty. They hadn't even had a chance to go into the house to get a drink of water and cool off, when Ruth flung the screen door open. "Nancy Lee was in the house!" she shouted, snitching on me.

I ran to the house to give my reason. But I never got the chance. Uncle Hank grabbed me by the arm, pulled me into the kitchen, through the living room, and down the hall. He pushed me into the bedroom and threw me onto the bed. His lips thinned as he tightened his mouth. His nostrils flared as he sucked in his breath. He looked really mad and had a silly grin on his face. "I'll teach you to do what you're told!" He took off his belt, and he whipped me, and he whipped me, and he whipped me!

"I didn't do anything wrong. I didn't do anything wrong," I cried out, over and over, sobbing in pain from the stings of the leather strap, gasping for air as I tried to catch my breath. I must have hyperventilated because I lost consciousness.

When I opened my eyes, it was dark outside. Looking out the bedroom window, I saw a blinking light off in the distance. It reminded me of an angel, all white and glowing. I ached and I was sore all over. I kept looking at the blinking light until I fell asleep.

On Sunday morning, I awoke and was surprised to find Ruth wasn't in the bed with me. That night, she slept in bed with her parents. Aunt Molly came into the bedroom, threw off my blanket and told me, "Get up, Nancy Lee. Wash your face and comb your hair, but be quiet about it. I don't want you waking everyone up. Your father is coming this morning." I was still wearing the dress from the day before. I got up and went into the bathroom. As I was looking at my body covered with red welts, there was a loud knock on the kitchen door.

"Where is Nancy Lee?" I heard my father ask when Aunt Molly opened the door.

I ran out of the bathroom and threw my arms around my father, but I didn't cry. "Daddy, I'm glad you're here," I said, giving him a big hug. I was happy he was there because, now, I was afraid of Uncle Hank, who was sitting at the kitchen table with his silly grin.

"I know, Nancy Lee," my father said, as he put his hands on my wrists and looked at my arms. He didn't say another word, even though he saw the red welts all over my arms and legs. If he had looked under my dress, he would have seen red marks there, too. While my father was still holding my wrists, he gave Uncle Hank a hard stare. Then, he looked at Aunt Molly.

Uncle Hank got up from the kitchen table and hurried down the hall into the bathroom and closed the door. That was the last time that I ever saw Uncle Hank.

"Ralph, I was outside the whole time, I didn't know he was hitting her," Aunt Molly told my father, as she handed him my jacket and a brown paper bag.

"I'll deal with this later." He took the bag and led me by the hand out the kitchen door. I didn't know I was going to leave with him until he put the bag on the back seat of his car, and said, "Get in Nancy Lee, I'm taking you to my friend's house."

I climbed in and sat in the front seat beside him. "Daddy, see what Uncle Hank did to me?"

"I know, I'll take care of it." He pursed his lips tight and turned the key in the ignition.

"Daddy, I just wanted to change Carol Jean's diaper, so I wouldn't get hollered at."

My father drove us to Morris Place, a street off Seneca Street. As we rode, he told me that his friend's name was Elmer and he also worked at Socony-Vacuum Company. My father parked his car and pointed at a two-family house. "That's the house where my friend lives. He lives upstairs with his wife. Your brother, Bobby, is staying with them." The lower flat had a front porch, but the upper flat, where Elmer lived, didn't. The houses and the neighborhood looked old and shabby. Morris Place didn't look like the two-family houses and neighborhood where Nanny and Grandpa lived.

My father picked up the brown paper bag from the back seat and we headed toward the house. Up the steps and through the opened door, we walked into a dimly lit front hall and went up the stairs. When we got to the top, my father knocked on the door. There was no answer. After a few more knocks, a woman opened the door. The first thing I noticed was that she didn't have shoes on. "Come in Ralph." Turning to me, in a deep, flat voice, not a soft voice like my mother's voice, she asked, "You're Nancy Lee, right?"

I didn't answer. I just smiled and nodded my head. She was younger than my mother, and sort of pretty. She wore a lot of makeup and I liked her long blonde hair, even though it was kind of messy. I thought her clothes were too small for her. Her black skirt was too short and her red blouse didn't fit. Two rounds of flesh peeked out from the top of her blouse.

When my father and I walked into the house, the smell of crushed cigarette butts in the ashtrays and the odor of dirty laundry assaulted our nostrils. The flat was a dingy and cheerless place. The floors were covered with linoleum. The wallpaper was a faded pattern of a design that I didn't recognize. I didn't like this place, but I didn't want to go back to live with Uncle Hank.

"Elmer isn't here, I don't know when he'll be back," she told my father, as we walked into the living room. "Howard, my boarder, is in his bedroom," she added, indicating a doorway leading off the living room. "We'll talk in the kitchen, so we don't disturb him."

Bobby was sitting on the dirty, white, linoleum floor in the next room, playing with some toys. When he saw us, he got up and ran to my father, who had a big smile on his face. He leaned down and gave him a squeeze. "Daddy, see my truck?" Bobby said.

The flat only had two bedrooms. One was where the boarder slept and the second was where Elmer's wife slept. Elmer slept on a daybed in what would have been a dining room, but it didn't have a dining room table and chairs; it had a buffet, a daybed, a big, stuffed chair with a table and a lamp next to it.

As we walked toward the kitchen to the back of the house, Elmer's wife pointed to the second bedroom and said, "You'll sleep in this room with me. Put your things into one of the empty dresser drawers." The room had a double-size bed, an old crib and a dresser. The first drawer I pulled open was empty. I took my clothes out of the brown paper bag, and put them into the drawer. There wasn't much in the bag but underwear, socks, and two dresses. Where were my pajamas and my Pick-Up Sticks that were in the bag when my father took me to Aunt Molly's house?

I peeked into the other drawers. One held Bobby's clothes. Another had fancy underpants and brassieres, some red and some black. I liked the red, silky panties the best. Someday, I'll have pretty panties, too, I promised myself!

After I finished putting my things away, I went into the kitchen. My father sat at the table holding Bobby on his lap, while he talked with Elmer's wife. As I walked in, he was giving her some money. Then, I realized Bobby and I weren't staying there just because Elmer was his friend. Bobby and I were boarders, just like Howard.

Dogs were barking from behind the kitchen door. "Do you have a dog?" I asked.

"Two dogs. They stay in the hall. I don't let them into the house," she emphasized, pointing her finger at me.

"But, can I just see them?"

Elmer's wife got up and opened the door. The dogs wanted to come into the kitchen. Elmer's wife said, "Sit! Stay!" and they obeyed. The two dogs looked like Brownie, the German shepherd dog we used to have. But, these dogs didn't seem friendly.

My father sensed that I was a little afraid. "All you have to do is show them you're not afraid and they won't bite you." Standing at the open kitchen door, I reached out and petted them. They licked my hand, and it worked. I wasn't afraid anymore! I took off my jacket and hung it over the back of the kitchen chair and sat listening to Elmer's wife and my father finish talking about registering me at school.

My father stood up and put Bobby down. I followed him as he walked toward the living room and the front door. "You'll be okay, Nancy Lee. You won't have to stay here too long. I'm working on getting us all back together."

"Goodbye, Daddy. When will I see you again?" I asked, watching him walk out the door and down the stairs.

"I don't know, Nancy Lee, I have a lot of things to do—maybe in a few weeks. You be good now." He walked out onto the porch, closing the door behind him. I hurried to the front window near Howard's bedroom. His bedroom door was shut, so I knew I wasn't disturbing him. I stood quietly watching my father get into his car and drive away.

"May I go outside for a walk?" I asked Elmer's wife when I went back to the kitchen.

"Yeah. Take your brother, I think he'd like a walk, too."

I put on my jacket and Elmer's wife put a sweater on Bobby. We headed down the front stairs and out into the September afternoon where the weather had changed, bringing a cool relief from the previous week's last blast of summer heat. We walked down the short block of Morris Place that dead-ended. Then we crossed the street and walked back, passing Elmer's house and came to Seneca Street. There wasn't anyone outside, sitting on a porch or elsewhere in the neighborhood. Bobby was getting tired, so we ended our walk.

After we went into the house, I went to the bathroom. When I came out, Bobby was sitting at the kitchen table, eating. I hadn't eaten anything at Aunt Molly's house before I left, so I was hungry. "Sit down, Nancy Lee. I hope you like corn flakes?" Elmer's wife said, as she poured some into a bowl. I didn't want corn flakes, but that was all she offered. "When you're done eating, wash up and get ready for bed."

Bobby got down from the chair. She took his hand and walked him to the bedroom where she got him ready for bed. I took my time eating the corn flakes. Then, I picked up the bowl and drank the milk at the bottom. When I finished, I placed the bowl in the sink with the other dirty dishes.

I didn't have a toothbrush. That was another thing Aunt Molly forgot to put in the bag she handed my father. I just rinsed my mouth, splashed my face and went to the bedroom. Bobby was in the crib and Elmer's wife was already in the double-size bed. I thought it was too early for bed, because it was still light outside, but I did what I was told. "I don't have any pajamas. What will I sleep in?"

"Just get into bed in your underwear, like I do. You don't need pajamas tonight. I'll get you some later." Watching me undress, she added, "How did you get those marks?"

"Uncle Hank hit me because I changed my sister's diaper."

"Your father should kill that bastard."

I was glad she said that, because I didn't like Uncle Hank, anymore. I was also glad that I didn't have to sleep with Ruth, anymore. "Here, you sleep on the outside of the bed," she said, patting the mattress. That was fine with me. I didn't like sleeping next to the wall. I got into bed wondering how it was going to be staying here until my father found a house where we could be all together again.

The next morning, I took my dress from the drawer, pulled it on over my head and tied the bow in the back. I took the socks out of my shoes where I had tucked them the night before and put them on. "Hurry up, Nancy Lee, we have to get you to school, and I have to get to work," Elmer's wife called out as I fumbled to tie my shoes. In the kitchen, I took my seat at the table and ate the corn flakes and milk that Elmer's wife put in front of me. "Eat up, I'll be right back. The woman downstairs is going to watch your brother." Elmer's wife came back and said, "Ready? Grab your jacket. Let's go. I haven't got all day. I've got things to do."

Down the stairs and out the door we hurried. "Pay attention to how we get to the school, because you're going to walk back alone," she told me as we hurried along down the street. When we got to the corner, we turned right on Seneca Street. Two blocks down, we came to an empty store and stopped.

"This is where you'll eat your lunch. Put this dime in your pocket. When you get out of school for lunch, come here and give the man the dime. He'll give you some soup. Do you understand?" I didn't understand, but I said I did. I put the dime into my pocket and we walked the rest of the way to school. Elmer's wife talked to the principal and the assistant principal took me to a classroom.

When the lunch bell rang, the other kids headed home and I headed to the empty store. When I opened the big, glass door and went in, I saw that it wasn't really an empty store. There were long tables and chairs in the front of the store. Some men were sitting there, eating the soup they must have bought with their dimes. I went up to the counter near the back wall where a man was standing. He wore a white apron and a baseball cap. I put the dime on the counter and looked up at the man.

"What do you want, little girl?"

"Could I buy some soup with this dime?"

"Where's your mother?"

"She lives with Nanny."

"Where is your father?"

"He's working."

"Sure, little girl, you can have some soup. What's your name?" The man asked, lifting the visor of his baseball cap.

"My name is Nancy Lee," I answered, with a smile.

"Well, Nancy Lee, you come back here behind the counter. I'll get a chair and you can eat your soup here at the counter."

I thought he was a nice man. I never asked his name. I just called him "Mister." I ate the soup and went back to school.

After school I came back to the house on Morris Place, walked up the stairs to the second floor flat and knocked on the door. Elmer's wife opened it and said, "I see you found your way back. That's good. Did you get the soup?"

"Yes. And, the man was nice to me."

"Be careful about that," she said, pointing her finger at me. "Men aren't nice unless they want something from you." What did she mean? My father was nice, and that man was nice—they didn't want anything from me.

As Elmer's wife, Bobby and I were eating supper two men came into the kitchen. They looked at me, but didn't say anything. One man sat down at the table and the other took two bottles of beer from the refrigerator, giving one bottle to the man at the table. I guessed they must be Elmer and Howard, but I didn't know which man was Elmer and which man was Howard until Elmer's wife said, "That's Howard," pointing to one of the men, and "That's Elmer, he's my husband," pointing to the other.

I smiled at them, but they didn't smile back. They just drank their beer from the bottle, puffed on their cigarettes and looked at me. They didn't look anything like my father. My father was always clean and smelled good, because he splashed his face with after-shave. I thought Elmer and Howard needed a bath and a shave. But, most of all, they needed to comb their long, oily hair.

The next day after school, I knocked on the door and Elmer's wife opened it, but this time she made me stand in the hall. "Now, you need to be able to come into the house if I'm not here," she said, handing me a key that was tied on a string. "Take this key, I'm going to close and lock the door. I want you to open it with the key." I did what she told me, and the door opened. That's good. Now, whenever you leave the house, wear this key around your neck. I won't be here when you get back from school tomorrow, so you'll have to use the key to let yourself in."

"Thank you," I said, feeling real important because she gave me a key. I never had a key to a house before.

"Remember, if you lose it, you'll have to sit on the steps until I come home, so don't lose it," she said, heading into the kitchen to get us something to eat. As I passed the bedroom on my way to the kitchen, I noticed the old crib where Bobby slept wasn't in the bedroom. Bobby wasn't in the house, either.

"Where is my brother?"

"He went to live somewhere else," she said, crushing out her cigarette in the ashtray on the kitchen table.

"Where?" I asked. She told me she didn't know the people.

The next Sunday, when my father came to pay my board, I asked him where Bobby went. "Bobby and Carol Jean are together at my other friend's house." My father called everyone his "friend." I was glad that Carol Jean wasn't at Aunt Molly's house anymore.

Every school day was the same. Elmer's wife woke me by saying, "Get up, Nancy Lee, eat your breakfast and go to school. I'll be home later." The door closed behind her and I would be alone in the house except for the two German shepherd dogs. Howard and Elmer weren't in the house. They were already gone by the time I got out of bed. I put on the socks that I had tucked into my shoes the night before, and pulled a dress over my head. I was already wearing underpants and an undershirt because that's what I slept in. Elmer's wife never got pajamas for me, as she said she would.

In the kitchen, I took the milk from the refrigerator, poured it into the bowl with the corn flakes, and ate my breakfast in silence. When I finished, I put the milk back in the refrigerator next to the bottles of beer, and rinsed the bowl, leaving it in the sink. I picked up the key with the string, put it around my neck, grabbed my jacket from the back of the chair, put it on and zipped it up. I took the dime from the table, where Elmer's wife left it, put it in my pocket and went to school. At lunchtime, after I ate my bowl of soup, I walked back to school. After school, I went to Elmer's house, put the key in the lock, went in and waited at the living room window for Elmer's wife to come home.

The following week, another thing was added to my daily routine. I was asked to let the dogs out. "When you come home from school, go to the kitchen door, open it and walk down the back stairs; the dogs will follow you. When you open the door at the bottom of the stairs, let the dogs out into the yard. They can't get out of the yard because the gate is chained shut. Don't try to open the gate!" she said, with her finger pointed at me. "Close the door and come back upstairs. When I come home, I'll bring them in. Can you do that?"

"Yes, I can do that." When the weather was rainy or too cold, Elmer's wife told me not to let the dogs outside, but to open the attic door and let the dogs go up there to "do their duty."

I was happy to discover that a girl lived in the lower flat. One day, when I came back from school, she was sitting on the porch steps. She was a little older, a little taller and a little heavier than I was. She had straight, black hair and dark eyes. When she smiled, her crooked teeth made it impossible not to stare at her mouth. "Hi, I'm Patty. My mother told me you lived upstairs; do you want to walk around the neighborhood with me?" she asked.

"Hi, I'm Nancy Lee; I have to let the dogs out. I'll be right back." I hurried up the front stairs, unlocked the door, and ran through the house, down the back stairs, with the dogs barking as they followed behind me. Then, I ran up the back stairs, through the house and down the front stairs. Patty wasn't sitting on the steps, anymore, when I got outside.

I waited for her on the porch near the front window, hoping she would see me and come back out. Finally, she did. "My mother told me you were here. Why didn't you knock on the door?" I shrugged my shoulders in a gesture that showed I didn't know why. We talked and walked around the neighborhood until it started to get dark. Then, we went back to the house where Patty went into the lower flat. I walked upstairs, unlocked the door, went in and waited for Elmer's wife to come back.

Elmer wasn't in the house. He was probably still in a bar. That's where he usually was. I knew that because when he did come in the house he always smelled like he had been drinking. Howard was in the house. I knew that because the radio was playing music in the front bedroom. Howard usually stayed in his bedroom and kept to himself, except for the times when Elmer's wife went into his bedroom to visit with him.

On one of the days that I walked with Patty, just before we headed back to the house, she said, "I have to see somebody. Do you want to come with me?"

"Sure." I readily agreed, hoping to meet a new friend. We walked down Seneca Street one block from Morris Place. We continued walking down the side street until we came to the house directly behind the one that we lived in. Patty rang the doorbell, and a man came outside.

"This is my friend, Nancy Lee."

"Hello there, Nancy Lee," the man said, sticking the tip of his tongue out to wet his lips.

"Hello." I smiled, wondering why he looked at me in such a strange way.

"Wait here, we'll be right back." Patty said, walking away, hand and hand with the man. They left me standing by the side door and walked to the back of the driveway where a car was parked. I wondered if they were going to go somewhere. Then I knew they weren't, because they both got into the back seat of the car. In a little while they came out. The man looked at me, licked his lips again, and went into the house.

"Why did you get into the car?"

"This is why," Patty said, holding out two quarters. "If you want some quarters, too, he'll give you some. He told me he has enough for both of us."

"Why would he give us quarters?" I asked.

"To play with his monkey."

"I didn't see a monkey in the car."

"It's behind his zipper, in his pants."

"I don't want to be your friend anymore," I said as I walked away. I knew what Patty did in the back seat of the car. I knew it was dirty and it was wrong! I hurried down the street, back to the house on Morris Place.

I decided to try to make friends with my cousin Esther. Aunt Mary Ann and Uncle Saul lived in the area. Esther and I were close in age and even looked somewhat alike; she had auburn hair and hazel eyes, like mine. I saw her in the playground during recess, but I don't think she recognized me, because she turned away when I called out to her.

One day, after letting the dogs out, I walked back to school and began walking the streets, until I found the house where Esther lived. It was a little, green house, with black shutters on the sides of the windows. I knew what her house looked like because when my father and I were staying at my grandparents' house we went there one evening after supper. I played the game of jacks on the sidewalk with Esther, while my father talked with his brother.

Aunt Mary Ann was a small, thin woman with long, dark hair. She was quiet and shy. Even though she didn't talk much, I still liked her and I think my mother liked her, too. "Nancy Lee, what are you doing here?" Aunt Mary Ann asked when she opened the door.

"I don't live with my grandparents, now. I live with other people until my father can find us a house," I answered, hoping she would invite me inside.

"I know that, but what are you doing here, now?"

"I want to know if Esther can come out and play?"

"Wait here, I'll get her," she said, as she closed the door. When Esther came to the door, I could tell she wasn't happy that she had to go outside. We sat on the porch steps and talked. I told her how our cousin, Ruth, was being a stuck-up and wouldn't play with me and how Uncle Hank hit me with his belt. Esther didn't seem to care. We told each other the names of our teachers and talked about the school and some of the kids at school.

I wanted to tell Esther that today was my birthday, I was nine years old, but she didn't give me a chance. She didn't want to stay outside any longer because she was cold and it was time for her dinner. Esther got up and went in her house. With misty eyes, I walked back to Elmer's house. I longed for my family to be together again in the housing project where we used to live; where I felt safe and loved. And, where I could take a bath!

"We can't use the bathtub because the faucets are broken," Elmer's wife said, when I first asked if I could take a bath and wash my hair. "You can bathe and wash your hair in the bathroom sink." Every Saturday night, before going to bed, I bathed by running the water until it was warm, washing my face, arms, legs, feet, and private parts with the bar of green soap setting on the dirty, bathroom sink. Then, I washed my hair with the same bar of soap.

Some days, after school, I also washed my clothes in the same sink, with a bar of green soap. After I finished squeezing out the soapy water, I carried my socks, underwear and dress upstairs to the attic, where the dogs lay on the dusty, wooden floor and watched me throw my wet clothes over the single, rope line strung from one end of the attic to the other. I had to be careful not to step on the fresh poop, because once when I did, it was hard to get all the stinky mush off the bottom of my shoe. It was all right if I stepped on the dry poop, because that would just crumble.

At the top of the attic stairs was one light bulb with a string to turn it on. It didn't do much to light up the attic. The windows, at each end of the dark, cold attic had boards nailed across the window frames without glass.

Some days, shafts of sunlight streamed in between the slots of the boards. When I reached my hand up to grab at the sunlight, the dust made swirls of tiny sparkles. The dust sparkles reminded me of shining stars. Standing in the attic by the window, I became transfixed on a moment in time when we lived on Duerstein Street. I remembered when Tommy and I sat on the front porch, with the many bright, sparkling stars scattered about in the dark sky. I remembered the coolness of the night air and the music coming from the open door to our living room.

I closed my eyes and softly whispered, "Star light, star bright, I wish I may, I wish I might have the wish I wish tonight. I wish I could be with Tommy again. I wish our family could be back together again." After a few minutes of remembering the fun I had playing with Tommy, I walked back down the attic stairs and into the kitchen to wait for Elmer's wife to come back.

Another wish I had was that Elmer wouldn't mumble so much while I tried to fall asleep. Sometimes, Elmer's wife, lying next to me, yelled out to him, "Shut up, you bastard." When I did fall asleep, despite his mumbling, her yelling would jolt me awake.

One night, when I was asleep, I was startled awake and it wasn't because of her yelling. I vaguely remember feeling a body lying next to me and smelling alcohol mixed with tobacco on someone's breath. A hand was on my tummy and it was sliding down into my underpants. I was startled and bolted up to a sitting position. It was Elmer's hand! Elmer's wife woke up. "Get out of here, you bastard!" she yelled at him.

He got out of the bed, mumbling something and went back to his daybed outside the bedroom door. Tired as I was, I fought off sleep for as long as I could, afraid Elmer would try to come into the bedroom, again. I didn't sleep well that night. What would I have done if Elmer's wife hadn't been there? I couldn't defend myself against a drunken man. After that experience, I never slept easily in another person's house.

Even though my life was filled with new experiences and events. I was surprised when my father said, "You have a new baby brother; his name is Jimmy." My father gave me the news the first Sunday in November when he came to visit and pay for my board.

Many years later, I heard the story of my brother Jimmy's birth as told by my father. My mother was in the early stages of labor. Nanny had notified my father so he could leave work and be with my mother. My father hurried to their house, arriving in the late afternoon. Nanny and Grandpa took Tommy for a ride in their car, so that my parents could be alone.

"Ralph, the contractions aren't really that bad, so let's wait a little longer before we go to the hospital." They sat at the kitchen table talking. It wasn't long before my mother said, "Ralph! I think my water just broke!" Then, she had a really strong contraction and slid from the chair to lie on the kitchen floor. She moaned, "Oh! Oh! Oh my God! Oh my God! The baby's coming!"

My father ran to the back hall and down the stairs to the neighbor below. He banged on the door. When it opened, he commanded in a loud voice, "Mrs. Huddle, Lorraine is having the baby, come quick!" He and Mrs. Huddle hurried up the stairs, and into the kitchen where my mother lay. The baby's head was crowning; my mother was about to give birth.

Describing the delivery in my father's own words: "The baby popped out like a ripe banana." My baby brother was born on Nanny's shiny, kitchen floor. My father laid the baby on my mother's stomach where she cradled him in her arms. Then, he twisted the umbilical cord tight around his finger to cut off the flow of blood between the baby and the placenta until it was delivered. The ambulance arrived and took my mother and baby brother to the hospital, with my father following behind in his car.

From the first day a child is born, it needs to be loved and cared for so the child may be happy. But, not every child is given that attention and not every day is happy. For me, Saturday was not a happy day. On Saturday, Elmer's wife, dressed in her short skirt, low-cut blouse and high-heel shoes, called to me from the bedroom, where she stood in front of the dresser mirror putting on her red lipstick and stinky perfume, "Hurry and finish your breakfast, Nancy Lee. I have to get to work. Grab your jacket and let's go!"

Gulping down the milk in the cereal bowl, I grabbed my jacket, and hurried down the stairs after her. We walked to Seneca Street, and waited for the bus that took us downtown, where the City Hall, savings banks, hotels, major department stores, theaters, restaurants and many office buildings were located. Downtown Buffalo, on Saturday, was always crowded with people, hurrying about, shopping or attending to business.

We got off the bus at a corner on Main Street in the heart of the city. On the corner was a newsstand. The walls inside had racks of magazines and a small blue, wooden box with a hinged lid sat nearby. The box held the *Courier Express* newspapers. "George, this girl is staying with me. She'll have to wait here. I can't leave her alone all day with Elmer being home and all." The man, at the newsstand didn't say anything. He just looked at me and nodded his head. I knew he wasn't happy about it.

George was older than my father, but not as old as my grandfather. He was tall and lean. Even with his long, black coat on, I knew he didn't have muscles like my father. He combed his shiny, black hair straight back, without a part. His face was clean-shaven, but I sensed his body wasn't kept very clean. Elmer's wife talked to George for a minute. He told her about some men named John who were waiting for her. Pointing her finger at me, she said, "Wait here and don't leave. I have to go to work. I'll be back later." Then, she walked away.

George didn't talk to me much. He didn't even ask me what my name was. If he did say something to me he called me "girlie." He kept busy selling magazines and talking to the men who stopped by the newsstand. Elmer's wife came back sometimes to talk to George for a few minutes and then she was off again, to do some more "tricks" for the people she worked for. I wondered what tricks she could do, but I never asked.

It grew dark and the wind picked up. In the streetlights, I could see tiny sparkles as the moisture in the air turned to snow. I was so very cold. At last, Elmer's wife returned and handed George some money. We rode the bus back to the flat where I ate the Spam sandwich she gave me, and hurried into bed to get warm. I didn't dream much, but when I did, my dreams were mostly about food, warm baths or the times when I was with my family. On some nights, I went to bed so hungry my stomach growled. Listening to it growl took my mind from how cold I was.

Every Saturday, we rode the bus downtown regardless of the weather. I stayed with George while I waited for Elmer's wife to come back. Sometimes she was gone for almost the whole day. I was cold. I was always cold. There was nothing I could do to keep warm. I wore dresses then, so my legs were exposed to the harsh winds, stinging and nipping at my bare legs. Elmer's wife wore real short skirts, but she didn't seem to mind the cold. I was glad that we didn't go downtown on Sundays, too. Sunday was the day my father came to pay my board.

Boxes of candy bars were lined up against the back wall of the newsstand. I was hungry, but I didn't have any money to buy one. George must have noticed me looking, because he picked up a Three Musketeers candy bar and handed it to me. He didn't say anything, he just handed me the candy bar. "Thank you George," I said, with a grateful smile, wishing he had given me a Butterfinger, Mars or Almond Joy candy bar. Then, I remembered that my grandfather once told me, "Beggars can't be choosers."

On a Saturday in December, Elmer's wife finished her work and returned to the newsstand earlier than usual. We walked down Main Street to one of the major department stores. As we walked, she said, "I want to get a picture of you with Santa. You probably know he's not a real Santa, but pretend he is and tell him what you want for Christmas. It's okay to pretend."

When my turn came, Santa asked, "What do you want for Christmas, little girl?"

Tears were beginning to wet my eyes. I knew if I started to talk, I would cry, and I couldn't do that with all the people around and Santa's helper about to take my picture. I bit my lip and shook my head, as if to say, "Nothing." I turned and faced the camera. "Snap!" the picture was taken and the ordeal was over.

Elmer's wife paid the three dollars for the photo. We left the store and headed for the bus stop. "Why didn't you smile?" Elmer's wife asked as she put the photo in her pocket.

On the Sunday before Christmas, I awoke and dressed in the better of my two dresses. I was excited, because my father would be coming. He came every Sunday afternoon except when he was too busy and couldn't make it. Elmer's wife, wearing a black, silk robe over her black bra and panties sat in the living room on the couch with the dirty floral-print slipcover, smoking a cigarette while I ate my corn flakes. There was a knock at the door. Elmer's wife got up to answer it. "Come on in, Ralph—Nancy Lee, your father's at the door." she called to me

I jumped from the chair and ran to the front door. "Why are you here so early, Daddy? Did you find us a house?" I blurted out as I ran into the living room not caring that Elmer was still asleep on the daybed and Howard was still asleep in his bedroom.

"No, not yet. We're going to Nanny's house, so you can see your mother and baby brother. Don't just stand there, get your jacket so we can get going." I hurried back to the kitchen, put the string with the house key around my neck, tucked it under the collar of my dress, grabbed my jacket from the back of the chair, put it on and zipped it up. What a surprise! I was going to see my mother, my baby brother and Tommy. Only four months had passed since my mother and Tommy left me and drove off with Grandpa, but it seemed so much longer.

Back in the living room, Elmer's wife was showing my father the picture of me with Santa. "I took Nancy Lee to see Santa, and for five dollars I got this picture. I knew you would want me to buy it." My father thanked her, gave her five dollars and put the picture in his jacket pocket. She lied to my father; she only paid three dollars for it, but I didn't say anything. Why didn't I say something?

We walked down the stairs, out the door and into the cold winter morning. "Daddy, where's your car?"

"Oh, I sold it. It isn't so bad taking the bus."

"But Daddy, it's cold taking the bus," I complained as we walked along the street toward the bus stop. I didn't have a hat or gloves, just my jacket to protect me from the harsh blasts of cold air. We had to take two buses to get to the corner of Genesee Street and Goodyear Avenue.

There we got off. Now the wind had really picked up and my father had to hold his brown fedora to keep it from blowing off. "Daddy, I'm cold, I said, as we began walking down the street to Nanny's house.

"Put up the collar of your jacket and keep your hands in your pockets. That'll help a little." I did and that gave me some protection against the bitter winds. With our mouths closed and our heads lowered to our chests, we hurried along without talking because the wind discouraged any conversation.

We reached the light-blue house with the white trim, walked up the porch steps, and my father opened the front door. Inside the hall, we were safe from the freezing cold of the winter day. My father shook the snow from his hat and stomped the snow from his shoes. I stomped my shoes, too, just like he did. That made him smile.

As we walked up the stairs, I smelled the familiar scent of lemon oil. I remembered Nanny's house; it was always spotless and not a thing was out of place. The cream-colored linoleum floor in the kitchen had a high wax shine and the ceramic tile floor in the bathroom was sparkling white. Everything in their house shined; the dining room furniture, the tables in the living room, and even the wooden floor around the rugs in the living room and the dining room were dust free and polished. When we reached the top of the stairs, my father knocked on the door to the second floor flat.

"Merry Christmas," Nanny said, when she opened the door.

"Merry Christmas, Ralph," Grandpa said, shaking my father's hand. "Hey, Squirt, Merry Christmas," he said, with his big smile.

"Merry Christmas, Nanny and Grandpa," I said, taking off my jacket and handing it to Nanny.

"Nancy Lee, come see your baby brother," my mother said, from where she sat on the couch, cradling a baby in her arms.

I was confused. My mother seemed very distant. She spoke to me as if I had just returned from school, or had come in from playing outside. Didn't she understand that I wasn't the same little girl she left behind? Didn't she understand that I just came from a world far removed from hers? Where was my mother, the one whom I knew so well? At that moment, I didn't feel connected to her anymore.

Tommy was on the floor, playing with the train that was going in circles under the Christmas tree, where Grandpa had set up a little village on the sheet of soft white cotton behind the train tracks. There was a blue church with a steeple, a red, brick schoolhouse, and a toyshop set among the little evergreen trees.

"Nancy Lee, how do you like where you're living? Dad said that you have the whole house to yourself and two dogs, like Brownie, to play with. You sure are lucky."

I didn't think I was lucky. "Hi, Tommy," was all that I said. I didn't tell him anything about Elmer's house. He might think I was a crybaby. Elmer's house didn't have any holiday decorations and it smelled dirty and musty. Nanny's house was decorated and it had a real Christmas tree, with bright, colored lights. Presents with red and green bows were piled near the tree and the Christmas song, *"Joy to the World,"* was playing on the radio. The alcove off the living room had a daybed; that's where Tommy slept. He could look at the Christmas tree as he went to sleep. He was the lucky one.

I sat on the couch next to my mother and looked at the baby in her arms. Jimmy was two months old, now. He was really cute. "Do you want to hold him?" My mother didn't wait for my answer; she put him in my arms and handed me his bottle. He smiled at me just before he opened his mouth to grab onto the nipple.

The house smelled so good. The kitchen was filled with the aroma of roasting turkey, with stuffing of dried bread cubes, onions, celery, walnuts, sausage and sage. "Come on everyone, it's time to eat," Nanny called, as she left the kitchen and headed toward the dining room with a bowl of mashed potatoes.

In the bedroom off the dining room was the crib that Carol Jean used to sleep in. It was against the wall, near a vanity dresser. My mother finished burping Jimmy and put him in the crib. Tommy stopped playing with the train and came to the dining room table with my father and me. When we were all seated, Grandpa brought in the platter with the golden-brown turkey and set it on the table next to the gravy. The turkey had white paper leggings on the drumsticks. We all bowed our heads. As everyone prayed, "Bless us Lord and these Thy gifts..." I silently prayed, *"Please God, help me, I don't want to live at Elmer's house, anymore."*

We feasted on the holiday meal, enjoying all of the traditional foods. Some of my favorites were sweet potatoes, acorn squash, and cranberry sauce. For dessert, we ate Nanny's homemade fruitcake and mincemeat pie with vanilla ice cream. I stuffed myself with as much as I could eat. I was happy to be with my family again.

After the table was cleared and the dishes were washed, we went into the living room and opened presents. I got a new blue sweater and a red mesh Christmas stocking filled with cellophane-wrapped candy and a big striped candy cane. There was also a coloring book and a small box of crayons in the stocking.

When it was time to leave, I put on my new blue sweater and buttoned it up before putting on my jacket. Proudly, I carried my red mesh stocking. This time, I made sure that I got a chance to hug everyone and say goodbye. "Goodbye, Mama. Goodbye, Tommy. Goodbye, baby Jimmy. Goodbye, Nanny. Goodbye, Grandpa."

I had mixed feelings, as I walked down the stairs and out the door. I was happy, but I was sad, too. I didn't want to go back to live at Elmer's house. I silently prayed again, "*Please God, help me. I don't want to live at Elmer's house, anymore.*" When we left, it was twilight and the winds had stopped. It wasn't as cold as it was earlier that day, or maybe it didn't seem as cold, because I was wearing my new sweater, or maybe it was because I felt a warm glow inside, after seeing my family again.

My father and I rode the two buses back. When we reached Elmer's house, my father opened the door and we walked into the hall. There was a smell of something burning. As we started up the stairs, we noticed smoke coming through the crack at the bottom of the door. My father hurried to the top of the stairs and banged on the door, but nobody answered. Elmer, Howard and Elmer's wife weren't there. In the back hall, the dogs were barking.

My father turned around, grabbed my hand and pulled me down the stairs after him. He was about to bang on the door of the downstairs flat. "Wait, Daddy, I have a key to open the door." I dropped my red mesh stocking, took the key from around my neck and handed it to him.

"Stay here!" he ordered, grabbing the key and running back up the stairs. I didn't obey. I followed after him. He unlocked the door and hurried into the house, running toward the kitchen where the smoke was heaviest. It was pouring out from above the stove and from the cracks around the oven door. My father flung open the oven door, grabbed the potholders near the stove and pulled out a pan with a burnt chicken. It was charcoal-black and still smoking.

He threw the pan into the sink, turned on the faucet and doused the pan and burnt chicken with water. As he turned off the oven, he asked, "Why do you have a key to this house? Who gave it to you?"

"I need it to get back in the house after school."

His face was red. He clenched his jaws tight. He was really angry! "Get your things; you're going to your grandmother's house with me!" He shoved me along into the bedroom. I took out the few clothes that were in the dresser drawer. He stuffed them into the front of his brown leather jacket and zipped it up.

We went down the stairs to the front hall, where I had dropped my red mesh Christmas stocking. Picking it up, I followed after my father, hurrying back down the street to catch the Seneca Street bus that would take us to my grandparents' house. That night, I slept on their little velvet settee in the dining room, where I had slept before. Snuggled under the blanket, I listened to the pendulum clock ticking away the hours as I dozed off.

My prayer had been answered. I wasn't going to live at Elmer's house anymore. But I wasn't going to live with my family either. The next day my father didn't go to work. After breakfast, we rode the Seneca Street bus to the downtown bus station and got on a second bus that took us to another part of the city. We got off and walked down one block. "This is it," he said, when we came to a brick building. Wide concrete steps led up to the front door. Inside, to the right was the office.

My father introduced himself to the woman standing near a file cabinet. She was short and stout, with dark hair. She directed us to an open door leading into another office and told us to go in. "I phoned you earlier this morning. This is my daughter, Nancy Lee," my father told the woman sitting behind the desk. He took a seat in front of the desk. I took off my jacket and new blue sweater and sat next to him.

"Hello Nancy Lee, I'm sure you'll like it here with us. We have a lot of girls your age living here." I returned her smile and sat quietly. She was about my grandmother's age and she had short hair like my grandmother's hair. My father began the conversation by asking about the cost and payment arrangements for me to live there.

"Let Mrs. Sawyer take Nancy Lee upstairs while we talk, shall we? Mrs. Sawyer, come in here, please?" The woman in the front office came into the room. "Mrs. Sawyer, take Nancy Lee upstairs."

"Come with me, Nancy Lee." Mrs. Sawyer said. She walked out of the office with me tagging behind. I followed her, thinking she was going to show me around upstairs and then we would go back downstairs so I could say goodbye to my father. I was wrong.

We walked up the wide staircase to the second floor. Mrs. Sawyer took me into a small bedroom and said, "Wait here, I'll be back shortly." The bedroom had a twin-size bed, a small dresser and a little table with two chairs. The room also had a door, which I thought was a closet door. When I opened the door, I was surprised to see it was a little bathroom with a toilet and a sink.

The windows facing toward the street had black bars on them. I stood at the window for a minute watching the people across the street. After a minute or two, I needed to use the little bathroom. When I came back to the window, I looked out again and saw my father standing on the other side of the street at the bus stop. Through the closed window, I called to him. "Daddy, Daddy, I'm here—Daddy, Daddy, I'm here, look up!" He didn't hear me. The bus came and took him away.

I ran to the door leading into the hall. The hall was empty. I stood there for a long while. I wanted Mrs. Sawyer or someone to come and talk to me. I wanted to know if my father was going to come back and say goodbye. I loved my father very much. I cried inside, because I didn't know when I would see him again. Finally, I gave up. Going back to window I looked out at the bleak winter day and let the hot tears flow.

After what seemed like a long time, Mrs. Sawyer came back with a tray of food. "Nancy Lee, I brought you dinner." She set the tray on the table and left the room. Slowly, I ate the mashed potatoes and meatloaf. My mother often made meatloaf and mashed potatoes; that was one of my father's favorite meals. As I chewed my food, I closed my eyes and pretended I was back home in the projects, eating dinner with my family.

After I cleaned the plate with the slice of buttered bread and drank the glass of milk, I went back to the window to watch the cars drive down the street and the people walking by. I stood there until the sky began to get dark.

The door opened and Mrs. Sawyer came in. "Take off your dress and get into bed, Nancy Lee." She picked up the tray and left the room, closing the door behind her. I climbed in between the two, smooth, white sheets and tucked the white blanket under my chin. My head sunk into the pillow like it was sinking into a fluffy white cloud. Soon, sleep overtook me and I was off to dreamland.

"Get up, Nancy Lee, the nurse is here to examine you." The voice was Mrs. Sawyer's, who was standing beside my bed with a woman in a white dress; the same kind of dress a school nurse wore.

The woman checked my head for lice and my body for any open sores. She looked in my mouth and in my ears. "You're in good shape, Nancy Lee. We just need to fatten you up a bit."

The nurse left and Mrs. Sawyer said, "Follow me."

"Where are we going?" I asked, following her down the hall.

"You're going to shower and wash your hair. After today, you'll shower and wash your hair on Saturdays with the other girls." We came to an archway. Passing through it we entered the shower room, which had a lot of showerheads coming out of the wall. Mrs. Sawyer turned on one of the showers and adjusted the water temperature, while I took off my undershirt and underpants.

Mrs. Sawyer handed me a tiny bar of white soap and stood there watching me as I washed. I didn't like her watching me, but there was nothing I could do about it. When I finished, I turned to hand her the soap. "No, you're not done. Wash your hair." When I finished, she turned off the water and handed me a towel. I dried off and held the towel up in front of me as I combed my wet hair.

"Follow me." Passing through another archway, we entered the locker room with square wooden boxes lining the walls. "This is your locker, Nancy Lee," she said, pointing to one of the square boxes. "There are some clothes in there, for you. Get dressed." In the locker were white underpants and undershirts, white socks, one white slip, two pair of pajamas and two cotton dresses.

After I dressed, I followed Mrs. Sawyer through another archway and into a room with toilets lined in a row on one side, and sinks lined in a row on the other side. Mrs. Sawyer handed me a toothbrush, "Wet your left hand and hold it palm up." She poured some white powder in it. "Now, wet the toothbrush and rub it into the powder to make a paste and brush your teeth. It felt good to brush my teeth with a toothbrush again, instead of with my finger.

When I finished, we walked down the wide staircase. At the bottom of the stairs, we turned and walked down the hall, coming to a room with another archway, which was the dining room. It was filled with rows of long tables and chairs pushed up tight to the tables. "Sit down, I'll get your breakfast." Mrs. Sawyer came back with a tray and set a bowl in front of me, "Here is your oatmeal." Then, she put a tablespoon of something thick and dark into a glass of milk, stirred it and told me, "Drink this, it's good for you." I drank the milk mixture but only ate a little oatmeal. I didn't like it. Mrs. Sawyer brought my jacket into the room, but my new blue sweater wasn't with it. Where was it? I wanted to ask, but I didn't. "We're going to register you in school today."

We left the orphanage through the front door and down the wide, concrete steps. It wasn't snowing, but it was cold. I put my collar up and my hands in my pocket. Mrs. Sawyer led the way, with me walking beside her. At a corner, we crossed the street and walked down another block until we came to a school. "This is where you'll go to school. You'll eat your lunch in school. After school, come straight back home." She called the orphanage "home." It wasn't a home—it was a red brick building! We entered the front of the school through one of the big double doors. I was registered in the fourth grade for the third time!

The day went as Mrs. Sawyer said it would. The school bell rang, signaling that school was over for the day. All us children got up from our desks and went into the cloakroom. I put on my jacket and zipped it up. We left the classroom together, walking single-file down the hall. We hurried through the double-doors out into the falling snow and cold blasts of winter winds.

Once outside, I didn't recognize where I was. I thought I was going to exit through the front of the school building with the double door that Mrs. Sawyer and I had entered. Instead, I had exited through the double doors in the back of the school building. I stood for a few minutes trying to figure out which way to go. Through the white falling snow, I saw a large brick building a few blocks away and headed toward it. On closer look, I realized that it wasn't the orphanage. I was lost, but too ashamed to ask anyone for directions to the orphanage. I wandered about the neighborhood trying to find my way back.

Hurrah! I finally found the orphanage. I walked up the wide concrete steps, opened the front door and went inside. As I passed the office on the right, Mrs. Sawyer saw me and called out, "You shouldn't use the front door Nancy Lee, and where have you been? We've been waiting for you!"

"I got lost," was all Mrs. Sawyer gave me a chance to say.

"You couldn't get lost, the school isn't that far from here. Come with me. Miss Dotty is waiting for you in the toy room," she said in a huff, grabbing my hand and pulling me along after her. Who was Miss Dotty? Where was the toy room?

We walked up the wide staircase and down the hall, stopping where a group of girls stood chatting and wandering about in a room. The room didn't have any windows. The ceiling globes provided the only light in the room. The walls were lined with brown, wooden benches. Inside the door, a woman sat at a small table. She was about the same age as Elmer's wife. She had short, brown hair with bangs, and she was plump. "Miss Dotty, this is Nancy Lee; she said that she got lost coming home." Mrs. Sawyer walked away and left me standing next to the table.

Miss Dotty changed from a stone-faced stare to a grin. She got up and walked over to me. Wham! She slapped me across the face! "We will have none of that foolishness. You didn't get lost." After she spoke and slapped me, she was stone-faced again. I was too shocked to cry. Besides, the other girls were watching, and I didn't want them to think I was a crybaby. "Now go and play, Nancy Lee."

I walked over to the wooden benches and sat down. The other girls just looked at me, but not one of them came over to me. I think they were afraid to talk to me, because they saw Miss Dotty was angry with me. I shut my eyes tight. For a moment, nothing existed.

A bell rang. It sounded just like the school bell. The girls and I lined up in a single row. We followed Miss Dotty down the wide staircase and into the room where I had eaten my breakfast. The room was filled with boys and girls of all ages. Each child stood behind a chair. I didn't know where I should stand, until Miss Dotty pointed to a chair. "Nancy Lee, this will be your chair."

A voice from a loud speaker said, "Bless us, Oh Lord, and these Thy gifts we are about to receive…Amen." Then, all the children and I pulled out the chairs and sat down. After the meal, we walked single-file up the wide staircase and back to the toy room.

There weren't many good toys under the lids of the benches. The dolls had missing hair and clothes, the games were all mixed up, the puzzles were missing pieces and the coloring books were all colored. Even if I could find a page to color, there weren't any red crayons. We stayed in the playroom until Miss Dotty said, "All right, girls, it's time to get ready for bed."

The girls took turns using the toilets. I hesitated when it came my turn, because the toilets weren't in stalls; there wasn't any privacy. "Nancy Lee, sit on the toilet! There will be no getting up once you're in bed!" Miss Dotty demanded. At the sink, I stood behind the other girls, and waited for my turn to wash my hands, splash my face and brush my teeth. As the other girls were doing, I cupped my hand to catch the water, lapping it up with my tongue to rinse my mouth and take a drink. I dried my hands on the rolling cloth towels in one of the machines on the wall.

In the locker room, I took off my dress, folded it, and put it into my square locker-box on the wall along with my shoes. Then, I put my socks and underwear into the cloth laundry bag setting on the floor. It felt good to put on pajamas again. All the other girls had the same yellow pajamas with long sleeves and long legs. Mine were a little too long, so I turned up the pant legs.

When we were all in our pajamas, we walked down the hall to the dormitory, another large room. Along two side walls and the wall with the entrance were twin-size beds, one for each girl. The beds all looked the same with white sheets and a gray blanket. At the far end of the room, opposite the entrance, was a row of windows that had black bars on them, just like the other room had. Miss Dotty pointed to a bed near the door, "This will be your bed, Nancy Lee."

On Saturday morning, naked, with my right forearm across my chest and my left hand covering my private area, I followed the other girls into the shower room. "Nancy Lee, come over here." Miss Dotty said. She stood near the sink, holding a pair of scissors.

"Please, Miss Dotty, I don't like short hair. I promise to keep it braided," I pleaded, knowing what she was going to do, because all the other girls had very short hair.

"It has to be cut. We don't want any place for lice to lay eggs, do we?" she said, with a big grin. Facing the mirror, I stood, naked and helpless. With every snip of the scissors, a tear rose in my throat, but I didn't cry.

The days and nights were all the same with a few exceptions such as the drills. After we were all in bed and I had just drifted off to sleep, I was startled awake by the bright, overhead lights coming on, and the shouts of a loud voice. "Get up everyone!" A female voice shouted again, "You know the drill. Into the hall!" I wondered what was happening? Was there a fire?

I jumped out of bed and went into the hall with the other girls who were forming a line with their backs about one foot away from the wall, making it impossible to lean against it. It wasn't Miss Dotty who woke us. This matron was very tall and thin with graying hair. Her skin was pockmarked and pulled tight against her high cheekbones. "There's no talking! You know there's to be no talking in the dormitory!" the woman shouted at us again. Then, she sat down at the little table in the hall. Every so often, she shouted something about not talking. We were all standing there quietly, drifting in and out of dreamland. She was the only one talking.

We stood there in a sleepy, unreal stupor for what I thought was a very long time. When my head fell to my chest, I snapped it back, waking myself. I tried to stay awake, but I couldn't keep my head from falling forward. Finally, we were allowed to go back to our beds and go to sleep. I dreaded the drills!

My memories and dreams were enhanced by my imagination. Some nights, before falling off to sleep, I imagined rising out of my body and floating through the sky. I imagined flying to a far-away place; where the sun shined bright and the fields below were filled with pretty, colored flowers. I imagined a pond of clear, blue water. On the far side of the pond, I imagined that I saw a man and I imagined that he spoke to me and told me that he loved me.

"Nancy Lee, who are you talking to?" a loud voice asked, jolting me awake one morning. I opened my eyes and saw Miss Dotty standing beside the bed.

"I wasn't talking. I was sleeping."

"Don't lie to me! You weren't sleeping. I heard you talking!" Miss Dotty said, throwing the cover off me.

It wasn't until many years later when I learned that it was true—I did talk in my sleep. The first person to confirm it would be my husband, Joe. He would tell me how he found it amusing that I would answer his questions while I was asleep.

In the mornings when I walked to school, the air was still cool and windy even though the snow had all melted. Soon it would be Easter. One day after school, when I went into the toy room, Miss Dotty said, "Everyone line up. Nancy Lee's grandfather brought you girls a treat." On her little table was a paper plate with small chunks of milk chocolate candy. I guessed that it must have been Grandpa Meyer who brought the chocolate candy because once he had brought a big chocolate bunny for Tommy and me to share. I stood in line with the other girls and took a chunk of milk chocolate.

We only got candy on Saturdays after our showers. Miss Dotty brought out a big covered tin, which held an assortment of cellophane-wrapped candy—little Tootsie Rolls, dark and light caramels, and Mary Jane chews. I didn't like any of them.

Sunday was the real treat day. Following the church service in the basement, we had the main meal at lunch. At supper, we were served a paper plate with a handful of potato chips, a big dollop of peanut butter and a scoop of vanilla ice cream. I thought Sunday suppers were the best meals of the week!

On Easter Sunday, a celebration was held in the orphanage basement. Some older women from a nearby church acted as adoptive grandmothers to us "forlorn" children. I didn't think the women really cared about us. I thought it was just a way for them to feel good about themselves. Each girl was matched up with one of the women, to sit next to for the celebration.

"I'll be your grandmother for today," the woman told me. I didn't like her. She asked me too many questions: "How do you like it here?" "How do you like school?" "Do you have brothers and sisters?" "Where do they live?"

My answers were the same to every question: "I don't know." "I don't know." "I don't know." I wouldn't tell her anything. She wasn't my real grandmother. She was only there for the day.

Neither did I like the spring winds that blew the rain into my face on the way to-and-from school, but the wind also brought a reminder that warm weather would soon bring school to a close. I don't remember much about the school, except the day when the teacher said, "If any of you children has a hobby or a collection, you can bring it into school tomorrow."

I raised my hand and asked, "What's a hobby?" The kids laughed at me. I asked the question because I thought a hobby was an object.

"It's something that you like to do: Do you play a musical instrument? Do you paint or draw? Do you make model planes?" she explained. "What do you like to do, Nancy Lee?"

I thought for a minute, then, I answered, "I don't know." The kids all laughed at me again. I had changed school three times. Despite that, I passed the fourth grade.

With school over, there wasn't much to do. The summer days were dull, not bright and sunny as I remembered them. I wished I could play with Tommy or Jeanie. I was beginning to lose hope of that ever happening again.

The playground was the only place I could go. We were told, "Everyone outside to the playground. You shouldn't be in the toy room on a day like this." The playground was in the back of the orphanage, facing a street that ran parallel to the street with the front entrance. It was enclosed with a tall, black, iron fence. There were always one or two matrons in the playground keeping watch on us. I didn't stand in line with the other girls waiting for a turn to swing. Usually, I just stood by the fence watching the people across the street. They did things like wash their car, cut the grass, or sit on the porch reading the newspaper.

In the early summer, a few days after the school year ended, I was in the playground standing at the fence, with my dress billowing in the warm breeze. One of the matrons came over to me, "Nancy Lee, go to the office." What did I do? My dress hadn't blown up to show my panties. Why did I have to go to the office?

I went inside, slowly walking down the hall and into the office. When I looked up, I was surprised to see my father standing in front of the desk. He had a big smile on his face. I ran up to him and threw my arms around him in a tight hug. I hadn't seen any of my family for so long. I burst into sobbing, uncontrollable tears.

"It's okay, Nancy Lee, we're going home," he said, with tears in his own eyes. My father brought a canvas bag with him, and Miss Dotty or someone had put my clothes in it. We walked out the front door, down the wide, concrete steps, and stood across the street to wait for the bus. It was the same bus stop my father waited at the day when I first came to the orphanage and I hadn't had the chance to tell him goodbye.

"Daddy, where is the house?" I asked where it was, but I really didn't care. I was going to be with my family again and no longer would I feel abandoned.

Reaching up to adjust his fedora, he answered, "In South Buffalo, above your grandmother's flat." Turning his head to look at me, he added, "As soon as I heard the people were going to move out, I called the owner and rented it right away."

It had been almost one year since my family had lived apart. I just wanted to be home again. I wanted to play outside the black, iron fence. I wanted to go to the toilet in private. I wanted my hair to grow long again. I wanted the sun to be bright and warm again. I wanted to feel excited and happy again. I wanted the child in me to live again. I wanted to be loved. These were my constant longings.

We rode the bus downtown to the central bus station where we got off and boarded the Seneca Street bus. Sitting in a window seat, looking out, I gazed at the different stores and houses as we passed them by. Soon, I began to recognize the area. We were getting closer to the house where my grandparents lived.

The bus stopped in front of Cazenovia Park. We got off, waited for the green light, and walked across the street. It was a warm summer day and the sun was high overhead. I tried to be happy, but I just couldn't make my face smile.

CHAPTER THREE

A Family Together

As trials and hardships increase and the hopes and dreams of a better life drift away, despair comes quietly like a thief in the night, stealing whatever is left of self-respect.

SENECA STREET, WHERE MY grandparents lived in the lower flat and where my family would now live in the upper flat, was a commercial area, with only a few other families living above the shops. Drug stores, grocery stores, shoe stores, dry cleaners, banks, taverns, movie theaters, and an assortment of shops lined the street.

Our house was also partly commercial, because it had a beauty salon in the front half of the basement, with a long, narrow window facing the street. The gray two-family house was built close to the street and straight up, without any space between the front of the structure and the concrete sidewalk. The driveway between the house and the next building was paved completely with asphalt. The driveway led to the back of the house and a two-car garage, where my grandfather and Uncle Harold parked their cars. The asphalt covered the whole back yard. There was no grass, just a dirt area at the side of the garage.

When my father and I reached the house, we walked into the driveway and entered through the second door, near the center of the house. That door led up the back stairs. It was the same door I had always used when I went to see my grandparents.

We walked up the few stairs, passing my grandparents' door, continuing up another set of stairs that turned the corner mid-way, ending at a narrow hall at the top of the stairs where there were two doors. One door led up to the attic, where laundry was hung during bad weather. The other door opened to the kitchen. My father opened the door and we walked in. Inside, on the immediate right, was a bathroom. Straight ahead was the kitchen. The flat was laid out the same as my grandparents' flat.

"Honey, you're home. Come here and give me a big hug." My mother was sitting at the table, dressed in a cotton housedress that she covered with her ever-present apron. She stood up with arms wide open, waiting for me to come to her. Quietly, I walked over and stood with my arms at my side while she hugged me.

Music was coming from the radio in the front of the house where children were playing. I walked toward the front sunroom and saw my younger brothers, sitting on the floor, playing. "Hi, Nancy Lee," Billy said, with a little stutter. He was out of the hospital, but still had bandages across his neck, chest and arms. Bobby didn't say anything. He just looked at me with his shy smile.

Carol Jean was sitting on a daybed. She scooted down and walked toward me. "See my dolly?" she said, in her little-girl voice, holding her doll out to me. I took the doll from her, held it for a minute and put it down on the daybed. The sunroom had old broken blinds covering the windows that made up the outer three walls.

I left the room and walked back to the kitchen where my mother and father sat at the table smoking cigarettes and drinking coffee. "Mama, where's Tommy?"

"Oh, he's over in the park, he'll be here soon. He knows you're coming home today." She got up and walked down the hall toward the bedrooms where baby Jimmy was crying. "Your baby brother is finished with his nap. I'll get him and you can feed him."

Everyone was here; I was the last to be brought back! Why? I used to daydream about how happy I would be when I came back home, but now that I was here, I wasn't happy. I felt a lump in my throat and couldn't say the two words I longed to say: "I'm home!"

I looked around the house. The dining room had a new dining room set. On the buffet was a sweet potato plant in a glass of water. The table was covered with a lace tablecloth. Six matching chairs were placed around the table. The china cabinet was filled with pretty dishes and a cut-crystal water pitcher.

The kitchen table wasn't the same as the table that was put into storage. It was much bigger. The flat came with a wooden icebox and a drip pan like the one in my grandparents' flat. There was a gas cook-stove that sat on iron legs, Two side-by-side windows were dressed with white, tied-back curtains and the windows were held open with wooden sticks, letting the fresh, warm air of the summer day into the kitchen.

The living room had our same maroon-and-dark-blue couch with matching chair and the same floor lamp that sat behind the little table near the chair. The same gray rug that Tommy and I sat on when we listened to our favorite radio programs was on the floor. The tables at each end of the couch and the coffee table in front of the couch were new. On the wall, over the couch, hung a painting of Jesus standing in a boat, with some of his disciples sitting in the boat, clinging onto the sides. The waters were turbulent, and Jesus was reaching his hand out to calm the waters. That was also new. Where did all these new things come from?

My mother had put Jimmy in the wooden highchair and was feeding him as I walked past, going down the narrow hall to look into the three bedrooms. One bedroom had a double-size bed and dresser, shared by Tommy and Bobby. Another had a double-size bed and the vanity dresser that used to be in Nanny's house. Carol Jean and I would share that bedroom. My parents' oak bedroom set was in the third bedroom, along with a baby crib where Jimmy slept. My parents didn't sleep together. Billy was still in bandages from a recent surgery; he slept in bed with my mother. My father slept on the daybed in the sunroom.

"Nancy Lee, do you want to feed your baby brother?" my mother called to me. Jimmy was ten months old now and much bigger than the last time I saw him. He had strawberry-blond hair, the same color hair as Billy and Bobby. He smiled at me when I sat down near the highchair to feed him. When he ate the last spoonful, he held his own baby bottle of milk. He was so cute and he smiled all the time. When his bottle was empty, my mother took it away and gave him a teething cookie to chew on. Her lightheartedness made it obvious that she was glad we were all together again.

"Tommy, I told you not to slam that door!" my mother yelled, when Tommy came back, running noisily up the stairs, flinging open the kitchen door and banging it into the wall.

"Hey, Spooky, you're home! Did you see the bicycle Auntie Alice bought you? I got one, too." Tommy blurted out loudly with a big smile.

"What bicycle?" I asked, turning toward my mother for an answer.

"Auntie Alice and Uncle Will bought bicycles for you and Tommy. You remember Auntie Alice, don't you? You saw her at Nanny's house last year at Easter, or was it the year before?" my mother said, as she tilted her head back and looked up, trying to remember. "Auntie Alice and Nanny are best friends. She drove Nanny to our house and me to the hospital to visit Billy," she added.

"Yes, I remember Auntie Alice. Why would she buy us bicycles?"

"Auntie Alice and Uncle Will are very rich; they want to help our family out a little, until we get on our feet. Don't ask questions. Just be happy you have your own bicycle. Didn't you tell your father that you wanted a two-wheel bicycle, like Jeanie had?"

"Your bicycle is in the yard next to the garage. Want to see it?" Tommy asked, pulling me by the arm toward the kitchen door.

"No, not now," I said, pulling away from him. I didn't care about the bicycle. I didn't care about anything. I was tired. I just wanted to go to bed.

My mother opened the door of the wooden icebox and brought out a bowl of potato salad and a package of hotdogs, wrapped in white paper and tied with a string. She put the hotdogs in a pot of water to boil. "Come to the table, Ralph, and bring the kids. It's time for dinner," she called to my father who was in the living room listening to the radio.

I liked my mother's potato salad. She made it with chopped celery, hard-boiled eggs, and lots of mayonnaise. I ate some and asked, "May I be excused?" My father wanted to know why I was going to bed so early. "I'm tired, Daddy, I'll see my bicycle tomorrow, okay?" He didn't say anything; he just turned and looked at my mother with a quizzical look.

In the bedroom, I took my clothes from the canvas bag and put them into one of the drawers of the vanity dresser. At the bottom of the bag was a bank savings book. My name was at the top of a page with a list of dates and deposits, totaling nine dollars and fifty cents. Pushing the empty canvas bag under the bed, I changed into my pajamas and went into the kitchen to show my mother the savings book. "Mama, I found this in the canvas bag."

"Where did you get this money?" she asked, holding the book and carefully looking at it.

"I don't know."

"Maybe it's the money Nanny sent when I wrote to you."

"You wrote to me? I never got any letters."

"Nancy Lee, I wrote to you a lot and Nanny always gave me a quarter to send with my letters. What do you mean you didn't get my letters?" she asked, lifting her head and looking me straight in the eyes. I was puzzled. She wrote to me? Why didn't I get her letters? Opening the drawer of the vanity dresser, I put the savings book away and went to bed. Lying under the gray wool blanket, I tossed and turned, finally falling off to sleep. Not long after that, the light on the wall by the side of the vanity mirror came on. Carol Jean climbed into bed next to me.

On Sunday morning, I awoke with the sound of my mother calling to me, "Come on, sleepyhead, get up and get some pancakes before Tommy eats them all." I got up, went into the kitchen, sat at the table next to Tommy and ate a pancake. My father was in the living room, drinking a cup of coffee and reading the Sunday newspaper. My brothers and sister were dressed and playing in the room with the daybed, where my father slept. My parents didn't call it the sunroom; they called it the playroom.

"Nanny and Grandpa are going to be here soon, so get dressed, honey, and put on a happy face," my mother said, clearing the breakfast dishes from the table. I did one, but not the other. I just couldn't make my face smile. I was home, the place I longed for. I had every reason to be happy, but I wasn't.

It had been a long time since I had anything to read other than the schoolbooks. I was glad when my father came into the kitchen and handed Tommy and me the comic section of the newspaper. I took the page with the adventurous reporter, Brenda Star. Tommy took the page with the detective, Dick Tracy. We sat at the table taking turns reading all the pages of the comics. Then, came a knock on the kitchen door; it opened, and in walked Nanny and Grandpa. He was carrying a picnic basket. "Hey, Squirt, how's it going?"

"Hi Grandpa." I looked up for a second. Then, I went back to reading the comics.

"Are you all right, Nancy Lee?" Nanny came over to me and gently lifted my chin.

"Oh, she'll be okay. It's just the excitement of being home," my mother said, taking the picnic basket from Grandpa and setting it on the kitchen table.

After Nanny gave me a kiss on the cheek, she opened the lid of the basket and took out a bundle of fried chicken parts, wrapped in a clean kitchen towel, and a loaf of homemade bread and two pies. "Lorraine, I made apple pie for dessert. I hope Nancy Lee will like my apple pie; I know Tommy does," she said, giving me a sympathetic look. Nanny set the pie on the buffet, took the lace tablecloth off the dining room table, folded it and spread another tablecloth on the dining room table.

"Nancy Lee, help Tommy set the table with the dishes from the china cabinet. Be careful not to break any, you two," my mother said with a smile in her voice. When we were finished setting the table, Tommy and I went into the playroom.

Nanny, Grandpa and my mother sat on the couch in the living room, talking with my father. After awhile, my mother and Nanny got off the couch and went into the kitchen where they finished preparing our Sunday dinner. "Ralph, get the kids, we're ready to eat." A bowl of mashed potatoes, a bowl of corn, a platter of fried chicken and a basket of sliced bread were already on the table. Tommy and I brought in some more chairs from the kitchen and everyone sat down to eat.

After the meal was finished and the table cleared, we all went down the stairs and into the back yard. As I walked past my grandparents' door, I wanted to stop in and see them, but I knew my father's parents didn't like Nanny and Grandpa, and my grandmother really didn't like my mother. So I kept walking.

It was a hot day, without a breeze. The sun was shining brightly overhead when we went into the backyard for photographs. Grandpa liked to take photographs with his Kodak camera. The two bicycles that Auntie Alice bought for Tommy and me stood in the dirt area on the side of the garage. Mine was a shiny red bicycle, and Tommy's was a shiny dark green. Auntie Alice also bought a little red wagon and a tricycle for my younger brothers and sister to share.

I tried to sit on my bicycle seat, but it was too high. Going back into the side door, my father said, "I'll bring the seat down so you can reach the pedals. Wait till I get a wrench from Uncle Harold." I stood straddling the bicycle and holding onto the handlebars, wondering what Tommy was doing on his hands and knees.

"Tommy, don't do that to the ants," my mother said, when she saw he was burning them with a magnifying glass. My father came back, lowered the seat, and I began to feel a little happier. I rode the bicycle to the end of the driveway and back.

"Come on everyone, stand together over here, so I can take some pictures," Grandpa said. That day, Grandpa Meyer took several pictures of all six of us children. Unfortunately, those were the only pictures ever taken of all us children together.

I finally figured out why I wasn't happy. "Daddy, why did Tommy live at Nanny's house instead of me? Is it because Mama doesn't love me? She loves Tommy more. That's why she chose him to go with her to Nanny's, instead of me?"

My father looked surprised. "Is that what you think? No, Nancy Lee, Tommy went with your mother because he doesn't listen. He would get into trouble if your mother didn't watch him. Mama doesn't have to watch you."

"Why was I the last one to come home, if Mama doesn't have to watch me?"

"You came home last because you're a good girl, you had lots of girl's to play with and you were being well cared for."

"I came home last because I'm a good girl? That's not fair!" I complained. None of what my father said made sense to me.

"Well, Nancy Lee, life isn't always fair, but remember that whatever happens, your mother and I have tried our best to take care of all you children."

As the days passed, I began to come alive again and my smile returned. One of the first things I did was to walk down Duerstein Street to see Jeanie Hart and show off my new bicycle. It didn't have chrome fenders, but to me, it was the prettiest red bicycle in the world. Jeanie and I hadn't seen each other in almost a year, but we picked up as if we had seen each other just a few days ago, talking, laughing and playing games. Sometimes, we played hopscotch on the chalked markings that Jeanie drew on the sidewalk.

It was a fabulous summer that year in 1948, playing with Jeannie again. Also, Tommy and I joined in the celebration of South Buffalo Day at Cazenovia Park. There were band concerts, beauty pageants and swimming contests. Grandparents, parents, young lovers and children of all ages filled the park, from sun-up to sundown. Tommy and I went across the street whenever we wanted and saw it all. I especially liked the fireworks at dusk, with the intense flashes of the rockets, bursting intermittently with brilliant colors that quickly faded as the next cluster of spectacular sparkles appeared with a thunderous bang.

The park had a brick building that everyone called "Caz Casino." That was where refreshments were sold. It also had an open porch, which was used for shelter during an unexpected downpour. Caz Casino was a great place to gather and meet friends.

There were two public pools in front of Caz Casino enclosed within a fence. One pool was for swimming and the other for diving. A smaller shallow wading pool, with a fountain in the center spouting water into the air, was nearby.

Teeter-totters, slides, merry-go-rounds and swings were scattered among the tables and benches in the picnic area. Farther away, near the bandstand, were two baseball diamonds circled by a hill where people could sit to watch the games.

Cazenovia Park wasn't the only place Tommy and I played. I would like to think my mother was aware of Freud's theory that too much control wasn't good for children, but of course she wasn't. She was just too busy with the younger children and the housekeeping to worry about Tommy and me. She allowed us the freedom to look after ourselves as we explored the world. We did a lot of things together, but nothing that was dangerous or against the law. We played outside until the streetlights came on. Wherever we went, the streetlights were our signal to head for home.

Tommy and I rode our bicycles all over the city. Once, we rode to Humboldt Park near Genesee Street. When Tommy lived at Nanny's house, he discovered that the park also had a public swimming pool. We didn't have swimsuits, but we made do with a pair of shorts for Tommy and a pair of shorts and a T-shirt for me.

We rolled our swimwear into towels, tucking them under our bicycle seats, and peddled away. Reaching the park, after what was a very long ride, we parked our bicycles and locked them with the locks my father bought us. I was glad that I could lock my bicycle. I didn't want it stolen like my tricycle had been.

Walking toward the bathhouse, Tommy entered the swimming pool through the side marked "boys" and I entered through the side marked "girls." I changed into my swimwear, put my clothes into a locker and went into the pool area where I met up with Tommy. I didn't know how to swim. I just made my way around the pool by clinging onto the sides. We stayed at the shallow end and had splashing fights.

There were a lot black kids but hardly any white kids in the pool. The black kids looked at us as if we were trespassing. We felt we shouldn't be there, so we got out. Back into the changing rooms, out the doors and jumping onto our bicycles, we hurried home. The sun was setting low in the sky. We peddled as fast as we could through the city and down the busy streets, until we reached our house.

My father was already home from work and he was angry! Everyone had finished eating. Our plates of food sat cold on the table. "Where have you two been? Why weren't you home for dinner on time? You know you have to be here in time for dinner."

"We went swimming with the nigger kids, and didn't know it was so late," Tommy answered boldly, taking his seat at the table. He started to eat, without even washing his hands.

"What do you mean, 'the nigger kids'? And, where would that be?" my father asked.

"Humboldt Park, near Nanny's house," Tommy answered with his mouth full.

"Stay in your own neighborhood. I don't want you riding all over the city. And, don't say 'nigger,' the word is Negro. Those kids are just like you. Their color doesn't matter. In God's eyes we're all the same. Now eat your dinner and get to bed!"

Tommy was always looking for an adventure. At another time, after we finished our lunch, Tommy said, "Let's ride over to Aunt Molly's house and show them our new bicycles." Tommy liked our cousins and I liked them too, but I didn't like Ruth or Uncle Hank, anymore. "No, I hate Uncle Hank. He hit me."

"Oh, don't be a crybaby, he didn't hurt you." Tommy said, not knowing how badly Uncle Hank whipped me with his belt.

"Go if you want to, but I'm not going," I said, peddling my bicycle away from him.

"Okay, we don't have to go there. Come on back." That day, we rode our bicycles away from South Buffalo. When we reached the city line in the town of West Seneca, we rode up and down the side streets, looking for new kids to play with.

Tommy stopped, got off his bicycle, letting it fall to the ground. He hardly ever bothered to use the kickstand. He took a piece of chalk from his pocket and wrote on the sidewalk, in capital letters: KILROY WAS HERE.

"Tommy, who is Kilroy?"

"I don't know—somebody to be feared, I think." A lady on her porch started to yell at him for writing on the sidewalk. Tommy hopped back on his bicycle and peddled away really fast. I had a hard time keeping up with him.

"Tommy, wait for me," I called as he got farther away. We continued our search for kids, riding our bicycles to Cazenovia Park. Not finding any kids to play with, we rode home.

"I bet I can beat you into the house," Tommy yelled as he ran ahead of me. We raced each other into the house and up the back stairs, shouting and laughing all the way. Tommy won, of course.

Tommy didn't go to church with my grandparents, but my father and I did. On Sunday, after my father and I came back from attending the morning church service and our family finished eating the afternoon meal, I asked, "Daddy, may I go swimming? Jeanie gave me one of her swimsuits that didn't fit her, anymore."

"If you're going to spend time at the pool, you should learn how to swim. I'll go with you." My father took his old swim trunks out of the dresser drawer. With suits and towels in hand we walked across the street to the swimming pool.

I changed into my swimsuit and hurried out to the pool area. My father was already in the shallow end waiting for me. Slowly, I walked down the poolside ladder into the cool water. "Now, lie face down, and pretend you're floating. I'll hold you up—I won't let you drown." My father put his arms under my belly. I kicked my feet and flailed my arms. Then, he took his arms away and I propelled myself toward the edge of the pool.

"I'm swimming, I'm swimming!" I yelled loudly, so everyone could hear me. After a few more clumsy attempts, with a lot of splashing and huge gulps of the chlorinated water, I finally learned how to swim.

I went to the swimming pool almost every day. On some Sunday afternoons, my father came with me. He took me into the diving area where he taught me to dive. He liked the attention we got, when the people watched him showing me how to spring on the diving board. He was a very good swimmer. And, he was proud of his muscular body. I loved swimming, and I loved my father!

My big brother, Tommy, also taught me things. He taught me how to play "It." We often played the game in the park, before the streetlights came on and we had to head for home. "It" was a game where everyone ran and hid, while the person chosen to be it stood at the appointed home base with closed eyes and counted slowly to twenty-five. When the time was up, the person tried to find the others before they ran to home base. When someone got caught, the person tagged him and yelled, "You're 'it'!"

While I waited at home base, Tommy's friend, Jimmy Girdle, tried to kiss me. When Tommy saw what Jimmy Girdle was trying to do, he ran up to him and pushed him down. "Don't touch my sister," he yelled, standing over Jimmy Girdle with his fists clinched. Tommy, my big brother, my hero!

Tommy was not only brave—he was a great explorer. The alcove, off the living room, had a hall closet with a large shelf, where my mother stored some cardboard boxes. Tommy explored what was in the boxes. Pulling them down and tearing them open, he discovered they were mostly boxes of Christmas decorations.

The last box, far back on the shelf, looked familiar. It looked like the box my mother called "Anna Belle's box." Tommy took it down from the shelf and opened it. He took out a wide, white ribbon, with light-blue, foil letters that spelled out "Baby Anna Belle." Also in the box were a small teddy bear and a white baby dress. Who was baby Anna Belle? Why were these things in the box?

My mother was sitting at the kitchen table with my younger brothers and sister while they finished their lunch. Hearing us pulling the boxes apart, she came into the hall. "What are you doing?" What have you done?" she yelled at us, with tears welling up in her eyes. We watched her put the baby things back into the box. Tommy and I were puzzled. Why was she so upset?

We hurried away, running through the house, down the back stairs and outside, where we crossed the street and waited in the park. We stayed there playing with our Duncan yo-yos and watching the bus stop, waiting for our father to come home from work.

He got off the bus with his black lunch pail in hand. We waited until he walked across the street, then we ran to the corner, waited for the light to turn green and hurried across the street, into the driveway and up the stairs. Tommy ran into the bathroom, slamming the door shut. I quietly walked past my mother who stood by the stove, her head down, stirring something in a pot. I went into the living room where my father sat in his chair, smoking a cigarette. "Your mother told me what you did, and she's very upset."

"Daddy, who is Anna Belle?"

"Anna Belle was your baby sister. You wouldn't remember her. You were too young when she died. Now go get washed up for dinner." I was astounded! Anna Belle was my baby sister? I wanted to know more, but my father wouldn't talk about her anymore.

Many years later, I learned that Anna Belle was born in July 1940 on my parents' fifth wedding anniversary. That winter, when Tommy and I were seriously ill with whooping cough, Anna Belle contracted the deadly disease, too. On a bleak Saturday morning in February, my mother awoke to find Anna Belle dead in her crib. She had lived only seven months and fourteen days. She died on the day of Tommy's fifth birthday. Anna Belle was laid out in a tiny, white coffin at Nanny and Grandpa Meyer's house and was buried two days later, on the day of my father's twenty-fifth birthday.

September rolled around and I looked forward to returning to PS No. 70, my old school. I would be ten years old at the end of September. Mrs. Madera, my fifth grade teacher taught me the joy of reading. When we had recess from our studies, she read to us from the *Nancy Drew Mystery Stories.* They were a series of books written by Carolyn Keene.

The stories were about a girl detective who lived with her wealthy attorney father and a housekeeper. Her mother died when she was young, and her father let her have a lot of freedom. She could investigate an abandoned mansion or a haunted house without being afraid. She was my heroine! I often wondered: Did those stories influence me to become an investigator of haunted houses?

The Christmas of 1948 was wonderful. A red-and-green plastic sign with glittering sparkles spelling out the holiday greeting "Merry Christmas," was hung outside our kitchen door. An artificial plant of red poinsettia sat on the table in front of the couch. The few Christmas cards we received were taped around the French doors at the entrance of the playroom. In the corner of the playroom my father set up a real tree, with a fresh pine smell, and strung colored lights on it early Saturday morning, before he left for work.

Tommy and I hurried through our breakfast, because we both wanted to be the first to decorate the tree. We each wanted to put on the best ornaments. "You two, give your brothers and sister a chance to put some on, don't hog them all," my mother said, when she saw Tommy and me racing each other to the tree.

"Tommy, that's not fair, you pushed me," I complained, when he grabbed at the boxes of, colored glass ornaments.

"Stop fighting, you two, or neither of you will decorate the tree." When Billy and Bobby finished their breakfast they came into the playroom and sat on the floor near the tree. My mother followed behind them, holding baby Jimmy on her hip, with Carol Jean walking by her side. Carol Jean, who would be three years old next month, sat on the daybed next to baby Jimmy.

"Let's take turns; you can choose first, then it's my turn, okay?" I bargained with Tommy, thinking if I gave him first choice, he might agree to slow down and share the boxes with the pretty ornaments.

"You two put on the glass ones and let Billy and Bobby put on the plastic snowflakes," my mother said taking the snowflakes from another box and handing them to my little brothers.

Tommy decorated the upper branches, and I decorated the lower ones. "Tommy, you can put the angel on the top of the tree," my mother said, handing Tommy the angel. The angel was the same one with the beautiful white fiberglass wings that was put on the tree when we lived in the housing project. Tommy would be thirteen years old in a few months and he was already as tall as my mother. He reached up and secured the bulb under the angel's skirt. The tree was now ready for the silver strands of tinsel. Tommy and I tossed a few strands one at a time onto the branches. We were finishing the last strands when there was a knock on the door.

"Lorraine, open the door. We have our hands full," Nanny called from outside our flat. My mother hurried to the door, with all of us children following excitedly behind her. We knew Nanny always came with donuts or a coffee cake.

"Mother, Auntie Alice—Merry Christmas! What a surprise! Come in, Come in!" Nanny was wearing a blue coat with a large, blue, rhinestone brooch pinned to one side. A silk scarf around her neck kept her make-up from touching the collar. She and Auntie Alice both wore hats and doeskin gloves and carried pocketbooks. "Here, mother, let me take that." My mother said, taking the cardboard box from Nanny and setting it on the kitchen table next to the one Auntie Alice set down. We rushed to take our seats at the table, waiting to see what was in the boxes.

"Well, look at the good, little children, waiting for Santa. You are good children, aren't you?" Auntie Alice asked.

"Hello, Nanny, hello, Auntie Alice—Merry Christmas!" we all said together. That was the first time I had seen Auntie Alice since I came back home. I remembered her, as my mother told me I would. She wore a gray coat with a big, gray fur collar. Nanny and Auntie Alice took off their coats and put them over the dining room chairs. While they were doing that, my mother put baby Jimmy into the highchair and gave him a teething cookie.

"Thank you for my bicycle. I really love it. Mama said you bought it for me." I think what I said pleased her, because she gave my mother a warm smile.

"You're welcome, Nancy Lee. Well now, let's have a look at all the things that Santa's elves left at my house." One at a time, my mother took the things from the cardboard boxes and spread them out on the kitchen table. There were tangerines, a mesh bag of nuts still in their shells, candy canes, a box of ribbon candy, a jar of striped hard-candy, and some gift-wrapped packages.

The other box held a bag of sugar, a bag of flour, a tin of Hershey cocoa, two boxes of raisins, a few cans of Pet evaporated milk, Karol pancake syrup, chocolate pudding mix, six large oranges and a canned ham. "Oh, my God, you brought so much food," my mother said, with a smile. "Children, what do you want Nanny and Auntie Alice to tell Santa for giving us all this?" my mother said, hinting for us to say thank you.

"Thank you! Thank you! Thank you!" we said all together. Good manners were something we children learned early. My father insisted we say "Please" or "Thank you", and "May I be excused?" Adults must be addressed as "Sir" or "Ma'am." If they were very close friends of our parents, we called them "Auntie" or "Uncle." Neighbors were called "Mister" and "Mrs." Only children were called by their first names.

"Well, Lorraine, I have to drive your mother home and get back to the Christmas shopping. Tell Ralph that Uncle Will and I wish him a Merry Christmas." Auntie Alice put on her coat and my mother gave her a cheek kiss.

"When you see Loretta and Art, wish them a Merry Christmas for me, will you?" Then, my mother told Nanny, "Goodbye, Mother, we'll see you and Dad on Christmas Day." She gave Nanny a cheek kiss, and thanked them again, as they walked out the door. Billy, Bobby and Carol Jean went back to the playroom to look at the Christmas tree. Jimmy, still in the highchair, chewed on his teething cookie. Tommy and I each took a tangerine and sat at the table enjoying the juicy section of the orange fruit while my mother put the rest of the food away.

A few days later, my mother made Christmas cookies. "Wash your hands and you can help," she said, as she rolled out the dough. Tommy and I used the cookie cutters to cut out trees, bells and Santa figures. Billy and Bobby sprinkled red and green sugar on the cutouts before they were placed on the cookie sheets and baked. My mother also made chocolate and vanilla pinwheel cookies, and a fruitcake with citron and raisins. I helped by stirring the fruitcake batter; my mother couldn't do it very well with her injured hand.

Two days before Christmas, I looked in the icebox and there wasn't much there, except milk, cheese, baloney, ketchup, mustard, relish, a bowl of margarine and the canned ham that Nanny brought. I wondered if that was going to be our Christmas dinner.

That afternoon, a man brought a box of food. There was a big turkey, a giant, green squash that was almost as big as the turkey, a bag of potatoes, a bag of onions, and two bags of cranberries. The man was from the Salvation Army. It was the best Christmas ever!

That winter, when I went out to play, I wore my jacket that zipped up the front and the brown leggings with the shoulder straps that Tommy outgrew. In one of the gift-wrapped packages that Santa's elves brought was a red hat, gloves and scarf set. They were almost too nice to play in, but my mother said, "Honey, you have to wear them, that's why Santa gave them to you." To keep my shoes dry, I wore black, rubber galoshes, with the metal buckles in the front. They were too small for Tommy, so they were mine now. My mother stuffed crumpled newspaper in the front to make them fit. All bundled up and ready for the snow, I walked down to Jeanie's house. "Oh Jeanie! Oh Jeanie! Can you come out to play?" I called, as I walked up the steps of her back porch.

The door opened and Mrs. Hart said, "Jeanie will be out in a minute, Nancy Lee. Wait on the porch." The snow was clean and white, the sun was shining, and it wasn't very cold. While I waited, I watched the water dripping one drop at a time from the melting icicles that were hanging on the edges of the garage roof.

Jeanie came out of the house, bundled up in a pink, one-piece snowsuit. The attached hood and matching gloves were sure to keep her warm. On her feet, she wore white boots that zipped up the front. She was really bundled up! "Jeanie, look how high the snow is by your garage."

"My father piles it there when he shovels the driveway," she said, as we walked down the steps.

"Jeanie, let's jump from your garage roof to the one next door. They're close enough. Tommy told me that he and his friends jumped garage roofs and it was fun." Jeanie agreed to try it. After many failed attempts to get on top of the garage roof, we finally made it. Now that I was on the rooftop, it was a lot higher from the ground than I thought.

"You go first, Nancy Lee."

"No, you jump first."

"I dare you. I double dare you! It was your idea." Jeanie said, giving me a little shove.

I reasoned that one of us had to go first if we were ever going to get down. I didn't take a running jump. I just jumped. I felt the back of my head hit the wall of the garage. I saw stars. I was lying on the ground with the wind knocked out of me and I felt a pain in the back of my head. Jeanie was standing in front of me. I don't know how she got down. "Are you all right?" she asked.

"That was fun," I lied, as I got up and brushed the snow off my face and smiled. I decided against trying to jump the roof again. "Let's make snow angels."

We found some clean, flat snow. Lying on our back in the snow, flapping our arms from over our heads down to our sides to make wings, we competed to see who made the best angels. The snow got down the collar of my jacket in my boots and up the cuffs of my leggings. My pretty red hat, scarf and mittens were coated with chunks of snow and ice.

After a day of play, I came home frozen stiff. "Take off your clothes in the hall. Don't come into the house with that snow," my mother said when I opened the kitchen door. She saw my teeth chattering and told me, "Get into the bathtub and take a hot bath. That'll warm you up." My mother was right; the hot water felt good.

"Mama, may I have a towel? I'm ready to get out."

"You'll have to make do with this. The towels hanging in the attic haven't dried yet," she said, handing me a ragged, old towel.

My younger brothers and sister didn't go outdoors to play in the winter. They usually stayed indoors and played in the playroom. Tommy came home when he should. It was a good thing that he did because my father had been drinking and he wasn't in a good mood when he came in the house.

After supper, I was ready for bed. Playing in the snow all day made me sleepy. When I laid my head on the pillow, it hurt. I reached my hand to the back of my head. There was a large goose egg—a reminder not to jump off roofs anymore.

The next day, I came down with a runny nose and a sore throat. "This will cure those sniffles in no time," my father told me, as he rubbed Vicks VapoRub on my chest and neck. He even stuffed some into my nostrils.

On Saturdays when it was too cold to play outside, I went to either the Maxine Theater or the Seneca Theater. There were black-and-white movies about Tarzan, serials of Buck Rogers and the future and always Technicolor cartoons. I often spent the whole day at the theater. One of my favorite movies was *Snow White and the Seven Dwarfs*. Snow White sang *"Some Day My Prince Will Come."* The Dwarfs sang the happy tune *"Hi ho, Hi ho,"* as they went off to work in the mines. I loved all the sparkling gems, the red rubies, green emeralds, and blue sapphires that the Dwarfs pick-axed out of the mines. Someday, I will marry a prince. I will have sparkling gems. I promised myself!

That winter, the winds blowing off Lake Erie made it very cold in South Buffalo. I was happy when spring arrived. It was a new beginning for me in the spring of 1949. I was baptized by total immersion at Cazenovia Park Baptist Church. The small pool of water was behind the curtain of the raised, podium platform, where the congregation could witness the baptisms. The class that I was in was scheduled for baptism in a Sunday evening service.

We prepared for the immersion by removing all our clothes, except our underwear. We each wore a long, white robe provided by the church. The robe had a long zipper up the front, and the hem was weighted so it wouldn't float up. After everyone in my class was dressed in his or her robe, we stood in line, near the steps leading up to the platform. One at a time, we walked up the steps onto the platform and, then, down the other steps into the water.

Reverend Palmer Muntz was already standing in the baptismal water, dressed in his robe waiting for us. "Do you accept Jesus Christ as your Savior? Do you want to be washed clean of your sins?" Reverend Muntz asked when my turn came.

I answered, "Yes" so loudly that my father, grandparents and the rest of the congregation burst into laughter. I closed my eyes, pinched my nostrils and Reverend Muntz dunked me backward into the water. When I came up, I was washed free from all sin, including the sin of hating Uncle Hank!

At the end of June, I passed fifth grade and eagerly waited for the opening of the swimming pool. There wasn't much to do except bicycle riding with Tommy or lingering around the house, waiting for Jeanie to finish her lunch so I could go to her house and play with her. One day, while I sat at the kitchen table working at a puzzle, there was a knock on the door. "Mama, someone's at the door," I called out to my mother, who was in the playroom with my younger brothers and sister.

"Well, open it and see who it is," she called back.

When I opened the door, a tall, slim, blonde lady was standing there, dressed very elegantly in a crisp white blouse and navy-blue skirt. "You must be Nancy Lee. I'm Aunt Loretta. Is your mother here?" she asked, with a kind smile on her perfectly made-up face. How did she know my name, and who was Aunt Loretta?

"Oh my God, Loretta, what a surprise! What are you doing here?" Excitedly, my mother brushed her hair back from her face and ran her hands over her dress and apron, as if she were trying to press out the wrinkles. "Come in, come in," she told the pretty lady. My mother led the way and they sat at the dining room table. "Would you like some coffee, Loretta?"

"No, thank you, Lorraine, I stopped by to see how you are doing. I haven't seen you since you left your mother's house. It's been a year, now. How is the baby? He must be big, now."

"Nancy Lee, go and get Jimmy, so Aunt Loretta can see how much he's grown."

I knew Aunt Molly was my father's only sister and that my mother grew up as an only child. This pretty lady must be someone my mother thought of as a close friend, I reasoned. When I brought baby Jimmy from the playroom, Carol Jean followed. Carol Jean was a happy little girl. She would go up to anyone and make one of her happy faces and that's what she did when she saw Aunt Loretta.

"Nancy Lee, you're probably wondering who I am. Auntie Alice is my mother and your Nanny's friend. Your mother and I have been friends for a very long time. Do you have girlfriends, Nancy Lee?" Aunt Loretta asked.

"Yes, Jeanie is my friend."

"Would you like to have another friend? My daughter, Elaine, is around your age. Would you like to meet her and stay at our house for a few days? Would you like that?"

"Yes, I guess so. When would I go?" I wasn't sure if I wanted to, but I could tell my mother wanted me to; her smile told me she was pleased with my answer.

"Today. You can ride back with me. Is that all right with you, Lorraine?"

"I think that would be wonderful." My mother and I went into my bedroom, where I pulled the canvas bag out from under the bed. As she packed some clothes into it, she said, "Now, don't forget your manners. And be helpful," she emphasized as she pulled hard at the zipper on the old canvas bag.

"I'll take good care of her, Lorraine, and I know she'll have a good time playing with Elaine," Aunt Loretta told my mother before she said goodbye.

We walked down the back stairs and out to her car that was parked on the street, in front of the house. I climbed onto the front seat and clutched the canvas bag tight to my chest as we rode away. On the ride to Aunt Loretta's house she told me about some of the things she and my mother had done while they were growing up. Before I realized it, I wasn't nervous anymore. I let the canvas bag rest easy on my lap.

"When did you and my mother walk to the big waterfall?"

Aunt Loretta stopped smiling. The look on her face became serious. "What do you mean, Nancy Lee? Why do you ask? Did your mother tell you something about a waterfall?"

I didn't know what to say; I didn't know why I asked her that question. "No, my mother didn't tell me anything. I just imagined seeing a path to a big waterfall. That's all."

Slowly, Aunt Loretta said, "As a matter of fact, we did. My parents and your mother's parents had many picnics together in Letchworth State Park. And, yes, your mother and I always enjoyed walking to the waterfalls. It's interesting that you should say that."

We rode through the city until we reached the little village of Williamsville. The Main Street was lined with quaint little shops and a movie theater. Aunt Loretta turned down a street not far from the movie theater, pulled into the driveway, parked her car and we got out. I carried the canvas bag, and followed her into the side door, through a sun porch, and into the kitchen.

"Elaine, come meet Nancy Lee," Aunt Loretta called out. I stood in the kitchen, while Aunt Loretta walked away. She came back with a girl who was a little older and a head taller than I was. She had long, blonde hair and a dazzling smile. "Nancy Lee this is Elaine." Walking to the sink to wash her hands she added, "Elaine, Nancy Lee's mother agreed to let Nancy be our guest for a few days. Isn't that nice? Show her where she'll sleep, while I make lunch."

Elaine, with a grown-up voice said, "Hello, Nancy Lee, I'm glad you could come. My mother told me she was going to ask your mother if you could." Elaine was very friendly. I liked her immediately. I wished she were my real cousin and not just my pretend-cousin.

I followed Elaine from the kitchen, passing through a large dining room with a large table, china cabinet and sideboard. Portraits of Elaine and her family hung in ornate, golden-colored frames on the walls. We passed the living room where there was a baby-grand piano in one corner. A huge, brick fireplace with built-in bookcases on either side filled one wall. I stood for a moment and imagined a fire crackling in the fireplace on a snowy winter night.

"Nancy Lee, aren't you coming?" Elaine asked, from the hallway to the bedrooms, where she waited for me. Her bedroom had twin-size beds. Elaine slept in one, and I would sleep in the other. Down the hall was a bathroom and three other bedrooms; two had twin-size beds, like Elaine's bedroom; the third was where Aunt Loretta and Uncle Art slept. Their bedroom had a bathroom next to the mirrored, double-door closet. Aunt Loretta's home was the biggest house I had ever been in. I envied Elaine. She had her own bedroom where she could go whenever she wanted to be alone. She could play with the many dolls on her bed, or read the many books on her bookshelf. She had a closet filled with clothes and shoes. Her splendid assortment of beautiful clothes overwhelmed me with a sense of shame about my own shabby clothes. Someday, I'm going to have a bedroom and splendid clothes like hers, I promised myself!

Elaine and I had lots of fun together playing endless games of Jacks on the shiny, kitchen floor. It was perfect for swiping up the jacks and making the ball bounce high and straight up. We played dress-up, with some of Aunt Loretta's evening gowns, which were too big for us. We pinned the sides with safety pins to make them fit. Elaine wore a beige-and-white print gown, and I wore a rose-colored gown. We posed with bouquets of flowers that we picked from the garden. Elaine pretended she was Miss America and I pretended that I was Miss South Buffalo. Aunt Loretta brought out her camera and took our picture.

Outside, in the backyard, we enjoyed the warm rays from the sun. We rested together on the green hammock, strung between two tall trees. We shaded our eyes with our hands, while we watched the ducks swim about in the pond in back of the house. The sweet fragrance of the rosebushes drifted by in the slight breeze. Someday I'll have a hammock and a backyard like this, I promised myself!

Aunt Loretta took Elaine and me to a theater where we saw the movie *Mighty Joe Young*. It was about a giant gorilla, named Joe, who was wild, but became calm when he heard the song *"Beautiful Dreamer"*. After the movie, we went to a Howard Johnson's restaurant for ice cream. It was the first time I was in a restaurant and the first time I sat in a booth. Aunt Loretta unfolded her napkin in a graceful gesture and placed it on her lap. Imitating her, I did the same. Someday, I'm going to be a lady just like Aunt Loretta, I promised myself! What a wonderful day that was. Even now, whenever I hear *"Beautiful Dreamer"*. I reflect for a second on all that Elaine had while growing up: two caring parents, a secure home and all that goes with making a young girl secure and happy.

Back at her house, Elaine and I played with her paper dolls. "Mother, Nancy Lee is taking all the pretty dresses for her doll and leaving the ugly ones for me," Elaine said as she walked into the living room to complain to her mother.

"She's your guest, so she gets first choice," Aunt Loretta replied, as she continued to play a soft melody on the piano. Now I liked Aunt Loretta even more. At bedtime, Aunt Loretta tucked me in and said, "Good night, Nancy Lee." Then, she went over to Elaine's bed, tucked her in and gave her a kiss on the forehead and said, "Love you," as she left the bedroom.

"Love you, too," Elaine answered back. Nobody had ever tucked me in or kissed me good night. It didn't seem fair. I used to envy Jeanie's life until I realized that, although, Jeanie had more than me, her life wasn't grand like Elaine's life. I decided to wish for the life that Elaine had.

Just like what happened to Cinderella—the clock struck the midnight hour and the magic ended! The week was over and I had to return to the imperfections of my life. I put my clothes in the canvas bag and Aunt Loretta drove me back to my home on Seneca Street.

Many years later, I visited Elaine and her husband in their Florida home. Elaine and I reminisced about the days of our youth. Elaine was tall, slim and beautiful, just as Aunt Loretta had been. Before the visit ended, Elaine surprised me with a gift of the photo that Aunt Loretta had taken on that day, long ago, when we played dress-up and I pretended that I was Miss South Buffalo.

I had seen Miss South Buffalo at the celebration of South Buffalo Day at Cazenovia Park. Although we lived across from the park, we didn't picnic there, like other families did. As a matter-of-fact, we didn't picnic anywhere; we always had our meals at home. The only picnic our family went to was for the employees and the families of the Socony-Vacuum Company where my father worked.

My father borrowed Uncle Harold's car and drove our family to the picnic grove. Everything was free: hotdogs, hamburgers, French fries, pop, beer, potato chips, pretzels and even the ice cream sandwiches that were kept on something called "dry ice." The man handing out the ice cream sandwiches told me that dry ice is so cold that it would burn me if I touched it. That didn't make sense, but I thought it must be true, because he wore leather gloves when he put another block of dry ice into the cooler.

I competed in the children's contests and won most of the prizes. I won the three-legged race, the wheelbarrow walk and almost every other challenge, probably because I was older than the other kids. My father entered me in the women's contests, too. He told the judges that I would be twelve next month, which was a lie. I would be eleven next month. I don't know if they believed him, but they let me compete anyway.

I ran the peanut-on-the-spoon race faster, blew up the balloon faster and sucked the water out of a baby bottle faster than any of the women did. I even outlasted all of them in the egg-toss contest. I won almost every prize. The women complained, but the judges gave me the prizes anyway. I won new tires for Uncle Harold's car, cases of motor oil and certificates, redeemable at various suppliers throughout the city.

A band played music in the pavilion and people danced. Even my parents danced. They sang to the music, laughed and had fun. I was happy to see them like that. They drank a lot of beer. My parents didn't seem to mind the stinky smell or the taste of it; they seemed to actually like it. They weren't drunk, but close to it.

The sun was setting. My parents gathered together my younger brothers and sister. Tommy and I hurried and stuffed ourselves with the last of the hotdogs and French fries, knowing we were going to leave for home. We all piled into Uncle Harold's car just in time because, as we left the picnic grove, big, heavy raindrops splattered on the windows. We got home safely. That night, I went to bed feeling proud of myself for winning all the prizes. At my young age, I wasn't concerned with my parents' drinking. I thought of it as being occasional and harmless. But it wasn't.

The next morning, when I opened the icebox door, the smell of food going bad filled my nostrils. We didn't have any ice in the icebox. My mother had forgotten to put the cardboard sign in the window, the sign that let the iceman know how much ice she wanted. "Tommy, Nancy Lee, take the wagon and get some ice. Go up Seneca Street; you know where the icehouse is," my mother said, handing Tommy some money and me an old blanket to cover the ice. Tommy hurried down the stairs and I followed behind.

We took turns pulling the wagon up Seneca Street. Tommy cheated, because I pulled the wagon most of the way. When we got to the Ice House, Tommy rang the bell and a grumpy old man came to the door. He wouldn't sell us any ice. He said the ice had to be delivered to the house.

"But, my baby brother still needs a bottle. The milk will be sour if we don't have any ice," Tommy pleaded.

"Humph," the man gave a grunt after a short moment of silence spent looking us over. "Wait here, I'll get you some ice."

When he opened the door again, he had a big block of ice that he carried between the two points of huge ice tongs. He set the ice on the blanket and Tommy wrapped the blanket over the top. "I don't know where you kids live, but you better hurry home before it melts." He didn't ask for any money and Tommy didn't offer any.

"Thank you, mister," we both said, as we hurried away. We took turns again, pulling the wagon down Seneca Street. This time, I made Tommy pull it most of the way.

"You cheated before, so now you have to pull it more than me," I said, dropping the handle and running ahead. When we got to the driveway I yelled up to my mother, "Mama we've got the ice!" She came down the stairs, took one side of the blanket and Tommy and I grabbed onto the other side. We walked upstairs backward, facing our mother and managed to get the ice block into the icebox.

A few weeks later, I wanted to play with Tommy and his friends, but he wouldn't let me. I didn't want to ride my bicycle alone, so I thought for a moment and remembered there was a bus that took people to the zoo. I had never been to a zoo. I wanted to see the animals, especially the monkeys like the ones in the Tarzan movies.

The day I left the orphanage and waited with my father at the bus station, he explained that when people got on a bus they paid the fare. For my age it cost a nickel. If any of the people needed to take two buses, they asked for a "transfer." With two cents and a transfer a person could get onto a second bus. That was the day I saw the words "Buffalo Zoo" written above the front window of a bus.

"Mama, may I have some money? Tommy gets money. May I have some?"

"What do you mean Tommy gets money? I don't give your brother any money," my mother said, looking up from the sink where she was washing dishes.

I didn't know where Tommy got the money either, but I saw some in his dresser drawer one day when I took a pair of his socks because I didn't have any in my drawer. I tiptoed into his bedroom and quickly took a quarter, hoping my mother wouldn't catch me. I left the house, waited at the corner for the Seneca Street bus, got on and paid the nickel. With the transfer and two cents, I got on the next bus with the words "Buffalo Zoo." "Mister, will you tell me when you get to the zoo?" I asked the bus driver.

He told me it was the last stop before the bus turned around. I sat down in the front of the bus near the driver. After a short ride, the bus came to the last stop. "End of the line—everybody off," the driver said, looking at me with a questionable glance as I got off the bus and crossed the street.

The gates were opened and rested against the wall at the front entrance. Excited, but hesitant, I walked through the entrance and along the paths, gazing into the pits and through the fences that surrounded the areas where the animals were kept. I entered the buildings and was amazed to see the many different animals. Lions, tigers and leopards were behind black, iron bars. Monkeys were behind black, iron bars. Eddie, the ape, was behind black, iron bars. The elephant, in the elephant house, was behind black, iron bars.

The zoo was a strange but sad place. I wanted the animals to be where they lived, before they were captured. I didn't like seeing them behind the bars. I knew how they felt. I walked out the front gate, not caring if I ever went to the zoo again. I crossed the street, waited for the bus, and found my way back home in time for dinner.

"Where have you been? Why weren't you home for lunch?"

"I went to the zoo."

"Don't you be sassy—answer me!"

"I did, Mama, I took the bus to the zoo and saw the animals."

"You better not tell your father that you went to the zoo on your own." My mother didn't ask where I got the money for the bus. She was drinking a glass of wine, so I think she forgot to ask. When my father came home, I didn't tell him that I went to the zoo and neither did my mother. They were too busy arguing.

Summer was coming to an end when I found a folded piece of paper on the sidewalk. I didn't know what it was, but it looked important. It had amounts of money and the words "payable to." My mother said it was a paycheck and the man had already signed the back. "If you take this to the bank they'll give you the money."

"I don't think they'll give me money for this piece of paper, and besides, it's not ours."

"God probably wanted us to have the money, or you wouldn't have found the paycheck."

I went to the bank and told the teller what my mother told me to say. "My uncle is home sick, and he sent me to cash his check."

The teller looked at me, paused a second, then said, "Sign here, under your uncle's name." I signed my name and took the eighty-seven dollars and change home.

My mother didn't ask if I signed my name, she only exclaimed in a surprised voice, "They gave you the money?" She handed me a twenty-dollar bill, as a reward for finding the paycheck. I ran to the corner drug store, and had the twenty-dollar bill changed into smaller bills. I waited for the Seneca Street bus and rode it to the downtown station. Then, with a transfer and two cents, I took the Main Street bus to the theater district.

After choosing a theater, I purchased my ticket and entered along the marble floor of the long hallway. It led to a thick, plush carpeted area. A delicious aroma aroused my hunger as I approached the refreshment counter. It was the aroma of hot roasted nuts in bins behind a glass display. The saleslady weighed the pound of nuts that I pointed to and handed me a white paper bag. I paid her and walked away with my treat of hot salted cashews.

It was magnificent inside. There was a wide, carpeted staircase leading up to the second level mezzanine and the balcony loges. But, I chose to sit downstairs. A uniformed usher with a flashlight led me to a seat in one of the many rows of burgundy-colored, upholstered seats that filled the theater. Overhead, above the seats, the center of the huge, domed-ceiling glowed with a design of multi-colored glass. Decorative lights were evenly spaced along the sides of the outer aisles. Covering the huge screen were heavy, velvet drapes that magically opened when the movie began.

The movie was a boring, black-and-white film. I sat front and center and ate the whole bag of cashews. When the movie ended, I rode the two buses back.

My father was already home from work and arguing with my mother. I hurried up the stairs and into the kitchen. He wasn't happy to discover that my mother had bought herself a bottle of wine to celebrate her new windfall. She was really tipsy.

"Where have you been?" my father yelled at me.

"I went downtown to the movies," I said, explaining how I got the money. I was sent to bed without supper and my parents continued to argue.

Several weeks after that, on a Sunday afternoon when my father was home, a man came knocking on the kitchen door. The knock on the door turned the bright, sunny day into a gray cloud of gloom for both my mother and my father.

I came out of my bedroom, where I had been sweeping the dust out from under the bed, and saw that my mother's face had drained from pink to pale white. The man told my father he wanted his money. My father promised to pay it all back if the man would keep the police out of it. The man agreed. Eventually, my father paid the man the full amount of the check I cashed.

Summer was over and it was time to go back to PS No. 70, which only went up to sixth grade. Tommy, who was now in seventh grade, went to another school. The day I turned eleven years old, I began to realize how insignificant I was. My birthday fell on a Friday. It began just like every other school day. Tommy ate peanut butter toast and I ate cinnamon and sugar toast for breakfast. Neither Tommy nor my mother wished me a happy birthday. I was disappointed and sad that they didn't even mention my birthday, but I didn't say anything.

I left the house and walked down Seneca Street, feeling sad. There was a small grocery store near the corner of Buffum Street, but it wasn't open. It had a *Courier Express* newspaper box in the alcove. The newspaper was paid for by the honor system. The loose change lying in the newspaper box was tempting. I took three nickels and ran away as fast as I could, getting to school just as the school bell started to ring. At lunchtime, I treated myself to a ten-cent hot dog and a five-cent root beer to celebrate my birthday.

There wasn't a birthday present or a birthday cake for me at dinner, just a heated can of Franco-American spaghetti. Usually, on Fridays, when my father got off the bus, he stopped at the local tavern before coming home. He was drunk when he walked into the house and began arguing with my mother, who was also tipsy, because she had been drinking her wine. I covered my head with my pillow to soften the noise. Finally, the arguing stopped. My father went into the playroom to sleep on the daybed and my mother went into her bedroom to sleep.

Lying in bed next to Carol Jean, I was having a hard time falling off to sleep. The moonlight shined through the bedroom window without curtains. It had only a torn window shade rolled halfway up. I gazed about the room at the wallpaper; it was old, faded, dried-out wallpaper. Some of it was already torn off the wall, exposing the bare plaster. Quietly, I got out of bed, found a loose piece of wallpaper, and very carefully, pulled it away from the wall. With a pencil, I wrote "HAPPY BIRTHDAY" on the dry plaster, letting the wallpaper fall back into place. With tears in my heart, I got back into bed where I lay awake for a long time, longing to be loved.

When and how did my parents become the two people I hardly knew anymore? What changed them? Where were the mother and father that I loved and felt safe with? Why couldn't my parents be like they were when we were living happily in the housing project?

Tommy was always going somewhere, or doing something with his friends and he wouldn't let me go with him. He didn't spend any time with me like he used to. "You stay away from my friends or I'll tell Dad you're following me. He won't like it." I was on my own, and had to find things to do on my own. On Friday nights, if Jeanie couldn't come out to play, I walked the streets. As it grew darker, the lights in the houses were turned on and I could see inside. I stopped in front of the houses and peered in the windows.

I imagined things about the people who lived inside: What were the mother and father like? How many children lived there? Did they have a refrigerator or an icebox? Sometimes, I imagined what their bedrooms looked like. I could almost smell the bedroom. After awhile, the crescent moon and a scattering of stars in the sky made me realize it was past the time the streetlights went on. I took in a deep breath of the cold night air and headed home.

I believe that was when I began to actively develop my higher sensory perception. The practice of wanting to know and asking myself to tune into something causes my mind to create images, sounds or thoughts that sometimes were imagined answers and sometimes they were true answers. Knowing how to discern the one from the other took me years of practice.

As my higher sensory perception increased, my family life became more dysfunctional. Or, was it the other way around? My mother was becoming less and less capable of caring for all of us children. Growing up as an only child whose parents doted on her could have been why it was difficult for her to keep up with the housework, the meals, the laundry and six young children. My mother often had a blank look in her eyes. I knew when she looked that way she was trying to block out her feelings. Drinking was the only way she knew how to deal with her sorrows.

I think she dreamed of having a better life, a life like Aunt Loretta had. Some nights when my father didn't come home until late at night, my mother sat at the dining room table, drinking wine and listening to the music on the radio. Vaughn Monroe singing, *"Dance Ballerina, Dance"* always made her sad. She was only thirty-one years old, but she stopped taking care of herself, putting on make-up, or fixing her hair pretty. She gained a lot of weight.

My father had a full-time job and earned enough to pay the bills, but because of all the money he spent on booze and cigarettes there wasn't much left. When my father came home drunk on Friday nights, after spending the evening at the local bar, he always argued with my mother. My father didn't want my mother to drink and my mother didn't want my father to, but neither of them would stop. I tried to believe their drinking and arguing would stop, but it didn't. It only got worse.

One Friday night, while I was in bed trying to sleep, my father came into my bedroom and handed me three twenty-dollar bills saying, "Nancy Lee, hide this in a safe place and don't give it to me. This is the rent money, so I can't spend it." He walked out of my bedroom, out the kitchen door and went back to the tavern, where he went every Friday night. I took the three bills, rolled them up tight and hid them in the rim of the wall lamp by the vanity dresser. I got into bed next to Carol Jean, and fitfully fell off to sleep.

Later that night, my father came into my bedroom, again. This time, he was really drunk. "Where's the money I gave you? I need it," he said, with slurred speech and the smell of beer on his breath.

"Daddy, I can't give it to you." I pleaded. "You said not to give it to you."

"I know I told you that before, but now I'm telling you to give it to me!" he said harshly.

"No, Daddy! It's the rent money. I can't give it to you." I began to cry. I think he was stunned by my refusal.

He looked at me without saying a word. He just stood there staring into my eyes for what seemed like a long time. Finally, he turned away. "Oh, Jesus," he said, and slowly walked out of the bedroom. The next month, he did the same thing and I refused again; that's how the rent got paid.

At school, Mrs. Stanton, the homeroom teacher, told the class that a woman was looking for someone to wash her floor. "If any of you children are interested, see me after class." I was interested. So, after class, I asked Mrs. Stanton for the woman's name and address. Her name was Mrs. Quinn and she lived above the drug store at the corner of Seneca and Duerstein Streets.

After school, I went to the side door of the brick building and rang the doorbell for the upper flat. A woman, a little older and a little heavier than Nanny, came down the hall stairs and opened the door. "Hello, Mrs. Quinn, I'm Nancy Lee. My teacher told me that you wanted someone to wash your bathroom floor."

"Yes, let me show you what I need you to do." We walked up the stairs to her second-floor flat. "I'll pay you ten cents to wash this floor on your hands and knees, and I want it spic-and-span clean. I need it done every Friday. Do you want the job?"

Of course, I said, "Yes." Washing the floor for Mrs. Quinn on Fridays would be a blessing for me. I could use the money for the movies. To me, the movies were the most wonderful reality of what life was really like.

I didn't have nice clothes like Jeanie or the other girls at school had. My clothes were Tommy's hand-me-downs or they were bought at the local thrift shop. That's one reason the girls at school didn't think of me as one of them.

Just before Thanksgiving, when I finished washing her bathroom floor, Mrs. Quinn asked, "Would you like to come with me to a church dinner this Sunday?"

The memory of the orphanage and the woman pretending to be my grandmother flashed through my mind, but I said, "Yes," because Mrs. Quinn wasn't a total stranger to me.

"Come to my house tomorrow. I want to buy a dress for you to wear to the dinner." I was excited that I was getting a new dress. I told my mother what Mrs. Quinn said. She agreed to let me go to the church dinner with Mrs. Quinn.

I went to Mrs. Quinn's flat on Saturday morning, just as she had told me to. We walked down Seneca Street to the Jarhaus & Brown department store and up the wooden staircase to the second floor where the girls' dresses were sold. The saleslady and Mrs. Quinn looked through the racks and selected a few dresses for me to try on.

After modeling the beautiful dresses, Mrs. Quinn chose a light-blue dress and paid the saleslady. She picked up the bag with the dress that had been carefully placed in a box with white tissue paper and handed it to me to carry. I was thrilled that she bought the dress.

"Mrs. Quinn, I really like that dress. Thank you for buying it for me," I said as we walked back down Seneca Street.

"I'll take the dress, now. Come to my house tomorrow at eleven o'clock. You can put it on there," she said, when we reached my house. I went into the driveway, pushed open the door and ran up the stairs so happy. I could hardly wait for tomorrow to come.

At eleven o'clock Sunday morning I was at Mrs. Quinn's door, anxiously pressing her doorbell, then I hurried up the stairs. I was excited about wearing the pretty new dress. I went into her house, took off my old dress and put on the new one. "Be careful eating; don't let anything get on the dress," Mrs. Quinn said, fussing with the big, wide bow tied in the back.

We got into her car and she drove us to her church. After the dinner we returned to her flat, where I took off the pretty new dress and put on my old dress. Mrs. Quinn said, "Leave the dress here. I'll take care of it." I was disappointed that she didn't give me the dress to take home. I never saw the dress again! Mrs. Quinn took it back to the store for a refund. Why did she do that?

More disappointments were to come. We didn't have a television set. Sometimes in the evenings before it got too dark, I walked down Seneca Street to stand in front of the Western Auto store, where there was a black-and-white television set in the window. It was kept turned on to interest customers into buying one.

The winter winds whipped the newly fallen snow into the air and about my bare legs as I stood at the window watching whatever was on the television. It didn't matter that I was cold or what program was on. Even the test patterns were exciting, and it didn't cost anything to stand outside and watch.

On one of those nights, I noticed a doll in the window. She was dressed in a pretty, pink dress, with sweater and bonnet, and she had life-like brown eyes with lashes of real hair. She looked just like a real baby. I didn't believe in Santa, but just in case, I hoped he would bring me that doll. Even if he didn't, I was happy just to look at her through the window and pretend she was mine. I wanted that doll with all my heart. There wasn't anything I wanted more.

Two days before Christmas when I walked back to the store to watch television and see the doll, she wasn't there! Where was she? Slowly and sadly, I walked home. In bed that night, I put my head under the gray, wool blanket and quietly cried myself to sleep.

Unlike the Christmas past, my mother had little interest in baking cookies or decorating the house. Auntie Alice and Nanny came with the boxes of food and a man from the Salvation Army came with a turkey and a box of toys, which included a spinning-top, Checkers, a Parcheesi board game, coloring books, a paint-by-number set, and a few stuffed toys for the younger children.

Santa brought some things, too. Jimmy got a wooden Snoopy Dog. It walked along on jointed legs when he held the string and pulled it behind him. Carol Jean got a rubber doll without clothes. Billy and Bobby got toy trucks. The toys looked like they were from the local thrift shop. Tommy and I each got a sweater. It wasn't a happy Christmas like last year.

I was disappointed that Santa didn't give me a pair of sneakers to wear for my gym class. When the sole tore on my old pair, my mother told me I had to wear the sneakers that Tommy outgrew. She said I didn't need new gym sneakers because gym was only once a week. I didn't like wearing boy's sneakers, so I took gym class in my socks with the holes in the toes.

I was ashamed to tell the gym teacher that I didn't have sneakers. I kept telling her that I forgot them. The gym teacher gave me a last warning, "Don't forget your sneakers next time, Nancy Lee!" Now, she was out of patience with me. I had to get sneakers from somewhere. I lingered in the locker room until all the girls went into the gym. Then, I searched the lockers until I found a pair. I only borrowed the sneakers, putting them back after gym class.

The next week, I hurried to the same locker, took the sneakers and put them on. I didn't know that the sneakers I took from the locker belonged to a girl in the same class. She was absent the week before when I borrowed them. When the girl couldn't find her sneakers, she complained to the gym teacher, and pointed to the sneakers I was wearing, "Those are my sneakers, not yours."

"Why did you take her sneakers?" the gym teacher asked.

"Because, I don't have any sneakers," I had to finally admit.

The gym teacher let me take gym in my socks after that day.

I didn't have any more problems in school until a chilly March day when shortly after taking my seat in the homeroom, I was called to the principal's office. "Please, Nancy Lee, take a seat," the principal said. "This is Mrs. Berg. She has a few questions to ask you." The gray-haired woman in the tan suit, with the briefcase on her lap didn't smile; she was very serious. I thought she was going to talk to me about the sneaker incident. I was nervous, as she began to question me.

"Your brother, Thomas, tells me he eats peanut butter on toast for breakfast; what do you eat, for breakfast, Nancy Lee?"

"I don't like breakfast."

"What do you eat for lunch?"

"Sometimes, I eat a hot dog or a candy bar."

"How do you pay for your hot dog or candy bar?"

"My mother keeps a ragbag on the attic stairs. Tommy and I sell them to the ragman when he comes with his truck. We get three cents a pound." I didn't tell her that Tommy puts rocks in the ragbag to make it heavier. "On Friday, after school, I wash a lady's bathroom floor and she gives me ten cents. Sometimes, I wash her kitchen floor, too; then she gives me a quarter." I wasn't going to tell her that sometimes I took two nickels from the newspaper box.

"Do you wash your mother's floors, too, Nancy Lee?"

"My father mops the floors because my mother can't squeeze the water out of the rag-mop." Not wanting Mrs. Berg to think that I didn't help around the house, I added, "I peel the potatoes and I feed my baby brother when he's hungry." Who was Mrs. Berg? Why was she asking all these questions?

Mrs. Berg asked if I would like some new clothes. She must have thought I needed new clothes because my dress had a little rip on one side where I pulled my belt too tight. Hoping she would include a pair of sneakers, I answered a very loud, "Yes! Can my brothers and sister have some, too?"

"We'll see." She continued asking questions about our family life and I gave her answers that would make her think we were really poor. I hoped she might give us a food basket, too. "My mother has to make butter by mixing lard with paprika and we only have ketchup or mustard sandwiches. The baloney is saved for the sandwiches my father takes to work," I lied.

When I finished answering the questions, the principal said, "All right, Nancy Lee, you can go back to your class now." I went back to class excited, hoping that I was going to get new sneakers and new clothes. Back in the classroom, I couldn't focus on what the teacher was saying. I kept thinking about what kind of new clothes Mrs. Berg would give me.

At lunchtime, I took the fifteen-minute walk home. I flew up the two flights of stairs, and into the kitchen to tell my mother the good news. She was feeding baby Jimmy, who was sitting in the highchair. Billy, Bobby and Carol Jean were sitting at the table eating their lunch. "Mama, Mama, guess what? A woman is going to buy us new clothes and new shoes!" I blurted out loudly.

"What are you talking about? What woman?" my mother snapped at me as she cut up the hot dog that was on Jimmy's plate.

"Mrs. Berg is her name. She came to school today and asked me if I wanted some new clothes."

"Don't you go talking to any woman, do you hear me?" she snapped at me again. The news didn't make my mother happy, as I thought it would.

"It wasn't just me; the woman talked to Tommy, too," I said, running down the stairs and back to school. After school, nothing more was said about the new clothes.

I hoped that we would get them before Easter. Last Easter, Jeanie had a new Easter outfit, including a hat and white gloves. I wanted to show off the new clothes to Jeanie, like she showed off to me. Jeanie also had a real Easter basket; it was filled with lots of candy and a big, chocolate bunny.

For our Easter baskets, we had shoeboxes my father brought from the Liberty shoe store. My four brothers, my sister and I got multi-colored jellybeans, yellow marshmallow peeps, chocolate-covered, marshmallow eggs and a small chocolate bunny in our shoebox, with a little colored straw on the bottom.

On a Friday morning, a few weeks before Easter, my mother said, "You kids aren't going to school today. You have to stay home." Did my mother find out about the new clothes? Was this the day Mr. Berg would bring them? My father wasn't home. He went to work, as usual. Billy, Bobby and Carol Jean were at the table, eating cereal and milk. Jimmy had been fed and was in the highchair, drinking from his baby bottle. Tommy and I were eating our toast. My mother was busy in the bedrooms.

There was a knock at the kitchen door. My mother came down the hall and into the kitchen, looking sad and nervous. I hadn't seen her look like that before. She opened the door. It wasn't Mrs. Berg with the new clothes. It was a younger woman. This woman had dark hair and she wore a blouse and skirt, not a suit.

"I'm Mrs. Clarkson from the Children's Aid Society. Are the children ready?" she asked. Tommy and I looked at each other. We knew this wasn't good. My subconscious fear that someday we would be split up again was about to happen.

"Just let me get their things," my mother said, as she headed back to the bedrooms. "Tommy, Nancy Lee, come here, you two, and help me with these bags," my mother called to us. "Here take these. One bag is yours and one bag is Carol Jean's," she said, handing me two brown paper bags. Tommy had already picked up two bags from the bedroom he shared with Bobby. My mother carried two bags from the bedroom where Billy and Jimmy slept and handed them to Mrs. Clarkson. "Here are my children's clothes. I'll carry my baby." My mother lifted Jimmy from the highchair and took Carol Jean's hand. We all followed Mrs. Clarkson down the stairs and out to the driveway, where her car was parked.

I can still picture my mother standing in the driveway on that cold March day, looking sad, as we six children got into the car. Tommy and Billy sat in the front seat. Bobby, Carol Jean and I sat in the back seat. Jimmy was crying, as Mrs. Clarkson took him from my mother's arms and put him on my lap. She closed the door, got into the car and sat behind the steering wheel. My mother opened the rear car door and handed me Jimmy's baby bottle. It was filled with sugar-water. "Here, Nancy Lee, give this to your brother," she said, with tears streaming down her face.

As we drove off into the unknown with a strange woman, I calmed Jimmy by giving him his baby bottle. Carol Jean and Bobby were crying too, but only for a little while. I couldn't see how Tommy and Billy were taking this, but I'm sure it was just as terrible for them as it was for me. I squinted to shield my eyes from the sun's rays that reflected through the car window. They began to tear up and there was a choke in my throat. Quickly, I stopped myself from crying. I must not cry, because it might scare my little brothers and sister. I repeated over and over silently, in my mind, "I must not cry, I must not cry." Taking a deep breath, I settled back in the seat and steadied myself for what I couldn't change. One by one, we were driven to the foster homes.

I kept Jimmy safe in my arms where he slept until we came to his foster home. He awoke when Mrs. Clarkson took him from my lap. He began crying again, as she carried him to his foster home. She forgot his bottle, or maybe she didn't take it because it was empty. I was the last one to be placed. With a brown paper bag holding all that I owned, I stepped out of the car.

I would carry my clothes in a brown paper bag over the next several years. I don't know what my parents were told about us being placed in foster homes. Nobody told us children that we were going away. It was a complete surprise to us. Tommy had just turned fourteen. I was eleven, Billy was eight, Bobby was seven, Carol Jean was four and Jimmy was only two years old.

I felt that Mrs. Berg had tricked me. I felt betrayed. Why didn't she just ask me: "If you had a choice of new clothes or your old clothes and staying with your parents, which would you choose?" I would definitely have chosen to stay with my parents. If only I hadn't said all those things. I had given Mrs. Berg the story that I thought she wanted to hear—the story that we were poor!

CHAPTER FOUR
Foster Homes

"Foster Homes" is a misnomer because they were not homes to children like me! They were just a place to eat, sleep and store your brown paper bag. A home is a place where you feel connected to those around you; it can be anywhere or anything—even a shack in the wilderness.

MY FIRST FOSTER HOME was in the Ford's home in the town of Clarence, a suburb of Buffalo. The house was a small Cape Cod structure, with a living room, kitchen, bathroom and bedroom on the lower floor, where I slept. The staircase next to my bedroom led to two dormer bedrooms. Mr. and Mrs. Ford slept in one bedroom and Kelly, their five-year-old daughter, slept in the other.

The day after I arrived, wearing my shabby clothes that I brought from home, I walked into the sixth-grade classroom at the Clarence public school. It was obvious that I wasn't one of the privileged kids. I didn't belong in the nice suburbs of the city. I knew it and the kids knew it. They didn't talk to me or welcome me into their groups of friends. I wasn't used to having school friends when I lived with my family, but now, without my family and familiar surroundings, it was emotionally painful.

"Give them time; they'll like you when they get to know you," Mrs. Ford said, as she put her arm around my shoulder, when I told her why I was sad.

"I don't want them to get to know me. I don't want them to know I'm a foster child," I whimpered quietly, letting the stream of hot tears run down my face. My heart ached for my family. I loved them, I missed them, and I wept for them.

The Ford's were younger than my parents. Mrs. Ford was slim and tall, with short, blonde hair. She often spoke to me about college. "Nancy Lee, if you study hard and get good grades, someday, you can go to college." Or, "I met Mr. Ford when I was still in college." Or, "When I graduated college, I married Mr. Ford and little Kelly was born a year later." Almost every day she said something about college. I think she missed college.

Mr. Ford had an important job with one of the utility companies. He wore a suit, white shirt and a tie to work, and carried a briefcase. He was a kind man with a kind face and a soft-spoken voice. He never told me to do anything without starting with a question. "Don't you think it would be the right thing if you helped with the dishes?" Or, "Don't you think it would be the right thing if you finished your homework first?"

Although they seemed to be a nice couple, the house was strange to me, and Mr. Ford was a stranger to me. The first night, I lay in bed my mind turned to the memory of the night when a dark figure slid in bed beside me. I knew what it was like to be a young girl fearing the night—not because of the dark, but because of what could happen in the cover of darkness.

I was a long way from home, feeling vulnerable and very much alone. I longed for my father, mother, brothers and sister. I wanted us all to be back together again. My thoughts turned to my family. With sadness in my heart, my spirit reached out for them. Crying softly, I got out of bed, sat on the floor, held my knees tight to my chest and rocked back and forth. And, then something very strange happened! It is still vivid in my memory to this day! Through my closed eyelids, I sensed a brilliant, white light. Opening my eyes, I expected to see Mrs. Ford shining a flashlight in my face, but that wasn't what happened. No one was in the bedroom, except me!

The brilliant, white light was beside me. On my right side was a huge, bright, white light, in the form of a man. He was sitting next to me, the same way that I was sitting. My head was level with his knees. He told me, *"You are not alone ~ I will always be with you."* I don't know how I stood up, got back into bed or fell off to sleep after hearing that message. My next awareness was waking up in the bed the next morning, filled with a peace that I had never felt before.

What did I experience? Was it an angel? I can't say for sure, but I believe it was a form of spiritual energy, often referred to as an "angel" or "spirit guide." The only thing I can say for sure is that since that experience I have never felt alone.

The following week, Mrs. Ford drove me to the Children's Aid Society in the downtown area of Buffalo. "Hello, Nancy Lee, I'm going to ask you some questions so I can get an idea of your IQ; is that all right with you?" asked the woman sitting at the desk, tapping her pencil on the white pad in front of her.

"What's an IQ?" I asked her, as I sat down.

"It stands for intelligence quotient."

The woman got up from behind the desk and sat on a chair near the couch where Mrs. Ford and I sat. She asked me a series of questions, mostly questions that involved numbers. After the session of puzzling questions, the woman went back to her desk. Mrs. Ford and I sat quietly, waiting for her to look up from what she was writing to talk to us. We didn't have to wait long. She looked at me with a smile and said, "The results of the test put you at 138, which is equivalent to a sixteen-year-old." I felt a sense of pride, but thought she must have figured wrong, because I didn't feel any older than my eleven years.

Mrs. Ford was given permission to take me to Boston, Massachusetts during the Easter break. On a Saturday, before we left town, my father came to their house to visit me. Mrs. Ford told me to go outside and watch for him. I put on my jacket and zipped it up to protect me from the sting of the cold wind. I hurried out the front door and began the walk down Shimerville Road toward Main Street. I was excited and happy when I saw my father get off the bus, way down at the corner.

"Daddy, Daddy—Hi, Daddy!" I yelled, waving my hand and running to meet him. There he was with his big smile, wearing his brown, leather jacket that zipped up the front, and his ever-present fedora. He didn't go anywhere without his hat.

"Slow down, you're going to fall," he called back.

"Where's Mama? Why didn't she come too?" I asked when I reached him and threw my arms around him in a tight hug.

"It's easy for me to take the buses. You know your mother doesn't like to ride the bus." I took his hand and we walked back to the Ford's house. He waited by the door while I went in to tell Mrs. Ford he was there.

"Well, bring him in, Nancy Lee—don't let him stand outside in the cold."

"Daddy, Mrs. Ford said to come in."

Mrs. Ford was standing behind me and I bumped into her as I turned around. I was so excited about seeing my father that I didn't notice she had followed me to the door.

"I don't mean to be a bother to you," my father said, as he came in with his fedora in his hand.

"Nonsense, you're not a bother. I'm glad to have the chance to meet Nancy Lee's father. You have a lovely daughter. Come into the kitchen; you can sit and visit with her there," she said, leading the way toward the kitchen, adding, "This is my daughter, Kelly. Mr. Ford isn't here now; he's at work. Enjoy your visit while I finish some things I have to do."

"You have a lovely daughter, too," my father told Mrs. Ford as she and Kelly walked away. He took a crossword puzzle book from his jacket pocket and handed it to me. "Here, this will give you something to do." I had never done a crossword puzzle before. My father explained that it was easy to do. "Just answer the questions and put the answers in the numbered boxes."

During our visit, we talked about how I liked it there and how things were back home. "You're getting a lucky break going to Boston. These must be nice people taking you with them," my father said, when I told him about the trip.

"Daddy, when can I go back home?"

"Your mother and I are trying to work it out." Taking a seat at the kitchen table, my father helped me with a crossword puzzle and we talked about my schoolwork. The visit was over all too soon. My father ended it saying, "It's hard trying to get to see all you children, but I'll come when I can. I have to go now, or I'll miss the bus." I walked him to the door and hugged him goodbye. He didn't want me to walk him back to the bus stop because the March winds were still blowing and it was bitter cold outside.

During the first week of April, we left the house for the trip to Massachusetts. I walked out the door, into the pre-dawn morning and the cool mist of the gray fog wet my face, bringing me fully awake. Mr. and Mrs. Ford put the suitcases into the trunk. I took my place next to Kelly who was already settled in the back seat.

It wasn't long before the sun brightened the sky and the day began. As we passed the farms, I looked out the window at the cows in the pastures. Some were eating the grass and their baby calves were in the pasture, too, next to their mothers, trying to chew the grass like she was doing. As we rode through the towns, we ate the lunch that Mrs. Ford packed for the trip. I enjoyed looking at the different stores and the people as they went about their business, walking along the streets, going in and out of the shops.

Near the end of the long ride, we stopped at a Howard Johnson restaurant to eat dinner. "This restaurant has the same name as the one my Aunt Loretta took me to once; it's on Main Street, near a movie house," I said, trying to show off that I had eaten in a nice restaurant before.

"Yes, there are a lot of Howard Johnson restaurants all over the country," Mrs. Ford casually replied. She wasn't impressed. After the meal, we got back into the car and continued on until we arrived at a hotel in Boston, where we stayed overnight.

The next day, we took the ferry to Martha's Vineyard off the coast of Massachusetts, staying for several days in Edgartown. One day, Mrs. Ford parked the car and we walked down to the beach. "These cliffs were created by six separate glaciers," Mrs. Ford said, as we looked up at the multi-colored layers of clay and sand that made up the Aquinnah Cliffs.

We watched the ebb and flow of the ocean on the face of the cliffs. Circling above were flocks of white and gray seagulls. They very cleverly swooped down and picked up clams in their beaks. Then, they flew above the cliffs, dropping the clams on the rocks, cracking them open so they could enjoy the tasty morsels.

We walked down a staircase to the beach. I took off my shoes and socks and walked barefoot on the pebbles and sand, down to the edge of the Atlantic Ocean, to fill a little bottle with water for a souvenir. As I held the bottle and dipped it into the ocean, a huge wave heaved up and splashed me, giving me a taste of the cold, salty, ocean water. Mrs. Ford and Kelly laughed when they saw me getting wet and the sea breeze blowing my hair about my face as I tried to spit the taste of the water from my mouth.

On another day, we drove across a bridge to Chappaquiddick Island, where we saw lobster traps and little weather-beaten dinghies along the coast. We walked along the narrow sidewalks of the shopping district of Oak Bluff. It was in that town that I met the movie star, James Cagney, when he came out of one of the little, gray-shingled cottages. "Hello, Mr. Cagney. Say hello to Mr. Cagney, Nancy Lee," Mrs. Ford said, as Mr. Cagney approached us.

"Hello," I said, with a curious smile.

"Good to see ya kid," he said, patting me on the head and smiling as he walked past.

"Who is Mr. Cagney?" I wanted to know.

"He's a very famous movie star." Mrs. Ford wasn't surprised to see him. I think she knew he was on the island and we walked past that house on purpose. The next day we headed back to Buffalo.

Unfortunately, after our trip, Mr. Ford's work transferred him to the Boston area, so I had to be placed in another foster home. Mrs. Ford packed my clothes that she had bought with the clothing allowance from the Children's Aid Society. Among my things in the brown paper bag were the silk, neck scarf and silver brooch that she bought for me in the store at Oak Bluffs. Whenever I look at those gifts, I remember her kindness. I will always be grateful to Mr. and Mrs. Ford for being in my life. They were good foster parents! This was not to be the case with some future foster parents.

A caseworker drove me to my second foster home in the Riverside section of Buffalo. Mr. and Mrs. Argus were middle-aged and had been foster parents for a long time, so they said. Mrs. Argus also said they didn't have any children of their own. Another foster girl about my age was living with them when I got there. We shared the attic, which had been converted into a bedroom.

I wasn't readily accepted at that school, either. When the kids teased me, I just had to put up with it, because I had no defense. I didn't belong in their school or their neighborhood and they knew it. While at this foster home I finished out the last two months of the sixth grade. I was glad that I was able to keep up with the other kids. I had gone to three different schools during the fourth grade, and now I was going to three different schools in the sixth grade.

There was a lilac tree in the small yard in back of the house. The lacy purple flowers smelled clean and sweet. The fragrance drifting about in the warm breeze of early summer made me long for home. Often, I closed my eyes and imagined that Nanny was near me.

One night, before getting into bed, I had the feeling I was being watched. I knew the eyes that were on me weren't those of the girl who shared the bedroom with me because her head was turned toward the wall. I lay in bed, puzzled at what I was sensing. I opened my eyes and saw the spirit of a boy, about ten or eleven years old. He appeared to be sickly and very sad. He stood at the foot of my bed, just looking at me; then, he disappeared. I wasn't afraid, but I was startled to see the spirit of that boy. In a little while I was able to put it out of my mind. I closed my eyes and eventually I fell asleep.

At the end of the week, when I took a towel from the linen closet for my Saturday bath, I saw a little silver bell. I shook it back and forth, listening to the sharp ring of the clapper, as it struck the sides. Mrs. Argus came hurrying from the living room where she had been sitting on the sofa mending a shirt.

"What are you doing?" she yelled at me, grabbing the bell from my hand.

"I'm sorry, I just wanted to hear the bell," I said, surprised that she was upset.

"That was my son's bell. He rang it when he needed me. I was puzzled. Hadn't she told me that she didn't have any children?

"Where is your son?"

"He's dead. He died when he was a young boy—that's none of your business!" she said, as she walked back to the living room. I went into the bathroom, with curious thoughts of the experience I had of seeing the spirit of a young boy. Could it have been her son?

Mrs. Argus wasn't only impatient with me; she was impatient with everyone. One Saturday morning she said, "Your father is coming to visit you, today."

"What time is he coming?" I asked, with wide eyes and a big smile, as I came down the stairs from the attic bedroom.

"How would I know? Sometime between one o'clock and three o'clock; those are the visiting hours."

I was happy because I hadn't seen my father since I got back from the Easter vacation with the Fords, and now I had passed the sixth grade. I had so much I wanted to tell him. And, I wanted to ask him when I would be able to go back home.

The doorbell rang, as we were sitting at the kitchen table finishing lunch. Mrs. Argus answered the front door and came back into the kitchen. "Your father's here. He's early. I can see he can't tell time. Go outside and sit on the front porch with him." I put my sandwich plate in the sink, ran down the back steps, out the door and around the corner. My father was standing on the front porch.

"Hi Daddy", I said with a big smile. "Did you see Tommy or baby Jimmy?" I asked, excitedly.

"Oh, they're happy and like it where they are." I wasn't sure if he was telling me the truth, but it was what I wanted to hear. "So, you passed all your exams, did you? You're going into seventh grade in the fall. You're really growing up, Nancy Lee."

We sat on the porch steps and I talked about how much fun I had on the trip to Massachusetts, and that I met a Hollywood movie star named Mr. Cagney. "Is he a real movie star, because I don't remember seeing him in any movies?"

"Sure he is, and a big one, at that. You got a lucky break meeting someone like him," my father said with a pleased smile.

"Daddy, when can I come back home?" I whined.

"I'm working on it, Nancy Lee. It won't be too long." Changing the subject he told me some things about his work and that he was trying to get some money saved up so we would have nice things when we got back together again. He wanted to buy an electric refrigerator for us.

Mrs. Argus opened the front door and said, "Your hour is up. You'll have to leave." Then, she closed the door—hard!

"Son of a bitch! What did she do—set a timer?" my father mumbled. I was sad that my father had to leave so soon. I gave him a hug and watched him walk down the street and turn the corner. I was angry with Mrs. Argus for making my father leave so soon. I went in the house and up to the attic bedroom where I worked a crossword puzzle.

Although Mr. and Mrs. Argus weren't Baptist, they still went to church twice on Sunday, just as my grandparents did. Mrs. Argus bought a "church dress" for me, but I was only allowed to wear it while at the church; between services I had to take it off so that I would keep it clean. It was a pretty dress with an eyelet bodice, but I didn't think there was anything special about it.

"You won't be needing your church dress anymore," Mrs. Argus said when she put my clothes into a brown paper bag for my move to the next foster home. Although she bought the dress for me, it wasn't mine to keep. Once again, what I thought was mine, wasn't. The dress stayed in the house when I left—it didn't make me sad to leave that foster home!

It was the beginning of July when a caseworker drove me to yet another foster home. "How far is this place?" I asked. She didn't answer. She must have thought I was complaining about the long ride. "How far is this place?" I asked, again, but louder.

"This house isn't in the city. It's in the town of Springville. You'll like it there." How did she know if I'd like it there?

Traveling down the long country road, we passed a few farms that had rows of corn stalks and other farm crops sprouting from the plowed earth. We were in the country, for sure. The caseworker turned off the main road and onto a tar-and-gravel road. Finally, we came to a big white house with a big, red barn. She turned into the dirt driveway and parked the car. I picked up my brown paper bag and followed her up the steps onto the front porch.

A woman came to the door in answer to the caseworker's knock. "Hello Mrs. Hughes, I'm Mrs. Burns from the Children's Aid Society. This is Nancy Lee, the new foster girl we spoke about."

Mrs. Hughes held the door open and we walked into a kitchen. "I hope you like it here, Nancy Lee. The sow just had seven piglets. They're the cutest little things." Pointing to a wooden rocking chair, she added, "Put your bag on the chair, go out to the barn and have a look while I talk to Mrs. Burns. I'll show you around the house later." Mrs. Hughes reminded me of my mother. She, too, was short and a little overweight, and, she wore an apron over her cotton dress.

I went outside to the back of the house where the barn was. The barn doors were open so I walked in. The hay stored in the overhead loft gave the air a sweet smell. I liked it. Two, young, American Indian girls were in the barn standing by the pigpen watching the mother sow nurse the little piglets. "I know your name is Nancy Lee. We knew you were coming," one of the girls said. The two young girls told me they were foster children, too. They were sisters, who had lived there since they were very young. I liked the little girls, but they were too young for me to enjoy playing with.

Mrs. Hughes came in the barn with a tall man wearing a pair of worn-out bib overalls. I assumed he was Mr. Hughes.

"Hello, Nancy Lee," he said, nodding his head in greeting.

"Hello, Mr. Hughes." The little, black-and-white dog that followed behind him ran over to me and wagged her tail as she sniffed around my legs, getting to know me. I reached down and she licked my hand when I tried to pet her.

"The dog's name is Lady. She follows Mr. Hughes everywhere. She even rides in the truck when Mr. Hughes goes into town, Mrs. Hughes said. Picking up the little dog, she walked out of the barn adding, "Ok, Nancy Lee, let's show you where you'll sleep." She put the dog down, and with her arm around my shoulder, walked me into the house.

Shortly after I had settled into that foster home, Mrs. Hughes said, "Your mother is coming to visit you today."

My mother, along with Nanny and Grandpa Meyer, Auntie Alice and Uncle Will, Tommy and Carol Jean, rode out to the farm in Uncle Will's big car. What a surprise seeing everyone! I didn't know what to do. Should I hug my mother first or Nanny? Should I say "Hello" to Auntie Alice and hug her first?

I didn't have to make the choice. My mother did it for me. She took my sister from her lap, walked toward me, and gave me a really tight hug. She looked pretty today, with her make-up on and hair done in a fashionable style. I smelled the Evening in Paris perfume she had on, remembering that she only used it for special occasions.

"Where is Daddy, Mama?"

"Oh, he couldn't come; there wasn't enough room in the car," she said, making her face into a playful frown.

Nanny and Auntie Alice brought boxes of cooked food from the trunk of the car. There were my favorite baked beans with brown sugar and molasses, potato salad, cold cabbage salad, fried chicken, buttermilk biscuits, brownies with chocolate frosting, and a big, thermos jug of red Kool-Aid. Grandpa held out the biggest watermelon I ever saw. "How about this? Think it's big enough for you, little squirt?" he said, setting it on the picnic table. The long table held plenty of food—a feast for everyone!

Grandpa also brought his Kodak camera and captured the events of the day. The family album holds the photos of the picnic visit. There is a photo of Tommy climbing a tree in the apple orchard; photos of me showing off doing cartwheels and handstands on the front lawn; and, a photo of Carol Jean, playing with the two little girls. The picnic visit lasted most of the day.

When it was over, I hugged my mother, Nanny and Auntie Alice, and said goodbye to Grandpa, Uncle Will, Tommy and Carol Jean. My mother took her purse from the back seat of the car, opened it and handed me two dollars and a crossword puzzle book. "Here, honey, I almost forgot. Daddy sent you some money and a book."

The car pulled out of the driveway and headed down the country road. I followed after it, waving my final goodbye, wondering when I would see them again. Walking along the road, away from the house so Mrs. Hughes couldn't hear me, with a choke in my throat, I sang the lyrics of *"Near You,"* one of my favorite songs.

Now I had two dollars and Mrs. Hughes told me that I could earn some more money by picking string beans at a local farm. I didn't have much of anything else to do, so I was eager to go. She drove me to a farm, not far away. We got there in mid-morning. A lot of kids around my age were already in the field picking the string beans. I hoped none of the kids would ask me where I lived. I didn't want them to know that I lived in a foster home. Picking beans was harder work than I thought it would be. I worked in the fields until late in the afternoon without talking to anyone or even taking a break, like some of the other kids did.

The pay was five cents for every quart picked. I don't know how the farmer determined how many quarts I picked, because as I picked the string beans, I put them into a cloth sling. When it was full, I took it to the farmer. He emptied it into a bushel and gave it back to me. I repeated the process until a whistle blew for us to stop. I waited with the rest of the kids, standing in front of the table where the farmer sat with a notebook and a cash box. "You're next," the farmer said, handing me one dollar and forty-five cents.

"I don't think you gave me enough; I know I picked more than that," I said, standing there, with beads of sweat rolling down my overheated, red face.

"That's all you earned today—now move along," he demanded. I didn't know what to say, I didn't have any proof that he cheated me.

When I got into Mrs. Hughes' car for the ride back, she asked, "How did you do; did you like picking beans?"

"I guess so," I answered, not telling her how I really felt. I decided not to do any more farm work.

I decided to just enjoy the summer. On a hot afternoon, for example,

I laid in the grass on the front lawn. It was so peaceful just to lie there, looking up at the blue sky, listening to the bees buzzing about the flowers near the porch, hearing the cooing of mourning doves and the mooing of cows from a farm somewhere down the road. The afternoon air was filled with warm sunshine and sweet fragrances. I was beginning to like the rural life. It wasn't too bad living at that foster home. But, I still wished I were back home with my family. I really missed them!

On another occasion, I walked down the road and picked some wild flowers. I made a bouquet with Queen Anne's lace, purple phlox, yellow buttercups and orange daylilies. Back at the house, Mrs. Hughes gave me a quart milk bottle for a vase. I put the bouquet on the dresser near the bed where I slept.

The house had indoor plumbing, but there was also a roughly built, two-seater outhouse on the farm. White lye was kept in a black bucket in the corner. I liked to take the black shovel, scoop up the lye and sprinkle it down the hole, pretending it was snowing. That was another way I amused myself until Mrs. Hughes said, "Nancy Lee you're using too much lye; you don't need to use that much." Actually, I didn't need to use any, because I never used the two-seater. I always used the toilet in the house.

There was a field next to the outhouse. On another day, dressed in shorts and a sleeveless blouse, I ran through the tall wheat growing in the field. I ran slowly at first, being careful where I stepped. Then, I ran faster, running in circles and zigzagging through the long shafts of wheat. When I reached the clearing on the other side of the field, I saw that I had little black leeches stuck to my bare arms and legs. I screamed, "Get them off, get them off!" as I ran down the road back to the house.

Mr. Hughes' dog, Lady, was across the road in another field. She heard me scream and came running. The mail truck drove past as the dog ran across the road. The truck hit Lady but it never stopped. Running into the house, I screamed, "Come quick! Come quick! The mail truck just hit Lady!" Mrs. Hughes ran out of the house and Mr. Hughes ran out of the barn. I picked the leeches off my arms and legs and flung them to the ground, as I ran behind them to where Lady lay dead in the road.

Mr. Hughes gently lifted Lady and carried her into the barn. He put her in the wagon hitched to the back of the riding lawnmower, tossed in a shovel beside Lady and sadly drove off into the orchard. Lady went to "dog heaven." When Brownie died, my grandmother told me, that's where all dead dogs go.

It wasn't long after that when August came to an end and I was told, "Get your things together, Nancy Lee, you're going to a new foster home tomorrow," I didn't ask why; I just did what I was told. I was getting used to being sent from one place to another, even though I couldn't understand why. When the day came for me to leave, it was a warm, sunny day in late August. I waited on the porch, looking up at the clear blue sky. A car pulled into the dirt driveway. I picked up my brown paper bag and was on my way.

My fourth foster home was in the Arno home in the town of Chaffee. The little, white farmhouse sat on top a hill that sloped down on one side toward a ravine with two barns in back of the house. The barn near the silo was where the cows were placed in stalls for milking. The other was for the farm machinery.

When I arrived, I was surprised to discover that my brother, Billy, was living there. I was almost twelve and Billy had just turned eight years old in June. Billy was a special concern for me because of all he had gone through after he was burned. "Hi, Nancy Lee, my foster mother told me you're coming to live here. Are you?" Billy asked, running up to me, with a big smile. I reached out and gave him a rocking hug, like brothers and sisters do.

Two other foster children, about my age, stood in the driveway with the foster mother. They just stood there looking at me and didn't say a word. One was a tall, skinny, American Indian girl with long, straight, black hair. The other was a blond-haired boy.

Mrs. Arno, the foster mother, was a heavy-set woman She looked to be a little older than my mother. She seemed neither stern nor friendly. She said, "Nancy Lee, meet David and Nora," adding, "Nora, take Nancy Lee in the house and show her where she'll sleep." With my brown, paper bag in hand, I followed Nora into the house. A kitchen, bathroom, living room and two small bedrooms were on the first floor. Mr. and Mrs. Arno slept in one bedroom. David and Billy slept in the other. From the living room, a staircase led to an attic bedroom. There were two twin-size beds in the attic. "That's your bed. You can put your clothes in this drawer," Nora said, pointing to one of the beds and the only dresser in the room.

After putting away my things, I went outside where I walked around the front of the house with Billy. "These people are really bad; Mister Arno will hit you with the strap, if he catches you doing something wrong," Billy said, in a low voice, as if he were telling me a secret. I was surprised when Billy said that!

"What do you mean, Billy? Did you get hit with a strap?" Billy went on telling me about the time he went down to the barn when he was told not to. One of the cows had just given birth to a calf. Billy wanted to see the new calf. Mr. Arno found out about it because Nora told on him. Billy got a bad whipping. I knew I wasn't going to like Nora, the snitch. I hadn't met Mr. Arno, yet, but already I knew that I wouldn't like him either.

I first saw Mr. Arno at suppertime. He came into the kitchen, washed his hands in the sink, and sat down at the table with us. He looked like a typical hard-working farmer with his stubby, brown-and-gray beard and the frayed-edge pant legs of his dirty overalls and rumpled, long-sleeve shirt. Mealtime was strange; not one word was spoken by anyone. We all ate in silence and left the table in silence. I sensed that this wasn't a happy place.

The very next Saturday I had my chance to avenge Billy! After breakfast, the Arno's got into their car and drove off, leaving us behind on the farm. They didn't say where they were going. I didn't know where they went or when they would be back.

Billy and Nora were in the house and David was in the barn. I waited outside, close to the house, hoping Nora would come out. Waiting for her gave me time to build up my courage. Finally, she came out. I grabbed her by the arm, swung her around and pushed her down. Sitting on top of her, I pinned her arms to the ground and yelled in her face, "Don't ever snitch on my brother again."

While I was still on top of her, the Arno's car pulled into the driveway. I jumped up fast. Nora ran into the house. Luckily, they didn't pay any attention to us. Nora got the message; from then on, she kept her distance from me. We shared the same bedroom, but didn't speak when we went up to sleep. For that matter, we hardly ever spoke to each other.

A school bus took David, Nora, Billy and me to school in the early mornings, when the sun was just peeking over the horizon. I sat in the front of the bus with Billy; Nora sat in the back with David. I was happy that Nora and I weren't in the same seventh grade class at school. I bet Nora was happy about that, too.

We weren't the only ones that got up at daybreak. The sounds of a tractor engine could be heard in the distance, as Mr. Arno went about his work. Roosters ran about, chickens cackled from the hen house and cows mooed in the pasture. This was a real farm!

When the bus brought us home from school, we had chores to do. One of my jobs was to get the flat-bottomed cart at the bottom of the slope near the barn, wheel it to the front of the driveway, put the empty, milk cans onto the cart, and return them to the barn. Then, I took them off and placed them near the milk cooler. It took me several trips to do the job.

The wooden handles of the cart were rough so I always got slivers in my hands. That was only one of my daily chores. Another job I had to do was gather eggs from the hen house and take them to the basement where Mrs. Arnold inspected them before putting them into the crates. The hens didn't like me taking their eggs. They cackled loudly and pecked at me with their sharp beaks, as I went about my work.

When it was time for killing the chickens, I had to wear shorts. "Put these on. I don't want blood getting on your clothes," Mrs. Arno said, handing me a pair of old, blood stained shorts. One at a time, Nora brought a live chicken to Mr. Arno. Its head was chopped off with a quick swing of his hatchet. Then, he handed me the chicken. With wings still flapping, and its headless neck dripping warm blood onto my bare thighs, I ran to where Mrs. Arno and David sat near a pot of boiling water. They dipped the chicken into the pot and quickly pulled it out. Feathers flew everywhere as they plucked the chickens until they were nothing but naked, pimply flesh. I detested my job, but I had to do it!

There were several plum trees in the orchard, with over-ripe fruit still on the branches. I asked Mrs. Arno if I might pick some of the fruit and sell them to people in passing cars. She said that I could. I picked the plums, put them into a basket and stood by the roadside, watching as the cars drove past. None stopped.

As I stood near the road, a bus passed. I watched as it went down the road and stopped not far away at the Cider Bee Restaurant. I didn't care about selling the plums after I saw the bus. I was too excited about the prospect of taking the bus back to the city to see my parents. I set the basket of plums on the ground and walked down the road to the restaurant. "When does that bus come by here?" I asked the lady behind the counter.

"Do you want the bus schedule for the Greyhound Bus? They're over there," she said, pointing to a shelf near the door. I knew buses ran on a schedule like trains. But, I didn't know that the schedule was printed on paper and the paper was free. I looked carefully through the papers on the shelf and found the Greyhound Bus schedule. Hurrying back to the foster home, I showed it to Mrs. Arno and asked if I could take the Greyhound Bus into Buffalo to visit my parents on the following Saturday.

"You'll get lost," was her answer. She didn't say "Yes," and she didn't say "No."

"I know how to take a bus, and I won't get lost. I have my own money to pay the fare. I promise I'll be back on Sunday night before it gets dark," I said, with a pleading look. I wasn't really sure how to get to Seneca Street, but I knew the bus driver would know. I quickly added, "I took the bus to the Buffalo Zoo by myself and I often rode the bus downtown by myself."

Mrs. Arno finally agreed that I could go on Saturday morning, but that

I had to be back before dark on Sunday night, or she would call the police and tell them I ran away. I asked if Billy could go, too. Mrs. Arnold said a definite, "No!"

All that week, I thought about going back home. When David, Nora, Billy and I rode the school bus to and from school, I closed my eyes and pretended I was riding the Greyhound Bus to Seneca Street. I imagined how happy my parents would be when they saw me.

Saturday morning, after I awoke, made up my bed, washed my face, brushed my teeth, combed my hair and dressed in jeans and a plaid blouse, I went into the kitchen, but I didn't take the time to eat breakfast. I was too excited about going home. I said goodbye to Mrs. Arno, who was putting a pitcher of milk back into the refrigerator. Nora was at the table, finishing her breakfast and didn't even look up when I passed her to walk out the door. Mr. Arno, David and Billy were already out in the barn. It was a beautiful morning. I ran down the driveway and hurried to the Cider Bee Restaurant. I didn't have to wait long. The bus came and I got on. "How much to downtown Buffalo?"

"How much money do you have?"

"I have three dollars."

"That'll be more than enough." I paid the fare and took a seat. The bus continued down the road, stopping to let people on and off. I looked out the window at the crops in the fields and the countryside, as we rode along. Six little signs placed in the ground one after another made a sentence reading, "The wolf / is shaved / so neat and trim / Riding Hood / is chasing him / Burma-Shave."

At the end of the line in downtown Buffalo, the bus driver told me where to stand to get the next bus. When that bus came, I asked the driver, "Do you go to Seneca Street?"

He told me he didn't but he would let me off where I could get on a bus that did. I sat up front and kept my eyes on the driver, waiting for him to tell me where I should get off. "This is it, little girl. Here's your transfer," he said, handing me a blue slip of paper.

I hoped my parents were home. Mrs. Arno couldn't call them to let them know I was coming because my parents didn't have a telephone. After riding on the second city bus, I reached the house on Seneca Street. My father wasn't home; he was working.

My mother was home. She was surprised to see me. And I was surprised to see that she looked as pretty as she did the day she was at the Hughes' farm. We sat at the kitchen table and talked about all kinds of things: the foster mother, the farm and school. I told her that Mr. Arno whipped Billy with a leather strap. Her eyes opened wide in shock. She exclaimed "Oh, no!"

After I ate a cheese sandwich, I hurried down Duerstein Street to surprise Jeanie. Nobody answered the door, so I hurried back to my house. My father had just returned from work. "How did you get here? Your mother told me you took the Greyhound." I thought he was angry with me and didn't like that I came back home. But, he wasn't angry with me; he was angry with Mrs. Arno for letting me come all that way, alone.

We ate supper together, and I slept in my old bed, again. The bedroom I used to sleep in with my sister was just as I remembered it. Maybe we were poor, maybe my parents did drink more than they should, maybe the house we lived in was shabby and didn't meet the approval of the Children's Aid Society, but I was glad to be home, even if it was just for a little while. The next morning I left early and returned to the Arno's farm as I promised.

The Arno foster home was where I lived when I changed from a girl into a lady. It came as quite a shock! None of the girls at school talked with me about such things. I guess they didn't think of me as one of them. When the gym teacher said, "Girls who have their 'lady time' still have to take gym, I don't want any excuses." I didn't know what that meant. Neither of the foster mothers nor my own mother gave me "the talk." I was like Maggie in the book *The Thorn Birds*, by Colleen McCullough. Maggie was never given the talk, either. It was Father Ralph de Bricassart who had to tell her about menstruation.

When I asked Mrs. Arno what I should do because I had this "problem," she only said, "Now you can have babies." What! What was she talking about? I didn't want babies. She explained, but with the least bit of information. Handing me a sanitary pad and an elastic belt she said, "Put these on, and that'll take care of it. When you need more, they're in my bedroom closet. Just ask for them."

In the beginning of this new experience, I didn't get it right because the sanitary pad kept popping up when I sat at my school desk. If I were a boy, I guess you would call it an erection. I was so embarrassed! Several months later, by the time the snows of winter came and went, I finally got the hang of it.

On a spring day, I was outside near the road watching the cars pass and longing to take the Greyhound bus again. Mrs. Arno called to me. "Nancy Lee, come here now! This minute!" She sounded upset. I hurried down the driveway and into the kitchen. "You were the last one in the kitchen this morning. Where is the letter that was on the table? I know you took it, now where is it?" she ranted, with her face beginning to turn red with anger.

"I didn't see any letter." I tried to tell her that I didn't even know what she was talking about.

"There was a letter I left on the kitchen table this morning. Where is it?" she demanded. When I couldn't give her a satisfactory answer, she said, "Get upstairs and don't come down until you give me that letter."

I hurried up the stairs and sat on the edge of my bed. I was hurt and upset because she blamed me, and I hadn't taken the letter. In a few minutes, I began to calm down, wondering who took the letter and where it was? A scene flashed in my mind of Mr. Arno picking up a letter from the kitchen table, taking it into their bedroom, placing it in the top drawer of the dresser. I wasn't sure if that was true or not, but I didn't want to stay in the bedroom all day.

I walked down the stairs and into the kitchen where Mrs. Arno sat, drinking a cup of tea. "Mrs. Arno, I think Mr. Arno put your letter in his dresser drawer."

She gave me a strange look, slowly got up and walked into the bedroom. When she came out, she had the letter in her hand. "How did you know Mr. Arno put the letter in the dresser?

"I don't know; sometimes I can imagine things, and they're true." From that day on, until I left their house, Mrs. Arno didn't boss me around anymore, but she often gave me strange looks. I think she thought I was spooky.

A short time later, I was at the kitchen table eating breakfast with Nora and Billy. Mr. Arno and David had already finished breakfast and were in the barn, working. Mrs. Arno said, "Nancy Lee, when you're finished, pack up your things. You're going to another foster home today." I was surprised and disappointed, because I had school on Monday and was going to get my mark for the math test. I was good at math and hoped I got all the answers right. Now, I would never know.

The caseworker came to the farm a little before noon. I don't know why they kept moving me and not letting me finish my grades in one school. I hugged Billy and said goodbye. I worried about him staying on that farm, but there was nothing I could do about it. "Billy, Daddy told me that we'd all be home soon. Be good and remember, I'll be thinking about you!" I called back to him, as the caseworker's car pulled out of the driveway.

My fifth foster home was in the town of Orchard Park. It was a foster home where Tommy had been living. He had recently been allowed to return home. Mr. and Mrs. Carr were the foster parents. They were old, but not as old as my grandparents. They had a son named Arthur and a foster girl named Maggie. Arthur and Maggie were both nine and I was twelve years old, too old to be interested in playing with them.

The Carr's foster home was also on a farm, but not as big as the Arno's farm. The house was almost hidden behind two large trees that stood in front, their roots running along the ground under the grass like snakes. The farm had one unpainted barn and several Black Angus cows in the pasture. A shed was attached behind the big, old, gray farmhouse. Mr. Carr came into the house entering the shed from outside, walking on the rough concrete floor past the wringer washing machine, tin tubs, gray metal buckets, rag mop, and broom leaning by the back door. There, he took off his muddy boots before walking into the kitchen. Everyone else used the side door, which also led into the kitchen. The front door, which led into the living room was never used.

Besides the living room and kitchen, the first floor had a pantry and a room with a twin-size bed and dresser. The stairs in the hall off the kitchen led to three bedrooms on the second floor. Mr. and Mrs. Carr had the large bedroom, Arthur had another and Maggie and I shared the third.

I came to this home in late April or early May. I'm not sure exactly, but it was in the spring. Early, on the morning of the day after I arrived, Mrs. Carr drove me to school. I was told the number of my homeroom and told to go there while Mrs. Carr took care of my registration. I found the room and took a seat in the front row. In a few minutes my classmates started coming into the room.

"Get out of that seat! Sit in the back," a girl ordered.

"Hey, Peggy, let her alone," one of the boys said.

"She's a foster kid; she doesn't belong here," Peggy answered. I got up and took a seat in the back of the room. That was my first day at school. How did she know so soon? Who told her?

During the last few months of the seventh grade, I didn't make any friends, because, Peggy, the most popular girl in my class, had made that comment about me not belonging there. Fortunately, the remainder of the short time that I was in the seventh grade was uneventful. I was able to pick up from where the other kids were in the lessons, and in June I passed the exams with good grades.

July began and I had no friends to talk with. Walking down the long road from the house to the corner of the main road, I turned right and continued walking until I reached the quaint little shopping district about a mile away. A restaurant, drugstore, bank, and various small shops lined both sides of the street. It was nice to be able to walk into stores again. I especially liked the little drugstore with a variety of things on the shelves. There were assortments of candy, make-up, fancy shampoo, and even some boxes of inexpensive costume jewelry.

On a Friday in August, during one of my many excursions about the town, I saw a Greyhound Bus parked at the corner by the drug store. I hurried to where it was parked. The door was open, and the driver was in the driver's seat reading a newspaper. "Mister, does this bus go into the city of Buffalo?" I asked, hoping he would say, "Yes," and he did. "Does it go all the way down Orchard Park Road?" I asked, hoping he would say "Yes" again, and he did.

Walking back to the Carr's farm, I stopped in the grocery store at the corner where I lived and asked, "Do you know what time the Greyhound Bus passes by here?" I was happy to learn that it passed by every day around noon. I hurried down the road and into the house. When I asked Mrs. Carr if I could take the bus into the city to visit my parents, she didn't object.

The next day, before noon, I hurried down the road and waited at the corner in front of the grocery store. The bus stopped. I boarded, paid the fare, and took a seat. It wasn't a very long ride. Soon, the bus reached the city line between the town of West Seneca and South Buffalo. I got off and walked the several blocks down Seneca Street to my parents' flat.

When I walked up the back stairs, I heard music playing. That meant my mother was home. I opened the door and went into the kitchen. I was surprised to see an electric refrigerator where the icebox once stood. My mother and Tommy were happy to see me and I was really happy to see them. Tommy had been allowed to return home now that he was sixteen. He seemed much older than I remembered him. He had a job as a shoeshine boy at a downtown hotel. He wasn't called "Tommy" anymore; my parents called him "Tom." He was only sixteen, but he was already six feet tall.

We had dinner when my father came home from work. Then, Tom and I played the card game, Blackjack. I beat him almost every time. I wished I could have stayed home for good, but I had to go back. If I didn't, Mrs. Carr wouldn't let me visit again. From then on, I rode the Greyhound Bus home almost every weekend.

When school started again, Peggy, the girl who had called me a "foster girl," and I became good friends. We had a lot of fun together. Peggy and I hung around with Beverley, Frank, Chet and Roy. We got together on the weekends and walked around the town. I liked them, but I didn't let myself get really close because I knew Peggy was right; I didn't belong there.

Peggy was a little ball of fire. Everyone liked her, despite her temper. Beverly was quiet, like me. We rode the same school bus. She got off a few stops before I did. Roy was tall and he came from a socially respected family. Frank was a redhead with good looks and a great personality. Chet reminded me of my brother, Tom, always looking for an adventure and daring to do anything.

The school bus that took me to and from school didn't stop in front of the Carr's farm. It came down the main road stopping at the corners of various side roads to pick up the kids and let them off. When the school bus let me off, I had to walk the long country road, passing the woods, before I reached the farm.

I had a frightening experience while walking to the Carr's farm after the school bus let me off. A red pick-up truck with two men rode slowly past me and stopped. As I approached the truck, the back of my neck began to tingle and I got goose flesh on my arms. I was afraid and knew I was in danger. "Come on, girl, get in! We'll give you a ride," the man said, opening the door and blocking me from passing.

I stepped around the door and took off running down the road. The truck came after me. I ran faster, just making it to the end of the driveway as the truck sped past. I may have lived in the country, but I was city-smart about dirty old men.

I was also smart about taking care of babies. As I walked home from school on another day, at one of the few houses on the road, a young woman sat on the stoop of her porch next to a baby carriage. She smiled at me and said, "I see you live at Mrs. Carr's farm. She told me that you might like the job of babysitting. Would you?" I jumped at the chance to earn a few dollars.

Babysitting was an easy job; all I did was give the baby a bottle, burp her and let her fall off to sleep in my arms. After I laid her in the crib, I was able to sit on the couch and watch television or read my schoolbooks. I thought babysitting must be the easiest job in the world. It wasn't any different from everyday living. I saved my baby-sitting money, hoping to buy a new bicycle. My other one had been left outside all the time that I was gone. It was in bad shape and had to be thrown away.

At the end of the school year, Chet asked me if I would go with him to the school dance. It wasn't like a date, we were just friends. Chet's father was going to chauffer us. Mrs. Carr took me to a thrift-store to buy a dress. There weren't any young girl's clothes in the store, just women's clothing. I tried on a yellow chiffon gown. It was a little too big, but Mrs. Carr paid the four dollars and bought it for me to wear to the school dance. "Mrs. Carr," I protested, "My friends aren't wearing gowns; they're all wearing short dresses."

"You'll wear that gown or you're not going," she said in a way that told me it was useless to protest any further.

In sewing class, I asked the teacher, "If I bring a gown to school tomorrow, can I stay after and use a sewing machine to shorten it and make it fit?" She said, "Yes." I was glad that she agreed and rode the school bus home a little happier.

I went into the house and told Mrs. Carr about my plan. She wasn't happy about it. "You'll spoil the gown if you shorten it." She wouldn't allow me to take it out of the house.

On Saturday, when I visited my parents, I asked my father if he would buy me a new dress. "I don't have the money right now. Maybe next week, when you come back."

"But, Daddy, it'll be too late, then." That Sunday night, I rode the bus back to the Carr's farm in a gloomy mood. My hope of getting a new dress was shattered. There was nothing I could do. I would have to wear the yellow chiffon gown to the school dance.

I was self-conscious about everything, as any normal thirteen-year-old was, but more so now, because I looked frumpy and out of place at the school dance. Even though none of my classmates made comments, I knew they were thinking, "Look at the poor foster girl."

The Saturday after school ended, I visited my parents, again. I was surprised to see Nanny and Grandpa Meyer there. My father hadn't gone to work that Saturday, so he was there, too. "Well, well, Nancy Lee, look how you've grown," Nanny said when I walked into the dining room where everyone sat at the table drinking coffee and eating the donuts that she had brought.

I gave Nanny a cheek kiss and took a seat beside my mother. "Honey, how did the dance go?" she asked, expecting me to tell her all about it.

"It was okay," I answered, not wanting to think about that humiliating event anymore. It wouldn't have done any good to complain about it, now.

"Hey, squirt, how about those exams? Your mother said they were hard. But, you passed; that's all that counts."

"They weren't that hard, Grandpa." While we waited for Tom to come home, we continued light conversation about school, the weather and how grown-up I was.

It was a little after three o'clock when Tom walked in. My mother had baked a chocolate cake. She brought it into the dining room and placed it on the table. Tom washed up and joined us.

Nanny handed me a small gift-wrapped package, with a blue bow on top. "Don't just look at it—open it, Nancy Lee." she said, smiling her gentle smile. It was almost too pretty to open. I carefully pulled away the Scotch tape so the paper wouldn't tear and lifted the lid of the gray, velvet-covered box. Inside was a rose-gold Gruen wristwatch. "Now, put it on and see how it looks," Nanny said, delighted with my surprised look.

"How's that, Squirt? You've got your own watch, now. Do you like it?"

"Yes, Grandpa, I like it a lot." I was pleased to get any gift. "Thank you, Nanny and Grandpa," I said, getting up from the dining room chair to give them hugs.

After Nanny and Grandpa left, my father and I walked down Seneca Street to a dress shop where he was going to buy me a graduation present. "There is a limit, but I think you can find something you'd like," he said, as we entered the store. I couldn't help wishing that I had this chance to buy something last week, when it would have made the world of difference in the memory of my first and only school dance!

My father didn't like the Daisy Mae blouse I picked out. But, after a lot of pleading, he bought it for me, saying, "You can have it, but wear it right. I don't want you wearing it off your shoulders." I agreed, but I think he knew I was going to do as I pleased when he wasn't around. After all, that was the reason I wanted the blouse in the first place. What thirteen-year-old girl ever obeyed everything her parents told her? He also bought me a two-piece swimsuit.

I had such a nice visit with everyone that weekend. I even got a chance to sit on the couch in the living room and watch the black-and-white programs on the new television set that my father bought. The television, radio, and phonograph player were all part of the same floor-model cabinet. When it was time to leave, my mother gave me two dollars. I left with my new blouse, feeling happy, as I walked toward the city line to catch the Greyhound Bus to ride it back to the Carr's farm.

The following Saturday morning I got ready for my visit home. Mr. Carr was out in the barn. Mrs. Carr and her son, Arthur, left to do shopping and run errands, as usual. After I finished cutting the grass and making my bed, I washed up and dressed in my Daisy Mae blouse. "Goodbye, Maggie," I said, hurrying out the door.

"Nancy Lee, will you bring me back a candy bar again?"

"Sure honey, I'll bring back a Baby Ruth." Carrying the bag with my clothes for the weekend trip, I walked down the long country road, singing "Tra la la, tweedle dee dee dee" and the rest of the lyrics to the song *"Mockingbird Hill"* It was a happy song. I had heard it on the radio at my parents' house.

The Greyhound Bus took me to the city line and I hurried the rest of the way down Seneca Street, trying to get out of the heat of that hot Saturday in July 1952. In the house, my mother was in the living room sitting on the couch, listening to music on the radio and reading a romance magazine. "Honey, you look so pretty in that blouse, but don't let your father catch you wearing it like that." Then she looked closer. "How did you get the black-and-blue marks on your chest?" my mother asked.

"I always get black-and-blue marks when I cut the grass."

My mother didn't say anything more about the bruises. She just frowned and raised her eyebrows as she walked into the kitchen. "You must be hungry." Opening the cupboard she took out a jar of peanut butter and made a sandwich for me. While I ate the sandwich and drank a glass of milk, Tom came home.

"Hey there, Spooky, I see you escaped from the farm, again," he joked. Tom saw the bruises. "What happened to you?" Tom asked as he went to the refrigerator, picked up a bottle of chocolate milk and drank from the bottle.

"Tom, you stop that. Get a glass if you want some milk." My mother scolded.

As I finished my glass of milk, I asked, "Tom, do you want to go to the pool with me? It's going to be a scorcher today."

"Sure, let's go, I'll even pay the ten cents for your locker," he said, walking toward his bedroom to get his swim trunks. I opened the top drawer of the vanity dresser where I kept my new Greun wristwatch. Next to it was the pink two-piece swimsuit my father had bought me. I rolled it into a towel. Tom grabbed his swim trunks, rolled them into a towel, and out the door we went.

My mother smiled as she watched us leave. She was happy to see Tom and me together again. "Don't worry about us, Mom; we'll probably stay until the pool closes," Tom said, as we headed down the stairs. "Come on, I'll race you to the pool," he said, when we reached the park, reminding me that I was still his little sister.

Tom went into the boys' entrance at one end of the brick building. I went into the girls' entrance at the other end. I changed into my swimsuit and handed my clothes to the girl standing behind the counter. She put them into a numbered cubicle and handed me a safety pin with a numbered tab. I pinned it to the bottom part of my swimsuit. With my clothes safely stored, I walked out the door and into the pool area.

Another girl sat outside the door behind a small wooden stool. Her job was to check that anyone entering the pool area didn't have athlete's foot. I put my foot on the stool and spread my toes. "You're cleared," she said.

Hurrying into the diving pool area where Tom waited for me, I climbed the ladder of the high board. "Tom, want to see me do a swan dive?"

"Sure, go for it," he yelled up to me, as he climbed the ladder of the medium board. Tom didn't like to dive. He just ran and jumped. Me? I liked to show off my diving skills. I stood on the edge of the board, took three spring bounces, and off I flew, into the air with my arms spread out, bringing them together just before I hit the water. Splash! There I was in the pool. The top of my two-piece swimsuit was floating on top of the water ahead of me. Before I got out of the pool, I grabbed my floating top and put it back on.

That day, I learned not to be a show-off, or I might show off more than I intended. After I did a few regular dives and Tom did a few more cannonballs, we left the diving pool and headed toward the swimming pool. "Tom, want to race me? I bet I can beat you," I challenged, as I jumped into the pool.

"Nah, we can't race, there're too many kids in the pool. Let's see who can hold their breath underwater the longest," Tom challenged. I pinched my nose shut and went under. When I came up for air, Tom's head was still under the water. He won! Then, we stood on our hands and stuck our legs out of the water. The challenge was to see who could stand on them the longest. I won that contest!

We played at the pool and enjoyed cooling off in the water, while the bright sun shined above us. At five o'clock, when the pool closed, we headed home, with our fingertips all wrinkled and our eyes red from the chlorinated water. My father had come home from work and my mother was preparing dinner. "Hi Daddy. Look, I'm wearing the new blouse you bought for me last week."

How did you get hurt?" he asked when he saw the black-and-blue marks on my chest. Why were these bruises such a concern? They didn't hurt.

"The handle of the Carr's push lawnmower hits me in the chest when I hit a rock or a bump."

"Why do you cut the grass?"

"It's my job now that Tom isn't there anymore."

"What other jobs do you do?"

"I wash my own clothes on the washboard with the brown bar of soap, and I hang them in the back room to dry. I set the table for dinner and help Maggie do the dishes. I sweep the kitchen floor and I sweep the mud out of the back shed."

"Son of a bitch, you're not her maid!" My father was angry. "You're not going back tomorrow, you're staying here until I get this straightened out."

That night after supper, Tom and I played Blackjack, as we usually did during my visits. Before going to bed, I took a nice bubble bath. After letting the water out of the tub, I leaned over the edge of the side of the tub to shampoo my hair. Lying in bed, I worried about what was going to happen if I didn't go back on Sunday afternoon. Finally I drifted off to sleep.

On Sunday afternoon, after we finished our meal. I knew my grandparents would be back from church and finished with their meal, so I went down to the lower flat. I rapped on the door and my grandfather opened it. "Well, look who's here; it's my little Dutch girl. Come on in and have a piece of candy." I closed the door and followed my grandfather into the living room.

I liked my grandfather because he was funny and kind. He also had a love of Irish whiskey. I suppose that's because he had Irish heritage. My grandmother wouldn't allow alcohol in the house, but I suspect my grandfather had some hidden.

My grandmother sat on the couch, under a wall plaque that read, "Jesus Saves."

"Hello, Grandmother."

"Hello, Nancy Lee, you're home again for a visit, are you?" she asked, looking up from reading her Bible.

"No, Grandmother, I'm home for good."

"What do you mean, you're home for good?"

"Daddy is angry that I cut the grass. I can't go back."

"I hope this isn't going to make trouble," she said, and went back to reading her Bible.

"Here, have a jelly slice," my grandfather said, taking the lid off the candy dish.

"No thanks, Grandfather, I don't like orange jelly slices, but I liked the maple nougat candy that was in the dish last weekend."

"I'll have to remember that," he said, with a wink of his eye as he set the candy dish back down.

I was glad that my grandmother didn't ask any questions about my not going to church. Even though they didn't have much money, she believed in "tithing," giving the church ten percent of whatever she earned. Two of her favorite sayings were, "The Lord will provide," and "Waste not—Want not." Another of her sayings was, "Poor? Yes—Dirty? Why?" I knew it was directed at my mother. She didn't like my mother and my mother didn't like her.

After a short visit, I went back upstairs and my mother asked, "Did you tell your grandparents that you were home for good?"

"Yes, and Grandmother thinks there might be trouble."

"Oh! She always thinks the worst, that woman. She's never happy about anything. She is who she is, and she'll never change. Never mind what she says," my mother said, crushing her cigarette out in the ashtray with determination.

"When will Daddy and Tommy come home?" I asked, changing the subject. I knew not to say anymore about the downstairs visit.

"Anytime now; the ball game should be over soon."

That night, after dinner, I took another bath before getting into bed. I didn't return on Sunday, as I should have. What was little Maggie going to think when I didn't come back with her Baby Ruth candy bar? We didn't have a telephone, so Mrs. Carr couldn't phone my parents to find out why I hadn't returned. It wouldn't be long before she did.

A few days later, my mother and I were in the living room watching television. There was a loud knock on the kitchen door. My mother got up from the couch to answer the door. I followed.

"Is Nancy Lee here?" a lady asked, when my mother opened the door. The woman was dressed in a dark blue suit with a serious look on her face, standing in the hall outside the kitchen door.

"Why do you want to know? Who are you?" my mother asked back, standing in front of the door, blocking the way.

"I'm Mrs. Watson form the Children's Aid Society. Is Nancy Lee here?" she repeated. "Well, I guess she is." Mrs. Watson said when she saw me standing behind my mother. "Why did you run away, Nancy Lee?" Before I could answer, my mother reached behind and pushed me back from the door.

"She didn't run away! My daughter has been coming home to visit every weekend for the past few months."

My mother went on to tell Mrs. Watson what I had told her about the living conditions at the Carr's house. I had told my mother that there was no bathroom upstairs where the bedrooms were. If we had to use a toilet during the night, we used the metal pail placed in the hall, specifically for that purpose. It was my job to empty it into the downstairs toilet when it needed to be emptied. In the daytime, if I had to use the toilet, I wasn't allowed to flush it. Mrs. Carr decided if it needed flushing.

I was not allowed to take a bath in their bathtub. Mrs. Carr told me that as long as I took a shower at school, after gym class, I didn't need to take a bath. I washed my hair in the same washtub that I used for washing my laundry.

Only once did I use their bathtub and that was by doctor's orders. Several months after I arrived at their house, I got scabies, caused by lack of bathing. "I haven't seen a case of this since the war. Soldiers in the trenches get this," the doctor had told Mrs. Carr.

The cure for scabies was for me to sit in the bathtub, lathering my body with soap and applying the prescribed liquid. Then, I wrapped in a sheet and went to bed. It worked. The mites that bore under my skin were killed and I didn't itch anymore. But, I still wasn't allowed to use the Carr's bathtub. I didn't want to get scabies again, so I dried my hands on my clothes and stopped using the dirty, old, towel that hung in the bathroom—Maggie and I weren't allowed to use the towels that hung on the outside of the bathroom door.

Further, Maggie and I weren't allowed in the living room. So, after Maggie and I finished clearing the table and doing the dishes, we stood by the doorway to the living room and watched *The Milton Berle Show,* Arthur's favorite television program. Sometimes, I teased Arthur by reaching my foot into the room and stepping on the rug close to where he was lying on the floor. "Mama, Nancy Lee's in the living room!" he shouted. Quickly, I pulled my foot back, so Mrs. Carr couldn't catch me.

Arthur was treated special compared to Maggie and me, because he was the Carr's natural child. He had butter–we had margarine. He drank milk–we drank water. He had dessert–we didn't. "You girls don't want to get fat, do you?" Mrs. Carr said when she gave Arthur a dish of ice cream. On Saturdays, he went shopping with her and we didn't. "You girls don't have any money to buy anything, do you?" she would ask.

I confided in my mother that Mrs. Carr wouldn't buy me sanitary pads. She gave me a bag of rags. "Here, you can use these. Wash them out when you do your laundry, but wash them separate from your other clothes."

After my visits home, before I returned to the Carr's farm, my mother always gave me a few dollars. "I thought you were using the money to buy candy bars or school stuff. I never thought you had to buy your own shampoo, tooth paste and Kotex," my mother said, after hearing my stories. She was angry with Mrs. Carr. There was no way Mrs. Watson was going to get me out of my parents' house and back to that farm.

"We will have to consider Nancy Lee as a runaway if she doesn't return," Mrs. Watson told my mother.

"Consider all you want! My daughter isn't going back to that hellhole."

Mrs. Watson never got a chance to step past the kitchen door. My mother wouldn't let her. She left, and I was home again. I don't know what my father did, but he got it straightened out, just as he said he would.

CHAPTER FIVE

The Teen Years

Hormonal changes in the teen years only add to the struggle of trying to walk proud with your head held high without being super-critical of everything and everyone..

WHEN I LEFT MY parents' house to live in the foster homes, I had the body of an average pre-teen girl, straight down the sides and a flat chest. Now, at the age of thirteen, I had a waist, hips and developing breasts. The few clothes that I had were left behind at the Carr's house. I wore Tom's T-shirts until my parents could get some more clothes for me.

The following Sunday was a hot summer day. My father and Tom went to the park to watch a baseball game, as they often did on Sunday afternoons. My mother and I were sitting at the kitchen table; she was having a cup of coffee while she smoked a cigarette, and I was working on a crossword puzzle. There was a knock on the kitchen door. "Barb, what a surprise! Come in, come in," my mother said, inviting the lady into the house.

The lady had the same auburn hair and blue eyes as my mother. She even looked a little like my mother, but older. They were about the same height, but there were major differences: she wasn't as heavy as my mother; she was dressed in nice clothing; she wore make up; and, her hair was done in a pretty fashion, the way my mother used to fix her own hair. Who was she?

"Hello, Lorraine, I heard that Nancy Lee is back home." They hugged and exchanged cheek kisses.

"Nancy Lee, this is your Aunt Barb," my mother said, casually with a big smile, as if this news wouldn't puzzle me. I had never seen this lady before. I knew my mother was raised as an only child, so I thought Aunt Barb must be another good friend that she knew when she was younger. I was wrong!

"Aunt Barb is my oldest sister."

"She's your sister? My real aunt?" I exclaimed, smiling a confused hello to the lady.

"It's a long story," my mother said, putting her finger to her lips, hushing me, as she poured a cup of coffee for her sister.

"Yes, I'm your aunt," my new Aunt Barb said, adding, "I brought you some clothes that Mary Lou outgrew." Mary Lou must be my cousin, I reasoned. Aunt Barb handed me a white box and a hunter-green coat that she had folded over her arm.

"Thank you, Aunt Barb," I said, still puzzled that she was my mother's sister. Setting the white box on the kitchen table, I opened it. Inside were two, freshly laundered, cotton dresses; one was pink, the other was light blue.

"Try them on, honey" my mother told me, smiling her approval of the dresses. I took the box into my bedroom and put on the pink dress with the scooped-neck bodice and full skirt.

"Oh, how pretty that dress looks on you," Aunt Barb said, when I came out of the bedroom. "They're both the same size, so you don't have to try the blue dress on, unless you want to," Aunt Barb said, with a warm smile.

"May I try on the coat?"

"Of course you can, it's yours now." I put on the coat and it, too, fit perfectly. I never had a long coat before. I had always worn jackets. When I put my hands in the pockets, I felt a hole in the silk lining of the pocket on the right. But, that didn't matter. I had a real grown-up coat, and I was thrilled! After a short visit with my mother, Aunt Barb finished her coffee, said goodbye, and drove back to the southern tier of Eden Valley, where she lived.

"Ok, Mama, tell me how Aunt Barb is my real aunt. She's not your real sister, is she?" I asked, as we both took a seat at the kitchen table again. My mother set down her cup of coffee, clasped her hands together, and began to tell me the story of her adoption.

"Yes, I have three sisters and one brother, all older," she answered hesitantly. "Barb is the oldest; she's ten years older than me; George was next and then Mildred and Margaret. I'm the youngest. My mother died when I was fifteen months old. Nanny is my birth father's sister and Grandpa is my birth mother's brother. They were married and didn't have any children, so my father let them adopt me."

Curiously, I asked, "How did your mother die?"

"She died of female problems, and that's all you have to know." I was hearing this family secret for the first time and I was very interested. I wanted more information. "What were your parents' names?"

"Margaret and Ed Goss. Why do you want to know?"

"No reason, I'm just curious. So, Nanny isn't your real mother; she's really your aunt?"

"Yes, she is my real mother. She raised me! Don't go saying anything to her, do you hear me! And, don't make me sorry I told you!" My mother was getting upset, so I didn't ask any more questions.

Years later, I learned that her birth mother died from the results of a self-induced abortion. The Comstock Law, prohibiting the distribution of information on birth control had resulted in thousands of women dying from trying to induce an abortion; some died by ingesting or douching with a variety of toxins; others by inserting knitting needles, crochet hooks or coat hangers into themselves. My maternal grandmother used knitting needles. She was twenty-nine years old when she died!

A short time after Aunt Barb left, Nanny and Grandpa came to the house. Nanny was dressed in a crisp cotton sundress, smelling as fresh as a bouquet of flowers. Grandpa was dressed as usual in a pair of slacks and a white, short-sleeved shirt. "Hey there, little squirt, how's it going?" Grandpa said, with a welcome-home smile.

"Hello, Nanny and Grandpa," I said with a happy smile.

"Hello mother, you just missed Barb. Did you call her and tell her Nancy Lee needed clothes?" My mother asked, getting up from the chair to greet Nanny.

"Yes, after you phoned telling me that she was home for good, I made a few calls."

"Go on in, and sit at the dining room table, I'll make some more coffee."

"You should never go to someone's house empty-handed." Nanny said, smiling at me and setting a box of jelly-filled donuts on the dining room table. She was forever teaching me good manners.

I sat at the table with Nanny and Grandpa, waiting for my mother to join us. "Aunt Barb brought me two dresses and a coat," I said, waiting for a reaction. I wanted Nanny to know that I had met Aunt Barb, my real aunt. And, I wanted her to know that I knew she had adopted my mother.

Nanny's only reaction was to say, "I know," as she patted the glow of perspiration on her forehead with her white handkerchief, which was trimmed with blue lace tatting.

My mother came into the dining room with cups of hot coffee on a tray.

I excused myself and let them visit. "Mama, I'm going to the park to find Daddy and Tom, okay?" I asked, getting up from the chair and heading toward the kitchen door.

"Say goodbye to Nanny and Grandpa first," she called after me. I did; then, I ran out the door.

Nanny had spread the word that I needed clothes. Aunt Loretta came with some clothes that Elaine had outgrown. She brought me a white blouse, two skirts, a cardigan sweater, two pairs of pajamas and two pairs of pedal pushers with matching tops. This was better than Christmas. Finally, I was back home again. This time, I hoped it would be to stay!

The flat my parents lived in hadn't changed much, except that now we had a refrigerator. My grandfather wouldn't have to yell up the stairs anymore for my mother to empty the overflowing drip pan. The gas stove was the same. The wooden, kitchen table and the mismatched chairs were the same, but the oilcloth that covered the table was new. It was white with bright red cherries printed on it.

The dining room set was the same, except that the glass in the door of the china cabinet was missing, and the handle was broken off the cut-crystal water pitcher that Nanny had given to my mother. No doubt this was the result of a fight my parents had when they were drinking. When they fought, it wasn't just with words.

The same maroon-and-blue couch, with matching stuffed chair sat in the living room on the gray rug. The brass floor lamp stood next to the chair. Lamps sat on each table at the ends of the couch and a coffee table sat in front. The room looked the same, just more timeworn. A few panes of glass in the French doors leading into the playroom were missing. The playroom still had the daybed placed against the back wall, with a small table at the end, and an empty pack of Pall Mall cigarettes, the brand my father now smoked.

The three bedrooms in the back of the house, near the kitchen, still had the doors missing. Even the doors to the closets were gone. Who had taken the doors off and why?

All of the floors in the house, except for the living room, were covered in the same old linoleum, with the worn spots and torn edges. The walls were covered with the same faded wallpaper, with pieces torn off in places. The house showed the many years of neglect and lack of maintenance.

I was happy and I wanted to tell Jeanie that I was back home for good. I walked up her porch steps and rang the doorbell. "Oh, my goodness! Is that you, Nancy Lee?" her mother said, holding the door open.

"Yes, Mrs. Hart, I'm back with my parents, again," I told her as I walked into the kitchen.

"Jeanie! Look who's here," she called up the bedroom stairs. How long are you staying this time, Nancy Lee?"

"I'm back for good."

"You're home for good. Are you sure?" Jeanie asked, as she came down the stairs into the kitchen still dressed in her pajamas.

"Jeanie, you sleepyhead, what are you doing in bed at ten o'clock in the morning?" I teased.

"How was it in the foster homes?" Jeanie asked.

"They weren't too bad," I lied. "I got a chance to meet a movie star," I bragged.

"Now, Nancy Lee, you know you didn't go to Hollywood" Mrs. Hart said with a sly smile, looking at me inquisitively.

"No, Mrs. Hart, I wasn't in Hollywood. I was on an island in Massachusetts. It was called Martha's Vineyard. The first foster parents took me with them during Easter vacation. I saw the Atlantic Ocean and watched the seagulls pick up clams and eat them. I really was there! We visited Oak Bluffs and Edgartown too," I added, because I wanted them to believe me. "I saw James Cagney when my foster mother and I were looking at the cute little houses."

"Oh, he's not a movie star. He's an old man," Jeanie remarked.

"Yes, he is a movie star!" I said defensively. So much for bragging, Jeanie wasn't impressed. Then, I told about the bruises, but nothing else. I didn't want Jeanie or anyone to know about the "pee bucket"—especially not Jeanie. I was worried she might make jokes about it later.

"Hurry up and get dressed, Jeanie. You don't want Nancy Lee to wait all day for you, do you?" I could tell Mrs. Hart was glad Jeanie had me to spend her summer with, instead of moping around the house all day.

Jeanie, my good friend, was still taller and a lot heavier. She had twinkling, blue eyes that gave her an angelic look; I had hazel eyes. Jeanie kept her strawberry-blonde hair short; I had long, auburn hair. Jeanie was a Catholic; I was a Baptist. Jeanie went to West Seneca High School; I would be going to South Park High School. Jeanie didn't like swimming; I loved swimming. Jeanie was the youngest in her family; I was second oldest in my family. Her family was middle class; my family was poor. We had little in common, yet we were best friends and enjoyed spending time together. We even swore an oath to always be friends. "Jeanie, let's make a pact that we will always be best friends," I said, as I held up my right hand to swear the oath, and she did the same. "I promise," we said in unison. Little did I know how fragile that pact was to be!

Jeanie knew about my life, so, usually, I didn't have to be too careful what I said or what she saw. I had a lot of fun spending time with her that summer. We took walks along Seneca Street, passing the meat market and the grocery store where my mother shopped for food. We passed the liquor store where she bought her wine and the tavern where my father drank his beer.

Jeanie and I often wandered through Morison's clothing store. We didn't have any money, but it was fun just to look at all the beautiful clothes. Someday, I'm going to be able to buy anything I want, I promised myself!

During that summer, I literally got my first taste of the Catholic Church. I was always curious about the Catholic religion because of the comments my grandmother made about the priests and the statues. One day, on our walk home from having a soda at Parson's drug store, Jeanie and I stopped at the corner of Duerstein and Seneca Streets for a last chat before parting. "Jeanie will you take me into your church tomorrow?"

"Okay, but you have to do everything I tell you. I'll meet you at the corner. Bring something to cover your head. You can't go in the church unless your head is covered."

"I don't have a hat, Jeanie." I didn't ask why I had to cover my head. I thought it was a secret ritual, making the experience even more mysterious.

"Just bring a clean hanky, you don't need a hat," she called back, as she headed home. I went into my house excited about the new adventure.

The next day, my mother didn't ask why I wanted a hanky. She just went into the dresser drawer and gave me one of my father's big, white handkerchiefs.

I met Jeanie at the corner, as we planned. We hurried across the street. I hoped my grandmother wasn't looking out the window. If she looked up from her work, she might catch sight of me going into this "heathen place," as she called it. As soon as Jeanie pulled one of the big, double-doors open, I hurried inside.

It was kind of dark inside. The only light came from the sun shining through the stained-glass windows. There were long rows of benches, called pews, not individual seats like in the Baptist Church. The Catholic Church had a sense of mystery and the air smelled sweet with the smell of burnt incense. My grandmother had been right; the church had a lot of statues. There was one with a man holding a little boy on his shoulder; Jeanie said his name was Christopher. And, there was one with a beautiful lady in a blue robe; Jeanie said her name was Mary. I recognized Mary because the Baptist Church had her in the manger at Christmas. These must be the statues my grandmother had said people prayed to.

"See the little basin of water? It's holy water. Before we leave, you have to scoop some water into the palm of your hand and drink it." This was a church, a holy place, so I thought Jeanie wouldn't lie to me in here. I believed that was what I had to do. So, I did it. I scooped a handful of water and drank it!

"You just drank a handful of germs." Jeanie said, laughing and pointing at me.

"Yuk! Why did you tell me to do that? I trusted you, Jeanie," I said, wiping my tongue over the back of my arm, trying to rid it of germs. Jeanie didn't trick me because she was mean. She just liked playing jokes on people.

When we went to the show on Friday nights. Jeanie always bought popcorn and candy bars to eat during the movie. She didn't just eat the popcorn. She threw it, one piece at a time, at the kids sitting a few aisles ahead of us. When they turned around to see who did it, she put an innocent look on her face.

Jeanie and I didn't go to the show every Friday night. The first Friday of each month we went to the CYO (Catholic Youth Organization) dances. We didn't dance, though; we just hung around and talked with some of the other teenagers. That was where I spoke to a priest for the first time. His name was Father Richard. He didn't seem like he was "perverted," as my grandmother had said all priests were. I thought he was a good man.

"If you would like to learn about the Catholic religion, we have classes, and you're welcome to attend. You're also welcome in the church, but you must not take our Holy Communion unless you're a baptized Catholic."

"Thank you, Father Richard, I would like to take classes someday." I didn't just say that—I meant it. I wanted to be a Catholic.

Sometimes, Jeanie and I made up secret codes that only we understood. Other times, we made up names for ourselves, and imagined we lived in another time and place. Two of my roles that I actually felt I once lived remain vivid in my memory. One is that of Marie DuVal, a girl living in the countryside of France. The other is that of Vickie Carlisle, a flapper of the Roaring Twenties, who died in a fire at the nightclub in California. Could these two characters be reincarnation memories?

On days when I wasn't with Jeanie, I went downstairs to visit my grandmother. She let me help her bake the four loaves of bread, one cake and two pies she made every Saturday. She let me roll out the extra piecrust and sprinkle it with sugar and cinnamon. Sometimes I spread apple butter on it, rolled it up like a jellyroll, cut it into slices and baked them. When they were finished baking, she gave me the piecrust cookies to take upstairs to share with Tom.

Another time, my grandmother helped me make a skirt from material she had left over from a customer's order. And, she showed me how to change the color of my white blouse to yellow by boiling it with yellow onionskins, or, pink by boiling it in beet juice.

My grandmother had eight sisters and two brothers. My grandfather had one sister and five brothers. Most of them still lived in central Pennsylvania, near Bald Eagle Mountain and Lock Haven.

In August 1952, shortly before I started high school, Uncle Harold, my grandparents, my father, Tom and his girlfriend, Judy, a tall, blonde-haired girl, and I were planning a weekend trip to visit my grandmother's sister, Adeline, whom my father knew as Aunt Addie. Our plans were to leave early Saturday morning, to spend the night with Aunt Addie, and to return on Sunday night. Tom and I hadn't been to Pennsylvania before; we were excited about going. My mother wasn't invited. She wouldn't have accepted even if she had been.

Very early on Saturday morning, we began our journey. Uncle Harold drove his car with my grandparents in the back seat. My father drove my grandfather's car, with Tom sitting next to him and Judy sitting in the back seat with me. We headed out of the city and onto Route 16, following behind Uncle Harold. "Dad, if we drive any slower, we'll never get there," Tom complained. Tom was right. Uncle Harold didn't drive very fast.

"Uncle Harold won't drive more than the speed limit, and that's something you'll have to learn to do when you get a car, or you'll get a speeding ticket," my father warned, adding, "I know how you can amuse yourself—play the future game."

"Hey, I remember that game. We played it when we were kids. We just close our eyes and say what we see ahead, before we actually see it," Tom explained to Judy. "I'll go first," he added. "I see a red car coming down the road. What do you see, Judy?"

"I see a bridge," Judy replied, after a moment's thought.

"I see a king's crown," I guessed. The two of them laughed.

"Is the king riding a big, white horse?" Tom teased. We rode for a few minutes and then, a delivery truck came from behind. As it passed, we looked at the side panel. There it was, my king's crown! The side of the truck had an advertisement for King's Food Market and it had a picture of a man wearing a crown.

"That was pretty good, Nancy Lee, how did you do that?" Judy asked, with a look of surprise.

"She's spooky like that," Tom said, smiling at me. We rode on playing the game a few more times, until I couldn't see anything more. Nothing appeared on my closed eyelids.

On the way to the little borough of Renovo where Aunt Addie lived, we ate the peanut butter sandwiches and chocolate cupcakes my mother packed for us, washing them down with bottles of Nehi orange soda. Connecting onto Route 44, we made a quick stop at a Texaco station. The station attendant filled up the gas tank, checked the oil and washed the windshield while we made a bathroom visit. Then we were on our way again.

I sat quietly, taking in the natural beauty of the steep, forested ridges along the Allegheny Plateau. It wasn't long before we crossed the state line into Pennsylvania. Passing the little village of Hyner, Uncle Harold and my father drove into a spot off the highway and parked so we could view the west branch of the Susquehanna River. "This section of the Appalachian Mountains is often referred to as the Grand Canyon of Pennsylvania," my father told us when we got out of the car. Uncle Harold got out of his car, too. Although the sun was bright overhead, the air was cooled by the blowing wind. It was too windy for my grandparents. They stayed in the car.

We arrived at Aunt Addie's house just before sunset. As we got out of the car, a woman opened the screen door of the little, brown house and stood on the narrow porch that ran the length of the house. She was dressed in a plain dress, the same style worn by my grandmother. Her graying hair was cropped short like my grandmother kept hers. It was easy to see that they were sisters.

"Praise the Lord, Minnie and Ernie, you're here," she said, with her face beaming a smile. My grandmother's name was Laura but she was often called Minnie.

"Addie, you know Harold, and Ralph. You met them in Ebenezer, at Hanna's funeral."

"Welcome, Harold and Ralph; glad you drove safe to come here." Looking past Uncle Harold's car toward Tom, Barbara and me, she said something in a language that I didn't understand.

"Aunt Addie asked you what your names are," my grandmother said, knowing that we didn't understand the Pennsylvania Dutch or the Mennonite language.

"I'm Tom. That's my friend, Judy, and that's Nancy Lee."

"Ah, Nancy Lee," Aunt Addie said with a curious glance in my direction. "Ralph, that's your little girl making the ruckus at the funeral, is it?"

Tom and I looked at each other, having a hard time trying to keep a straight face because of the way Aunt Addie put her words together. My father didn't answer; he just smiled and walked onto the porch, carrying the overnight gear he had taken from the trunk. As we walked into the house,

Aunt Addie spoke in the Mennonite language, again, and my grandmother replied, "No, Ernie and the boys can't understand the Dutch talk. We'll talk the English."

Inside the house, the warmth of the summer day and an aroma of something wonderful to eat filled the air. The house was small and modestly furnished. It had a living room, bathroom and large kitchen on the first floor, and three bedrooms upstairs. Aunt Addie lived in the house alone. I don't know if she never married or if she was a widow. I never asked.

After we were settled in, Aunt Addie served us a delicious meal of roasted chicken and mashed potatoes. The evening passed with the adults talking, while Tom, Judy, and I sat on the front porch enjoying the slight breeze, giving us relief from the summer heat.

"Come into the house now, it's time to get ready for bed," my father said, holding the screen door open. The adults slept in the upstairs bedrooms. The couch was moved away from the wall, where Judy and I slept in our clothes on the bare, wood floor. We each had a pillow and a sheet covered us. Tom slept in his clothes on the couch with a pillow and a sheet to cover him.

The next morning, we took turns in the bathroom, washing and changing into clean clothes. After that, we enjoyed a breakfast of bread pudding and coffee. Packing our gear back into the trunk of the car, we said our thank you and goodbye to Aunt Addie.

"I have the Bible with me, I'll read it on the ride back," my grandmother called to her sister, from the open car window. Tommy, Judy and I waved goodbye, as the cars pulled out of the driveway and headed down the road.

"Daddy, when did I make a ruckus at a funeral?" I asked, wanting an explanation why Aunt Addie had said that about me.

"Oh, that was a long time ago; you were just a little girl then. Don't worry about it."

"I'm not worried about it. I'm just curious, that's all. Tell me, Daddy, I want to know. The flash of memory that I have about going to a funeral with you, did it really happen?"

"Well, yes, you went to Aunt Hanna's funeral with me. You said she talked to you and told you her name was Nancy. At the time, I didn't know her real name was Nancy. We always called her Aunt Hanna. I often wondered how you knew her name."

Tom looked at me and said, "No more spooky stuff, you're going to scare Judy."

The funeral that I had attended with my father in the town of Ebenezer was the first time I remember having an experience with spirit communication. Why was I able to communicate with spirit, yet Tom was never able to? I suspect the answer is that Tom's personality is very different from mine. I can only guess that people like Tom, who are focused on the physical world, will not have the same experiences as people like me, who are relaxed in their thoughts and allow themselves to believe that anything is possible.

September rolled around, bringing with it an exciting new world for me. I began my freshman year at South Park High School. On the first day of school, with great anticipation, I jumped out of bed, hurried down the hall to the bathroom, brushed my teeth, washed, and put my hair up in a ponytail. My father had bought me a pair of brown-and-white saddle shoes and I wore them with white ankle socks. From the clothes that Aunt Loretta brought me, I chose a white blouse and navy skirt with the navy cardigan sweater.

"Bye, Mama, I'm leaving now," I called out, as I ran down the stairs and hurried across the street. I practically ran all the way through the park, crossing Abbott Road and McKinley Parkway, walking down a side street and finally reaching the school.

After going into our assigned homerooms to record our attendance, the freshmen were assembled in the auditorium, where the principal welcomed us to our first year of high school. I felt relieved that I didn't stand out; that I blended in with the other kids. I wasn't prepared for what was coming. "Let's give a special welcome to Nancy Lee, this year's youngest freshman." I was still only thirteen. At the end of the month, I turned fourteen—hurrah!

It wasn't long before I felt like I was on equal ground with the other teenage girls. I tried to be like them. I wore pink lipstick and black mascara on my eyelashes just like my new friends, Barbara, Ellie and Arlene.

Barbara was short with blonde hair and blue eyes; she had elfin features and an upturned nose. I liked her the best. She was a lively, good-natured girl, and we hit it off right away. I don't know how she got the nickname "Slushie." Ellie was an attractive blonde with delicate features. I thought she was really pretty and she had a lot of nice clothes. Arlene was tall and had chestnut-colored hair. She had an ordinary face, neither pretty nor unattractive, just the typical face of any teenager.

I envied something about each of them: Barbara's quick wit; Ellie's delicate features; and, Arlene's self-confidence. I was still a little shy and insecure about my looks. I wished I could take all those admirable pieces of them and put them into me. I thought their lives were wonderfully simple and I envied them for that.

Miss Jenkins, my sewing teacher, was pleased that I already knew a lot about sewing. In her class, I made a dress from the pattern and material my grandmother gave me. After the dress was finished, I didn't like it. I thought it was too plain. "Nancy, how would you like to wear your dress and represent the class next week at Open House?" I thought the dress made me look like an old lady. But, I felt honored that Mrs. Jenkins asked me, so I agreed.

Sadly, neither my mother nor my father came to the Open House. I really didn't expect them to, because my mother wouldn't take a bus, and, on Fridays after work, my father went to the corner tavern to drink and play cards with his friends. Without complaining, I accepted my parents' behavior, but still, I was embarrassed at Open House, when Miss Jacobs asked, "Nancy, aren't your parents coming? I was hoping to meet them."

I didn't always go directly home after school. Sometimes, I walked with Barbara, Ellie and Arlene. They lived on side streets, off South Park Avenue. We often stopped for a Coke at Chat and Nibble soda shop. It was the favorite after-school hangout. The kids put their nickels in the tableside jukebox and we listened to the songs, while we drank our cherry Cokes.

Some of the boys that we sat with regularly were Tony, Cippy and Joe. Tony was the shortest of the boys and slim. He definitely looked Italian. Cippy was husky and rather quiet. Joe had blond, springy curls under the baseball cap he usually wore, and was the clown of the group.

On Friday nights my friends from high school came to my side of town to see a movie. The Seneca Theater was a place where kids from the local high schools, including South Park, West Seneca, Mount Mercy, Bishop Timon and Father Baker, got together to meet and socialize. Jeanie, a year older and a year ahead of me in school, sat with her friends from West Seneca High, on the right side of the theater. I sat with my friends from South Park High on the left side of the theater.

I liked the Marilyn Monroe movies, especially *Gentlemen Prefer Blonds*. Marilyn Monroe lived in a foster home and she was shy and poor while growing up, just like me. I thought since she could make a success of her life, so could I. While searching for my own identity, I often identified with her and imitated her. She wasn't a real blonde, you know!

The Seneca Theater is where I met a boy named Zack. He was very handsome, with a muscular body and sand-colored hair. His facial features were distinctively masculine, with high cheekbones, a straight nose and a clean-cut chin. Zack went to Father Baker High School and was a year ahead of me in school.

After we got to know each other better, Zack sat next to me in the darkened theater. I was very conscious of the warmth of his nearness.

Gradually, he put his arm across the back of my seat and every now and then, his hand slipped down to my shoulder. I liked that, but it made me a little uncomfortable, knowing he was touching me. When the show was over, Zack walked with the other the kids, going back to the South Park area and I walked alone down Seneca Street to my house. It wouldn't be long before that would change.

The winter passed, the snows melted, and the cool, wet winds of springtime blew about the city, finally changing from a roar to a whisper of warm breezes. May turned into June. I passed my freshman year. When my report card came in the mail, my mother was pleased that I did so well. "What good grades you got, Nancy Lee. Oh, excuse me, I mean Nancy." I had told my mother I didn't want to be called Nancy Lee any more, to call me just Nancy. My classmates only used first names; they didn't use their middle name. I wanted to be like them.

"Didn't you know I have an IQ of 138 points?" I told my mother with a sense of pride.

"Who told you that?"

"A woman at the Children's Aid tested me."

"Well, don't let that go to your head, Miss Fancy Pants—your IQ could have changed since then."

I looked forward to being a sophomore in the fall, but for now I was going to enjoy the summer. I spent my days working in the park at the refreshment stand known as Caz Casino. The job was easy; I liked making cotton candy, pop corn and milk shakes. Every day during the lunch hour, when all of the kids had to leave the pool the lifeguards stayed. Two lifeguards always came to the back service counter that opened to the pool area, and ordered milkshakes. "Nancy if you make my milk shakes extra thick, I'll teach you some new dives," Peter, one of the lifeguards, bargained with me.

"How are you going to teach me new dives if I can't get into the pool?" I asked, putting an extra scoop of ice cream into the metal, milkshake cup.

"Just bring your suit tomorrow," he said with a smile, reaching for the milkshake. I smiled back and went to the front counter to wait on the kids standing there.

The next day I came prepared, hoping Peter would keep his word. At lunchtime, he and the other lifeguard came to the back service counter to get their milkshakes. "I brought my swimsuit, are you going to let me into the pool like you promised?"

"Of course, but make my milkshake first."

I put in four scoops of ice cream, making it super thick. After handing

Peter his milkshake, I hurried into the lavatory, where I changed into my swimsuit. That summer, Peter taught me the racing dive and let me practice speed swimming.

Mr. Lender, the man who ran the refreshment stand had told me he would pay me ten dollars a week, but I didn't get paid that every week. Some weeks, when it was time to get paid, Mr. Lender wasn't there, Louis, his son only gave me five dollars for the week's work. I didn't like that, but I didn't say anything. Why didn't I say anything?

My days were spent working at Caz Casino but in the evenings and on some weekends, I spent time doing things with Jeanie. We walked down Seneca Street to Parson's drug store and sat at the soda fountain, drinking root-beer floats and talking girl stuff. It was great to share secrets with her.

Unfortunately, my mother wasn't the kind of mother that I could talk to and get advice from. She never talked to me about the facts of life. I got some information about sex from Jeanie and my friends. I knew the basic stuff, like how babies were made and that it took nine months, but that was the limit of my sex education.

Sometimes, when I wasn't with Jeanie, I walked over to the South Park neighborhood. There I met up with Barbara, Ellie, Arlene and the boys in our clique. We just hung out, walking the streets and having innocent fun. That summer, when I went into the South Park side of town, Zack and I saw more of each other. We didn't have "dates," we were just part of the group that met and spent time together. One time, when it was getting dark, the streetlights came on and all too soon it was nine o'clock, the time of my girlfriends' curfew. They headed home.

Zack didn't want me to walk home alone. He insisted on riding me on the crossbar of his bicycle. My being a passenger didn't seem to matter; he didn't even struggle as he peddled. He was so strong and his wide shoulders seemed even bigger in the T-shirt that hugged his muscular torso.

I pretended my parents cared about me the way my friends' parents did. When my friends said they had to be home by nine o'clock, I said I did, too. The truth was, I had no set time, as long as I made it home before my father did. I wanted my friends to think my parents cared, so I made up rules that didn't exist and I even lived by them.

At a Friday night movie, Zack sat next to me and put his arm across the back of my seat, as he sometimes did. But, this time he played with my ponytail. His hand brushed across the nape of my neck, making me catch my breath. Before I knew it, our lips touched. It was my very first kiss. I liked it! It wasn't yucky at all, the way I thought a kiss would be. I was beginning to really like Zack and I think he liked me!

At the end of summer, Billy was allowed to leave the Arno's farm. The Children's Aid Society drove us away from our home, but they didn't drive us back. Tom told me that he had returned home on the Greyhound Bus that I took from the Carr's farm. Now, my father needed to find a way to bring my brother Billy back home.

On a Saturday afternoon, my mother and I had just finished putting away the laundry. She sat on the couch reading a magazine and I was listening to the radio; Kay Starr was singing *"The Wheel of Fortune"*. My father came home from work and walked into the living room with one of his friends. The man was taller and much younger than my father. And, he was handsome in a rugged way.

"Lorraine, meet Wally, he's going to get Billy next week."

"Hello, Wally, you're going to drive out to get my son?"

"Ralph's a good guy. It's the least I can do to help a fellow worker," Wally said, turning his attention from my mother to me.

"Wally, this is my daughter, Nancy Lee," my father said when he saw Wally looking at me."

"Just call me Nancy. Nobody, but my parents call me Nancy Lee, anymore," I said in a grown-up voice. My mother looked at me. I thought she was going to burst out laughing, but she didn't.

"You remind me of a girl I dated when I was at Purdue."

"What's Purdue?"

"It's a university in Indiana where I studied engineering." I wondered what engineering was, but I was too embarrassed to ask. "Your father tells me your brother, Billy, needs a ride to come home. I think your brother would like if you came along." Looking at my father, I knew he wanted me to go along for the ride, so, I agreed.

The following Saturday, Wally came, and we took the long ride to the southern tier. I didn't mind that I was sandwiched between Wally and my father in the front seat, as long as Billy could leave the Arno's foster home. When we arrived at the farm, my father went into the house. I stayed in the car. I didn't like sitting there next to Wally, but I didn't want to see Mr. or Mrs. Arno. I really didn't like them.

"Did you like living on the farm, Nancy?" The question surprised me! I didn't know my father told Wally I used to live there, too.

"It wasn't so bad," I lied.

"Do you have a boyfriend?"

"No," I answered quickly, hoping Wally wouldn't ask any more personal questions. I didn't talk about such things to anyone but Jeanie. Even my parents didn't ask me questions like that.

"A pretty girl like you, Nancy, must have lots of boyfriends."

"Do you have a girlfriend?" I asked, trying to turn the subject from me to Wally. I asked the wrong question!

"No, but I'd like to," he said, smiling at me.

"A nice man like you should have lots of girlfriends," I mimicked back. Again, that was the wrong thing to say! Wally was over six feet tall and very good-looking. I wondered why he didn't have a girlfriend.

"How old are you?" Wally asked.

"I'll be fifteen in September. How old are you?"

"I'm twenty-seven, too old to be your boy friend, but maybe we could be friends," he said in a low voice. Was he serious? I didn't know what to say. I was relieved to see my father and Billy come out of the house. Billy opened the back door and got in.

My father said, "I've got to get some of Billy's things, I'll be right back." That ended my conversation with Wally. He didn't ask any more personal questions and Billy was going home!

On Saturdays, Wally continued to offer my father rides from work, occasionally coming into the house, "Just stopped by to say hello," he said, every time. One Saturday, he brought a camera with him, "How about letting me take your picture, Nancy? I'd like to have a picture of a pretty girl. Okay with you?" he asked, pointing his camera at me. I didn't put up a fuss. After all, he was my father's friend. He took my picture. Then, he asked my father to take a picture of us together. I thought that was creepy! I didn't like the way Wally put his arms around me for the picture. After that day, I made sure I wasn't home on Saturday afternoons.

Shortly after starting my sophomore year, my girlfriends and I met up and took a bus to a roller skating rink. After a few hours of skating, we were getting ready to leave, when I saw Wally standing near the low wall that circled the rink. I skated over to him.

"Hello, Wally, what are you doing here?"

"Your father told me you were at the roller rink. I thought I'd give you a ride home."

Ellie saw us talking and skated over to the wall. "Aren't you going to introduce me, Nancy?"

"Ellie, this is Wally, my father's friend."

"You girls want a ride home?" Wally asked, smiling at Ellie.

"That would be great," Ellie said, flashing a quick smile and skating away to tell Barbara and Arlene.

We returned our rented skates, walked out with Wally and got into his car. Ellie sat in the front seat next to him and I sat in back with Arlene and Barbara. Wally dropped me off first, saying, "Nancy, be sure to tell your father I drove you straight home." That was the last time I saw Wally and I was glad about that. Even if he was my father's friend, he was a pest!

That summer, Tom found a full-time job as an elevator operator at the Hotel Statler. He gave me four dollars a week for doing various chores for him, such as taking his work uniform to the cleaners and picking it up, doing his laundry or going to the store when he wanted chocolate milk or apple pie. That was how I earned money for the movies or to buy more clothes.

Babysitting was another way I earned money. I charged fifty cents an hour. One of my babysitting jobs was on a side street, near Abbott Road, on the far side of the park. I didn't walk to and from the job using the sidewalks. I took a shortcut through the park. One very dark Saturday night, walking home after babysitting, I was about halfway into the park, when I almost tripped over something.

"Who's that? Who are you?" somebody yelled. I froze to a halt. A small group of teenagers were sitting and lying about on the ground. I was just as surprised as they were.

"I'm Nancy," I answered softly.

"Hey, you guys—hold it!" a voice called out to the others, who were making sexual remarks. "I know who she is. She's Tom's sister! What are you doing here?" In the blackness of the moonless night, I could barely make out the boy who stood up and walked toward me.

"I was babysitting and I'm taking a shortcut home."

"Come on, I'll walk you out of the park. It's not a good idea to be here alone after dark. Some boys could grab you. You don't want that. Do you?" he warned, as we walked through the park. When we got to the street, he said, "Remember what I told you, I might not be here the next time!" Back into the park he went, and I got home safely. After that night, I didn't take shortcuts anymore. I stayed on the sidewalks, out of danger.

From the money I earned, I bought a raspberry-colored, felt, poodle skirt, with a crinoline slip, and a black, elastic cinch belt. I wore it with a white, short-sleeve angora sweater and a little silk scarf tied at my neck. I was doing what the other girls were doing. Every morning before heading off to school, I put on pink lipstick and blotted my lips with a piece of toilet paper. I curled my eyelashes with an eyelash curler, and colored them with black Maybelline mascara. I felt so grown up as I opened the little red plastic box, took the tiny brush, wet it and rubbed it on the cake of mascara before brushing my eyelashes. All of us girls wore jeans, turned up at the cuff with white bobby socks and penny-loafers. I was just like them; I blended in.

We four friends, Barbara, Ellie, Arleen and I, thought of ourselves as the crème de la crème of the sophomore class and we were! I elected to take French, because they were taking it. When we met at the soda shop, we had fun trying to speak French. *"Allo, mon Cheri"* was the French way of saying, "Hello, my dear." And, always, when we parted, going our separate ways, *"Au revoir"* was the French way we said "Goodbye."

We also had study hall together, where we passed around the forbidden Juicy Fruit or Teaberry sticks of gum with our little paper notes. My girlfriends wrote about how far they had gone with their boyfriends. The three categories were: #1-kissing, #2-petting, and #3-all the way.

The dreaded Slam Book was a popular thing in the 1950s. Each page was headed with a person's name and passed around for anyone to write in and read. The anonymous comments could be either good or a slam, but usually they were a slam at the character of the person. On one girl's page someone wrote, "She's easy." The girl wrote under it, "It's a lie, I didn't go #3 with Tony." Under that someone wrote, *"touché."*

As I walked home from the theater with Zack on a Friday night, he said, "My mother invited you to dinner on Sunday." I didn't know how to respond. I never thought of meeting his parents and I hoped he didn't want to meet mine. "Can my brother come, too?" was all I could think of to say.

"I didn't know you had a brother. How old is he?"

"Tom will be eighteen in February."

"He's a year older than me. Sure, he can come, I'd like to meet your brother." Zack didn't have any brothers or sisters. He must have assumed that I didn't either. Now, he knew about Tom. But, he still didn't know I had three more brothers and a sister.

Saturday morning, after Tom woke up, I told him about the invitation. "You got yourself a boyfriend, and been keeping it a secret? Sounds serious to me," he teased. Tom was a good sport and he would do anything for me. He agreed to drive us. Tom had his junior license now and bought a fixer-upper the past fall. He and his friend, Ronny, had it up and running.

My mother and father may have thought that a boy liked me, but they didn't ask me, and I didn't tell them about Zack. As a matter of fact, I never had any discussions with them about any of my friends. When I told my parents about the invitation to Zack's house, they didn't object. "As long as your brother is going with you, it should be okay," my father said.

Sunday noon came and Tom drove us to the street where Zack lived. He pulled over to the curb in front of the house and parked. It wasn't necessary for us to ring the doorbell, because Zack was standing inside the hall behind the storm door waiting for us.

Zack lived in an upper flat, just as I did. But there were distinct differences in our two houses. The walls of his back hall were covered with brightly patterned wallpaper. The staircase had rubber stair treads covering the steps. At the top of the stairs in the hall, there was a place to hang coats, and a small table with a basket of artificial flowers in the corner.

I wished that the hall where I lived looked like this. In contrast my hall had dirty, torn wallpaper. The window at the staircase landing provided the only light. The bulb had broken in the light socket and the brass threads were stuck there.

Mr. and Mrs. Wahl, Zack's father and mother, were very nice. She was a small woman with a kind face. He was a tall, muscular, handsome man with a strong chiseled face. I could see Zack's resemblance to his father.

Zack's mother served food that I wasn't familiar with. I ate very little. Tom ate like he was starving. "I'm going to have to invite you back, Tom. I like a boy with a good appetite," Mrs. Wahl said, filling Tom's plate with more cabbage and sausage. After dinner, Zack's father invited me into the living room, while Tom stayed at the kitchen table and talked to Zack and his mother. Mr. Wahl sat in a stuffed chair and I sat on the couch, hoping Tom or Zack would come in and sit beside me.

"You have nice skin," Mr. Wahl said, smiling at me, trying to be friendly.

"Thank you," was my only reply. I remembered the pimple hiding under my bangs. He hadn't noticed that!

Mrs. Wahl finished clearing the table. Then, she, Zack and Tom joined us in the living room. I was relieved that the questions were limited to school topics and not questions about my family.

After Tom and I returned home, I realized how very different Zack's life was from mine. His house wasn't elaborate, but it had furniture newer than what we had. I was ashamed of everything in my life. I couldn't let Zack into my house or even go into the dingy hall. I didn't want him to see the shabbiness of the flat or know that on Friday nights, my mother sat at the dining room table drinking wine and listening to the music on the radio, while my father sat in the tavern with his friends.

It seemed I was unhappy about a lot of things. I used to wish I were back home, but now I didn't like living there. Maybe my mother was right; maybe I did live in a fantasy world. I pretended I didn't like something when I didn't have the money to buy it. I pretended I liked to walk, instead of taking the bus to school. I pretended a lot of things. I pretended not to need my mother, and didn't listen to her when she did tell me something.

I wanted my mother in my life, but resented her when she was. My life was so confusing!

Every Friday, when Zack sat next to me in the show, we kissed once or twice during the movie. Now, after the movie, he didn't walk home with the group of kids going back to the South Park neighborhood. He walked with me down Seneca Street. When we got to my house, we stood in the driveway by the back door. There, in the driveway, before saying goodnight, he held me in his strong arms and we kissed.

Zack was a head taller than I was. It felt so good reaching up and putting my arms around his neck as we embraced. Our closeness caused every inch of me to quiver with delight. One full body kiss and the magic moment ended. Zack hurried across the street to take the shortcut through the park. I hurried up the stairs and into bed where I replayed the kiss, over again in my mind, until I drifted off.

In December, on one of the Friday movie nights Zack gave me a friendship ring. "I have something for you," he said, when he reached into his jacket pocket, and took out the silver ring. "Why are you giving me a ring?" I didn't know what else to say.

"Because you're my girl." I put out my hand and he slipped it on my finger. It was a little big, but not so big that it would fall off. I never had a ring before. I thought it was the most beautiful ring in the whole world. Now, it was official. I was his girlfriend! I wore the ring to school, but I didn't tell Barbara or anyone who gave it to me—and they never asked.

Spring was in the air, but I didn't want to fall in love. The Friday night movies continued, and I began to realize how serious our relationship was becoming. I enjoyed the physical contact and the sensations that I felt when we kissed. But, these feelings also scared me. We were becoming too romantically involved. It wasn't Zack's fault. He hadn't even touched me in private places with my clothes on. It was his kisses that made me swoon.

In July of 1954, Bobby and Jimmy came home from their foster homes. Bobby was now ten and Jimmy was five. A short time later, Carol Jean came home. She was eight. She was so much like my mother, with her gentle nature and pretty smile. The seven-year age difference made it difficult for my sister and me to be close. We had nothing in common except a dysfunctional family life. I had a sister—whom I hardly knew—who shared my bedroom.

Now, Bobby and Tom shared the double-size bed, as they had before. And, once again, Billy had to share my mother's bed. Jimmy was too big for the crib in my mother's bedroom, but he had to sleep in it anyway. My father slept on the daybed in the playroom, as usual. Later in life, I learned why my parents didn't sleep together.

My mother would have her hands full taking care of the younger children, keeping them in clean clothes, with only an old, wringer washing machine to help her do the laundry. With all us children back home, it wasn't long before the house became a mess. My mother was never as neat as Nanny, but lately she had become lazy. The beds weren't made up and dirty dishes were always in the sink.

There were clothes strewn about, empty milk glasses left on the tables in the living room, the newspapers lay on the floor where my father dropped them. The seats of the dining room chairs were now spotted with food stains.

There were rings around the bathtub and dirty towels hung on the towel bar. The boys often came into the house with scraped knees, washed off the dirt and blood with the corner of a wet towel and hung it back on the towel bar.

Billy and Bobby also liked to roughhouse, running after each other up the back stairs with mud on their shoes, slamming the kitchen door to the back wall, racing through the kitchen, dining room, living room, and into the playroom, knocking over the coffee table on their way. "Boys, stop running through the house!" was a constant remark my mother made, while sitting at the kitchen table drinking a cup of coffee and smoking a cigarette.

My mother's nickname for me was "Miss Fancy Pants," probably because I was fussy about what I ate, or that I wouldn't wear clothes that weren't ironed, or that I didn't like the green soap my mother bought, or that I polished my nails and wore make-up, or that I didn't walk around the house barefoot.

I think my father made an average salary, but his wages were garnisheed and a lot of his take-home pay was wasted on Friday night drinking. I once heard my father say, "Son of a bitch! First they take away my children; now they're taking away my money."

"Mama, who's taking Daddy's money?" I asked, after my father left the room.

"We owe about $6,000 for when you kids were in foster care; now don't go blabbing that," she said, putting her finger to her lips and making a "Shush" sound.

I didn't want Zack and my friends to know my mother used wine to mask her feelings of sorrow. I didn't want them to know my mother was overweight because she drank too much. I didn't want them to know she wore the same old apron and didn't put on lipstick or try to make her hair pretty. She didn't seem to care about herself, anymore. I didn't want them to know she lost her "*joie de vivre*," her joy of living. Whatever happened she just accepted it, even losing all her contacts with the outside world. Aunt Barb and Aunt Loretta didn't come to visit anymore.

The same shame that I had for my mother, I also had for my father. I didn't want Zack and my friends to know he used drinking as a way to cope with his problems. I didn't want them to know that when he came home drunk, on Friday nights, he often argued with my mother. The man he had become was so uncharacteristic of the father I once knew. I was angry with him, too.

Whenever I heard my father come home drunk, I quickly got out of bed and tried to distract him with conversation to keep him from fighting with my mother. He told the most elaborate stories that were a combination of fantasy and his past recollections. "Do you know how I got this part in my hair? I ran into a goal post playing football and split my head. That made the part. It's been there ever since," or, "I would be six-feet tall if they didn't cut six inches off my legs."

"Why did they do that, Daddy?"

"Because I had rickets," he answered, flipping back the lid of his Zippo lighter and lighting a cigarette. Sometimes, he showed how strong he was by holding onto the overhead doorframe and doing pull-ups. I let him talk until he got tired. Then, I walked him into the playroom, where he plopped down on the daybed to sleep. What happened to him? Where was the father that I knew as my protector, the father that used to take care of me?

Nancy Lee, fifteen years old. My mother's nickname for me was "Miss Fancy Pants," probably because I was fussy about what I ate, or that I wouldn't wear clothes that weren't ironed, or that I didn't like the green soap my mother bought, or that I polished my nails and wore make-up, or that I didn't walk around the house barefoot.

I was embarrassed about almost everything in my life. I thought that Zack was too good for me. How foolish I was to think he could be my boyfriend. Zack had told me that he loved me and that he even talked to a priest at his school about his feelings. Zack said that his feelings weren't just a high school crush. I didn't know how to handle that. I couldn't let him love me.

That summer, before my junior year, I had to break up with him. I had to do whatever was necessary to keep him from learning my family secret. Zack was hurt when I told him that I didn't want to see him anymore and I couldn't explain why. Several times that summer, I spotted Zack at Caz Casino and the pool, but I hurried away before he noticed me. I missed him so much!

One very sad day toward the end of summer, I went into the bathroom and closed the door. I stood by the sink, staring into the mirror, as the hot tears ran down my cheeks. I opened the medicine cabinet, took out a razor blade from the little gray box and unwrapped it from the tissue paper. Slowly, I pulled the blade across my wrist, feeling a hot sting. Then, I did it again.

I wanted to feel the pain. I watched the blood dripping into the bathroom sink. I wanted to make the pain in my heart go into my wrist. It didn't do any good to cut myself. My heart still ached for Zack. I bandaged my wrist and went to my bedroom to lie down. Where was my guardian angel now?

Summer ended and I started back to school in my junior year. I didn't walk to the soda shop with my friends anymore. I was afraid I might see Zack and nothing at my home had changed. My mother could tell that I was sad. Trying to cheer me, she said, "I want to have a "Sweet Sixteen" birthday party for you. You can invite all your school friends."

Deep down, I knew I shouldn't put all my shame on my mother, but I had to blame someone. What was she thinking? "Are you crazy?" I screamed, letting all of my shame explode at her. "Just look at this house! Do you think I would bring anyone here?" Before that day, I had never considered sassing my mother. She looked shocked! I don't think she had any idea how I felt about her or my father and the way we lived. I don't think it crossed her mind even once in the two years I had been home that I never invited a friend to the house.

Tom had friends over all of the time. That, too, was one of the reasons the house was always a mess. I did chores for Tom, but I didn't clean up after him.

"Don't blame me. I don't like living this way either. I can't help it if things aren't the way you want. I'm doing the best I can. Why don't you ever blame your father for anything?"

I knew that my mother's right hand bothered her, but I thought she could try harder to keep the house clean. I guess that I was too occupied taking care of myself to help her. Besides, she never asked. She told me she would clean the house to prepare for the party and she did. She bought a can of Bon Ami cleanser, and I scrubbed the bathtub, toilet and sinks. I used all the cleanser and several rags to get the job done. We washed the windows with vinegar and water and dried them with newspapers. We dusted the furniture, swept and washed the floors. My mother even painted the old, chipped toilet seat. Unfortunately, she painted it the day of the party and it didn't completely dry before the party.

The party was set for Saturday at seven in the evening. Jeanie wasn't invited because she might slip and say something about when I used to live in the foster homes. Tom invited his friends, Ronny, Big Willy, and Ray. I invited the clique from South Park, including Zack. I didn't invite him personally, but told Barbara to tell him he was invited. I wanted to test myself. I wanted to find out if I could see him again, without wanting him. I still wanted us to be friends even though we had broken up.

"What do you want for a birthday present? Name it and it's yours," Tom asked, the day before the party.

"Are you sure, Tom? I can have anything?"

"Well, sure, if it doesn't cost too much."

"I saw a dress that I think is so beautiful, but it cost fifteen dollars; can I have that dress for a present?"

"Here, knock yourself out," Tom said, taking fifteen dollars from his wallet and handing it to me.

The bodice was black velvet and the bottom was patterned with black velvet over gray taffeta. It flared out when I swung around. "That's a pretty dress, but why didn't you get a dress in a different color?" my mother asked when I put it on.

I didn't want anyone to go into the back door. I wanted them to use the door that our family never used—the door that led to the beauty salon, my grandmother's sun porch, and to our front door.

Barbara let everyone know they should use the first door on the outside of the house. Inside, a wide staircase led to a landing where the second door opened to a narrow staircase leading directly into the alcove near our living room. "You can't have your friends come in the front door, Nancy. There's no doorbell and no key for that door." my mother insisted.

"I'm going to watch out the front window. When I see them coming, I'll go down and stand at the door."

Billy wouldn't cooperate and stay in his bedroom. He wanted to join the party. I made him promise not to say anything about foster homes. With my friends all in playroom at the front of the flat, I don't think any of them knew my younger brothers and sister were in the house. Bobby, Jimmy and Carol Jean stayed in their bedrooms and played. They only came out occasionally, to sneak a peek. A few times, I caught them standing at the dining room door. When they saw me looking at them with a stern look, they hurried away.

My parents were sober and in a good mood. We had snacks, Pepsi and a store-bought birthday cake with sixteen candles. Tom played his records and everyone joked around, having a good time. My friends brought birthday cards, and some had a few dollars in them. Zack handed me a small present. I unwrapped the pretty paper and lifted lid of the box. Inside, on a cushion of soft cotton was a Trifari bracelet with emerald-colored rhinestones. "Zack, thank you, it's so beautiful."

With Zack standing so close, smiling his warm smile, I realized that I wasn't over him yet! When the party ended, everybody said goodbye and left, talking and laughing as they walked down the front staircase. I must admit it was a nice party.

That fall, I had a very bad cold. I missed a few days of school and didn't go to the show on Friday night. Because my grandparents had the same last name and lived at the same address, Barbara assumed that my family had a phone and that my grandparents' phone number was my number. On Saturday afternoon, my grandfather called up the stairs, "Nancy Lee, you have a phone call."

I hurried down the stairs. It was Barbara on the phone, telling me to tune into a certain radio station for a surprise. I hurried back up the stairs and tuned into the station. I didn't have to wait long before the announcer said, "We have a request for Nancy from Zack." The song was the Hilltoppers, singing, *"P.S. I Love You".*

On the following Friday, I got up the courage to go to the movies again. I knew Zack would be there. I should have known better! I got to the theater before any of my friends and sat in my usual place. A few minutes later, they came walking down the aisle. Zack sat in his usual seat, next to me.

Neither one of us was happy about breaking up, but he was more in control of his emotions than I was. Tears began to come and my throat tightened. Quickly, I got up saying, "I'll be right back." I didn't go back. I almost ran out of the theater, sobbing to myself as I hurried home. That was the last time I ever saw Zack!

Adding to the misery of our poor life, my father had a hernia operation and had to leave his job at Socony-Vacuum, where he worked at moving fifty-five gallon drums of tar onto flatbed trucks. At the end of October, the gas company shut off our service. My mother had to cook our meals on an electric hotplate. To heat the house my father put a stove that burned kerosene in the dining room.

The shelves in the refrigerator were almost bare. Nanny and Auntie Alice brought food occasionally, such as tomato soup, pork and beans, Franco American spaghetti, crackers, a tin of cocoa and bananas. Billy loved bananas! My father stood in a line to get the surplus food that the government handed out to needy families, marked "U.S. Surplus." He brought home butter, blocks of cheese, tins of peanut butter, powdered milk, rice and corn meal. "Are we on welfare?" I asked my father, as he unloaded the food from the canvas bag onto the table.

"Don't ask questions that are none of your business," my mother said, taking the food and putting it into the cupboard. I was ashamed of my parents. I thought people who accepted handouts were people who couldn't pay their own way in the world. I would rather go without, but it wouldn't be fair to my brothers and sister to go without because of my pride. I had to accept the fact that we needed the government handouts.

My parents and I weren't getting along. Things were changing in the family and I was deeply affected by the changes. I wouldn't listen to anything they said. I wasn't sure what I wanted. I only knew what I didn't want. I didn't want my parents to drink. I didn't want them to fight. I didn't want to be poor. I loved my parents and I hated my parents at the same time. I was so confused!

On the long walks home from school, I didn't feel the cold; instead I felt a warm glow, while I thought about the times Zack had walked me home and we kissed with long lingering kisses that were painfully sweet. On weekends, I occupied my time by listening to songs on the radio and working crossword puzzles, or sitting and staring into the pages of my mother's romance magazines, while my mind wandered to the happier times with my South Park friends.

Was I ever going to get over longing for Zack? Was I ever going to be able to have a relationship with someone? Who would want me after finding out about my family life?

When I listened to the music on the radio and heard Joan Weber singing, "*Let Me go Lover,*" I couldn't stop my eyes from tearing. I hurried into my bedroom before anyone saw me crying. The gray shadows of sadness that followed me were turning into dark shadows of hopelessness.

On a dreary November morning, I awoke with Carol Jean still asleep next to me. I rubbed my legs together trying to warm them. Looking out the bedroom window at the cold, wet sky, It was hard for me to get out of bed and go to school, since I stopped going to the soda shop with my friends, not meeting them at the Friday night movies, anymore. I didn't want to get out of bed, but I did.

My bedroom was the only place I could go when I needed to get away from the noise of the television or my brothers rough housing. With the three bedrooms all at the back of the house, off the kitchen, I had little privacy, except for the old drape my father had attached to the doorframe to substitute as a door.

When I finished helping my mother clean the kitchen and wash the dishes, I went into my bedroom and pulled the old drape closed. Alone in my room, I sat down on the edge of the bed. The creaking of the bedsprings broke the bleak silence of the drab room. "I don't care, I don't care, I don't care," I repeated to myself in a low whisper over and over again.

I felt the hot tears beginning to fill my eyes and roll down my cheeks, as I looked around the room. The faded wallpaper was torn from the wall in places, exposing the gray plaster. The metal bed frame holding the coiled springs and thin cotton mattress had bare spots where the brown paint was chipped away.

Two sheets covered the mattress, along with a gray wool blanket. Next to the closet, without a door, stood the vanity dresser. It looked out of place in this room. The mirror reflected a pitiful face as I watched the hot tears fall. "I don't care, I don't care, I don't care," I kept repeating, in a low voice, to myself.

My heart ached. Why couldn't I have a normal home, a normal family and a normal life? I just wanted to be like all the other girls that I knew. They were carefree and happy. I wanted to be like them. I wanted to love and be loved. "I don't care, I don't care, I don't care," I told myself. But I did care!

I was feeling sorry for myself because we were poor. I couldn't buy a nice birthday present for someone, like the one Zack had bought for me. I had nothing to give. I only had me. The words of the song *"I Can't Give You Anything But Love"* played in my head. That was it! I had a good body. I was a virgin. Men wanted to marry virgins, didn't they?

I stood up and undressed, wanting to see if I would be desirable to someone, someday. Would my body be attractive enough for someone to overlook the way I'd been raised, or that I had nothing to give? I took the rubber band out of my ponytail and let my long hair fall down my back. Not too thin, although I could see my hip bones on either side of my flat tummy. Standing with my back straight, my breasts looked full and perky. Someone would want me, just for me. Yes, I was desirable. Hope was not lost. The gloominess was replaced with gladness. I realized I had a treasure. I promised myself I would value my treasure—my virginity—and keep it until the right moment, my wedding night. "I don't care, I don't care, I don't care," I said softly again, wiping my tears with the back of my hand.

I put my clothes back on. Then, I took my little, white diary with the tiny lock and key from under the mattress and wrote in shorthand, "The only thing I have to give is my virtue and I intend to keep it!" I took a sweater from the vanity dresser and put it on, because I was going to the cold basement to wash the clothes.

Saturday was the day I usually did laundry. I gathered the dirty clothes that lay in a heap on the closet floor. Picking them up, I put them on a bed sheet and brought the four corners together, making a bundle. I went into Tom's closet without the door, picked up his dirty clothes and gathered them into his sheet, making another bundle. Dragging the two bundles behind me, I headed down the stairs to the basement.

The basement wasn't very big. We only had access to the back half, which we shared with my grandparents. In front of each of the twin laundry tubs stood a wringer washing machine. One belonged to my grandparents, and one was ours. Taking our box of soap powder from the shelf, I saw it was empty, again. I put it back and reached for my grandparents' box of soap powder. I threw in two handfuls.

While the clothes washed, I went over to the basement steps and worked a crossword puzzle. When all the clothes were clean and in the wicker laundry basket, I carried them to the second floor, then up one more flight of stairs into the attic where my father had strung some clotheslines. My mother did the laundry for the rest of the family the same way. That may be why clean towels and face clothes were a rarity in our house. While I was in the attic, my mother yelled up to me, "Nancy, while you're up there, shut the attic windows, will you?"

I finished hanging the clothes and went for a walk down Duerstein Street to Jeanie's house. Jeanie wasn't home. I looked across the street to the house where I lived when I was a small child. I was overcome with the memories of the innocent days when I rode my little red tricycle along the sidewalk and seeing Tommy climbing the cherry tree with Brownie sitting in our driveway watching us.

That night, I took a pair of scissors from the kitchen drawer, went into the bathroom, closed the door, and without emotion, I cut off all of my beautiful, long hair.

Chapter Six

All Grown Up

A 16-year-old girl who still believes in fairy tales is no match for the desires and strength of a 23-year-old man, even if she does have a guardian angel watching over her.

I STILL CARED ABOUT Zack as much as I cared about anyone. His smile and the sparkle in his eyes remained in my thoughts and haunted my dreams. I needed to turn my attention away from him. Besides wanting to avoid seeing Zack, I realized that poor girls like me didn't make it to college.

"Mama, I'm sixteen and I decided I'm not going to school anymore. I'm going to get a job."

"No, you have to stay in school. You only have another year to go, then you can graduate and get a good job."

"Tom quit when he was sixteen. You can't make me go, because I won't!" I didn't care what my mother said. She didn't understand how hard it was for me to go to school and keep to myself, because I didn't want to hear anything about Zack. I quit school at the end of November. Neither my father nor mother had graduated from high school. I know they had hopes that their children would, but they allowed us to make our own decisions.

Tom's girlfriend, Rosie, a petite dark-haired girl was also looking for a job and said, "Adam Meldrum & Anderson is hiring extra help for the gift-wrap station." Together, we walked through the park over to the department store at the Southgate Plaza on Abbott Road to apply for the job.

"Can you girls start work tomorrow?" Mr. Telly, the assistant manager, asked while we stood near the office filling out the job applications.

"Yes!" we both answered. I didn't even ask how much the job paid. It really didn't matter. I was happy just to be working at a department store. Finding a job so quickly brought me a sense of peace. I was pleased to learn that as an employee, I got a ten percent discount on everything in the store and a twenty percent discount on personal clothing, including items on the sale racks.

The first few weeks my earnings were spent on clothes and toys for my younger brothers and sister. All the gifts that I had bought and wrapped in pretty paper were put under the Christmas tree, as gifts from Santa. As in the past Christmas, my parents gladly accepted the boxes of food and toys brought by the Salvation Army. The boxes of goodies that Nanny and Auntie Alice brought also added to our holiday joy.

On Christmas morning, I awoke and lay in bed watching the shimmering snowflakes outside the bedroom window, as Carol Jean slept peacefully next to me. "It's Christmas, it's Christmas!" Billy shouted, waking everyone as he ran out of the bedroom down the hall, through the house and into the front playroom where my father slept near the Christmas tree. That year, although we were still poor, we had a nice Christmas.

Following the Christmas holidays, extra help wasn't needed for the gift-wrap station. Rosie was laid off, but Mr. Telly asked if I would stay to work the end-of-the-year store inventory. I jumped at the chance. Inventory work put me at a desk, working with ledgers, purchase orders, and register receipts. I loved the job. My major focus in high school was bookkeeping and I was a good typist and I knew shorthand—it never occurred to me to look for an office job!

After inventory, Mr. Telly asked me to stay on as a "floater," to work in the various departments when someone didn't show up for work. It wasn't long before I was permanently assigned to the glove and cosmetic department, located near the glass double-doors and the display windows at the front entrance. I worked five days a week from nine in the morning until five in the evening, except on Thursdays; I worked from noon until nine at night.

Occasionally, after work, I spent time at Jeanie's house where we listened to her records. Other times, we just walked down Seneca Street, talking girl talk. Jeanie didn't understand why I quit school. "I'm glad that you like your job, but I know you could get a decent job if you went back and finished school."

I thought I had a decent job and I told her so. "Jeanie, there's nothing wrong with working as a sales girl. My grandmother said that any job is a decent job, as long as it's an honest job."

Tom paid my parents for his room and board. He even paid for the telephone that we now had. With my twenty-seven dollar weekly take-home pay, I put five dollars into a savings account and brought home ten dollars worth of groceries. My father didn't want me to buy food. He wanted me to give him the ten dollars in cash. We had several arguments about it. I wouldn't give in because I wasn't going to contribute to paying for beer and cigarettes. Every payday, before coming home, I stopped at the A&P grocery store.

One day, after picking up my pay envelope at the office, I was handing a customer her change when Billy came into the store and walked over to me. "Billy, what are you doing here?" I asked, with eyes and mouth wide open.

"Dad said he wants the board money. He's outside, do you want to talk to him?" Billy stood with his head lowered, waiting for an answer. I knew he was only doing what my father told him to do. I didn't want to make a scene, so I gave Billy the ten dollars. "I'll talk to you when I get home; now, get out of here."

When I got home, I warned Billy, "Never do that to me again!" He never did. My father couldn't be so easily convinced. We continued the arguments. Sometimes, I still stopped in the A&P and bought ten dollars in groceries to take home. If I didn't think we needed the food, I paid my father in cash.

Fortunately, it wasn't long before my father found a job working at the Bethlehem-Lackawanna Steel Plant. Tommy and I didn't pay board anymore, because my father earned enough money to pay all of the bills and put food on the table. I was able to put more money into my savings account.

On the morning of Thursday, August 11, 1955, I took my time dressing, because it was the kind of day where I just wanted to sit in the shade under a tree somewhere and hope for a cool breeze. I put on the pink, sleeveless dress that I bought with my last pay. Dressed as I was, wearing my white flats and white clutch purse, I felt as fresh as springtime walking through the park to Abbott Road where I would wait for the bus to take me to work.

When I reached my bus stop, I discovered that one half the length of Abbott Road was being paved. Dump trucks, asphalt spreaders and huge rollers were on one side of the road; a flagman directed the two-way traffic on the other half.

As I stood at the bus stop, a construction worker prompted one of the workers to go over and talk to me. The slimmer of the two workers—the one with black hair, dark eyes, and tanned skin, who was sweaty from the sun and hot asphalt—came swaggering over to me. I was nervous, knowing he was coming over to flirt with me, but I took a deep breath, steadied my nerves, and put on a serious face, acting real grown-up.

With a sly smile, jokingly the asphalt worker said, "My name's Joseppe, but you can call me Joe, I'm a smoother. I smooth the seams of the asphalt. What's your name and what do you do?"

My head held high, I responded with my best grown-up voice, "My name's Nancy and I work at AM&A's department store at the Southgate Plaza." Foolishly, I told him where I worked, because I was showing off that I was a working girl.

After a minute or two, I turned away, looked down the road, and was relieved to see the bus coming. I didn't want to answer any more questions and my face was beginning to flush from the embarrassment of the attention I was getting. The other worker called to him, "Hey, Joe, get back to work." I got on the bus, went to my job and didn't give the incident another thought.

At nine o'clock that evening I was closing down my register at the cosmetic department when a young man came into the store. With a swagger, he walked toward me. He looked like a young Frank Sinatra, except he had brown eyes, not blue eyes. He had a self-confidence that made me think he got whatever he wanted. "Remember me?" he asked, with a smile.

I didn't recognize him as the asphalt worker. He was cleaned up, wearing a white shirt and dress pants. He saw my quizzical look and added, "I'm Joe. I talked to you at the bus stop. I came to drive you home, so you don't have to take the bus."

I was taken off guard and said, "No thank you, I don't think my mother would like that." I used my mother as an excuse, I didn't know how else to refuse the ride.

"I'll wait for you outside by my Cadillac," he said with a cool arrogance. I walked away, heading toward the office at the back of the store to turn in the money pouch. Glancing back over my shoulder, I saw him walking out the door. I thought he left because I didn't accept his offer for a ride.

When I left the store, Mickey, the security guard, held the door open. With a sly smile, Mickey said, "I see you have a ride home. You be careful, now; the moon is full tonight and the wolves are out, looking for girls like you."

"I'll be fine, Mickey," I said as I looked in the direction that Mickey was looking. Joe was standing in front of a green Cadillac, smoking a cigarette.

As I walked toward him he said, I drove all the way from the West Side, twenty miles from here, just to take you home. Come on, I won't bite." He opened the car door on the front passenger side for me to get in. I was still apprehensive, but flattered that he drove so far. Hesitantly, I got in.

"I live on Seneca Street. Do you know where it is?"

"I thought we could have a cup of coffee before I dropped you off. Is that all right?"

"My mother will be worried if I'm late, but one cup of coffee should be okay." I said, still pretending that my parents worried about me and that I had to be home by a certain time. I wanted others to believe that I was loved and cared for.

We stopped at a coffee shop a few blocks from my house and Joe parked the car. We went in, sat at a little table and ordered coffee.

"How old are you?" Joe asked after a few minutes of conversation.

"I'm sixteen," I answered casually. The coffee came splattering out of his mouth.

"Jesus, you're jail bait!"

"What do you mean, I'm jail bait? I never heard that phrase."

"It means I could get into trouble if I mess with you. I'm twenty-three—seven years older than you," Joe said, putting his cup down in the saucer and wiping up the spilled coffee with paper napkins.

"I'll be seventeen next month," I said, trying to close the age gap between us. After we finished the coffee, we exchanged phone numbers and I said, "I can walk home from here." I had given Joe my phone number but I didn't want him to know where I lived.

"I'm not going to let you walk home alone at night; remember what that guy said, a wolf might jump out and bite you," he joked. He must have meant what Mickey said. Taking me by the elbow, he walked me to his car. Reluctantly, I got in.

A few blocks down the street, I pointed to my house and Joe pulled into the driveway. "Good night and thank you for the ride," I said, hurrying out of the car. I went into the back hall and waited until I heard his car pull out of the driveway.

After dinner on Sunday, the phone rang, "Nancy, it's for you," my mother said, with a smile from ear to ear like the Cheshire Cat. It was Joe, telling me he would like his friends to meet me next Saturday night.

"Are you asking me for a date?"

"Yes, I guess you could call it a date," adding "Stay on the line, I want you to hear something." I waited, with the phone to my ear for a few minutes. Then, I heard a trumpet playing, *I Can't Get Started,* a song recorded by Bunny Berigan.

"What do you think?" Joe asked, when the song finished and he came back on the phone.

"Why did you want me to listen to that record?"

"It wasn't just a record. I was playing my trumpet along with it." Of course, I told Joe he sounded great.

After a few more minutes talking about his trumpet playing, we said goodbye. I hung up the phone, turned around and saw my mother sitting at the kitchen table. She had been listening to my phone conversation. "Who was that?" she asked.

"His name is Joe. He drove me home Thursday night, and I think he likes me." I didn't want to waste time talking to my mother, I was anxious to phone Jeanie and tell her that I had a "date." Excitedly, I dialed her number. "Jeanie, you'll never guess what! I met a boy with a Cadillac and I think he likes me; he asked me on a date." I didn't care that my mother was still listening, I continued telling Jeanie what I knew about Joe—which wasn't much.

"He's too old for you. You don't know anything about him. What high school did he graduate from? Where does he live?" Jeanie asked. I didn't like her attitude.

"He lives on the West Side and you don't know him either. If you're my friend, you should be happy for me. I think you're just jealous because I have a boyfriend and you don't!"

"If he's from the West Side that's all I have to know. To him, you're just another conquest. All he wants to do is seduce you. I am your friend and I don't want to see you get hurt, but I know you won't listen to me!" With that, she hung up the phone.

On Saturday, the day of the date, I phoned Jeanie and told her, "To ease your mind, I want you to meet Joe. If you still think he just wants to take advantage of me, I'll stop seeing him. I don't want anything to break up our friendship. Can he pick me up at your house? I don't want him to come into my house. Besides, I never know how my parents will be."

"Sure, you know he can pick you up here, but won't he wonder why?" I knew she was right. I knew I couldn't keep Joe or anyone that I dated away from my parents forever. I knew it was just a matter of time before I would have to end this relationship, too. I phoned Joe and gave him Jeanie's address. He didn't like the idea of picking me up there, but he said he would.

I was eager to make a good impression on Joe's friends. I wore the black dress that Tom bought for my sixteenth birthday. I combed my hair back like Kim Novak, the Hollywood movie star, polished my nails with red polish, used dark mascara and red lipstick, added Chanel No. 5 perfume in all the right places, and walked down to Jeanie's house in my black high-heeled pumps.

Jeanie, dressed casually in her jeans and a T-shirt, answered the door. Her parents were out for the evening. "Wow! You look great," Jeanie said, as I walked into her house. We went into the living room, sat on the couch and waited for Joe. Kay Starr singing *"The Wheel of Fortune"* was playing on the radio when Joe rang the doorbell. Jeanie opened the front door. I could tell immediately that she and Joe didn't like each other.

"Hi, I'm Jeanie," she said with a forced smile.

"Hi," Joe said, then turning to me with a quizzical look, asked, "Are you ready to go?"

"I'll call you later, Jeanie," I said, walking out the door. Joe got in the car and sat behind the steering wheel. He reaching across the seat and pushed the passenger door open for me to get in.

"Why are you friends with her?" Joe asked with disgust as he backed out of her driveway.

"Jeanie and I have been best friends all of our life."

"The next time, I'm not picking you up at that fat girl's house. I'm picking you up where you live. I want to meet your parents." I was shocked that Joe insisted on meeting my parents! This was only the second time I was with him. I didn't think he had to know anything about my parents, my brothers and sister, or how we lived.

"Look, when you meet my friends, if they ask, don't tell them you're only sixteen. Tell them you're nineteen; you look it. They'll believe you." We rode to a nightclub on the West Side where Joe and his friends went to dance. Inside the nightclub, we walked into a room with small tables and a live band, near a dance floor. The room was filled with confident, adult males and females who all seemed to know Joe. We sat at one of the small tables with another couple. I was glad they didn't ask how old I was, so I didn't have to lie.

A girl, perfumed and wearing a seductive red satin dress, came over to our table, grabbed Joe's hand and said, "Come on, Joe, dance with me." The music was loud and the dancing was fast dancing, something I didn't know how to do. As a matter of fact, I didn't know how to dance at all.

Joe was a great dancer, so great that everyone stood back on the outer edge of the dance floor to watch the two of them dance. Joe let go of that girl's hand and grabbed another girl who was standing on the edge of the dance floor, and started dancing with her, while the band continued into another fast song. When the music stopped, the crowd cheered him as he came back to the table.

The waitress asked for our order. Joe said, "We'll have two Seven-

Sevens." I didn't know what a Seven-Seven was. When the glasses were brought to the table, I took a sip and wrinkled my nose. "What's wrong? It's just Seven-Up with a little whiskey," Joe said with a chuckle, putting his cigarette out in the ashtray. My glass sat there without another sip. I didn't like the taste.

I pretended that I wasn't nervous, but I was, with all his sophisticated friends looking me over. Joe finished his drink and asked me to dance. The band was playing Glen Miller's hit song, *"In the Mood"*. Joe took my hand to lead me to the dance floor. I pulled back. I was embarrassed because I couldn't dance. What was I doing here? Joe must have wondered the same thing. "If you're not going to dance, let's go!" Joe turned his back on me and headed out of the room, toward the door. I grabbed my clutch purse and followed him, not knowing what else to do.

On the ride back to South Buffalo, Joe and I didn't talk; we just listened to the jazz music that played on the car radio. Pulling into the driveway, he stopped the car, reached across me and pushed the car door open. I didn't understand why he was so mad just because I didn't know how to dance. Jeanie was right. I didn't know him at all.

"Get out," Joe ordered.

"What's wrong? Why are you so angry?"

"You made a fool of me! When I ask a girl to dance, she dances! Get out!" Joe ordered again.

I got out and went into the back door. Joe drove off, spinning his tires as he pulled out of the driveway.

Joe didn't phone me on Sunday, but I didn't care. I didn't care if I ever saw him again. I was hurt and angry. When Jeanie phoned me and asked how the date went, I lied, "It was okay, but he was disappointed that I didn't know how to dance."

"Where did you go to dance?"

"It was a nightclub where all his friends go."

"He took you there because he wanted to impress his friends with his new conquest."

"Jeanie, you don't know him. So, you can't judge him!"

"You don't know him either! You're blinded by the glitter of a man with a car!" Again she hung up on me.

The following Thursday, when I worked until nine o'clock, Joe was outside the store, standing next to his Cadillac. I was taken by surprise, when in a gentle tone he said, "Come on, Nancy, get in, I'll drive you home." I got in and waited for him to say he was sorry for how he acted. But, he didn't say anything.

Before we reached my house, Joe pulled into a parking lot and turned off the engine. "Let's talk. I want to know you better." We talked and told each other about our families. Joe had two married sisters. He also had an intellectually challenged brother, Sammy, who lived at home with Joe and his widowed mother.

"I have four brothers and a sister. And, my parents drink too much." There, I said it! I didn't care what he knew about my family because I was going to tell him that I didn't want to see him again! Joe didn't show any reaction. It was as if he wasn't even listening. He took a last puff of his cigarette and tossed it out the car window. I felt relieved that he knew about my family and it didn't seem to matter to him. I was going to tell him that I didn't want to see him anymore—but I didn't.

When Joe pulled into my driveway, he put the car in park. With the engine still running and the radio playing jazz, he leaned over and I let him kiss me several times. Joe's wet kisses didn't make me tingle like Zack's kisses and I didn't like the taste of cigarette breath.

On a Sunday in September, before I turned seventeen, Joe phoned and invited me out to dinner. "Friday night, I'm going to take you to Lyon's Tea Room, where there's no dancing. Would you like that?"

"Yes, I would," I answered with enthusiasm.

"I'll pick you up at seven o'clock and meet your parents then."

I hung up the phone and went into the living room where my parents sat watching television. "Mama, Joe, the boy who drives me home from work, wants to take me out for my birthday and he wants to meet you and Daddy. Why do you have to always wear that old apron? Why can't you fix yourself up like you used to do?"

I had begged my mother to stop drinking. She didn't think she drank too much. "I only drink occasionally," she would say, quietly. That was true, she didn't go out to taverns; she only drank wine at home. But, too much, I thought!

"Daddy, I'm ashamed of this house. There's cardboard in the French doors where glass should be. The wallpaper is old and dirty and the house is always a mess. What if you're drunk when he comes to meet you, or fighting with Mama? You know you get drunk every Friday night. It's not fair! Why can't this be a normal house? Why can't this be a normal family?"

Tom, who was standing in the dining room listening to my tantrum, went into his bedroom and came back with his camera. "Nancy, look up." Snap! Tommy took a picture of me sitting on the arm of the couch, with tears rolling down my cheeks. "Cheer up, Nancy, if the guy really likes you, he won't care if there's cardboard in the French doors instead of glass."

My father chimed in, "Nancy Lee, this house isn't that bad, you just want things to be perfect. Well, life isn't like that." My mother was quiet.

She looked at me and didn't say a word. I knew her feelings were hurt because of the things I said, but they needed to be said. I wanted her to be the mother she was when I was younger.

When Friday came, I hurried home from work, straightened up the house, bathed, washed my hair and dressed, putting on my make-up and my blue, full skirted, taffeta dress. I answered the door when Joe knocked. He followed me into the dining room where my mother sat at the table. She had made an effort to fix her hair and she put on a clean apron. She was very charming when she met Joe, "So, you're the young man who has all of my daughter's attention? I can see why!" Then, she took a sip from her glass of wine.

Joe was wearing a dark suit, white shirt and bow tie. Now, he really looked like Frank Sinatra. "You don't have to worry about your daughter. I'll take care of her," he said with a charming smile.

My father wasn't home. He was drinking and playing cards with his buddies at the tavern, like he did every Friday night. But, I didn't tell Joe that; I lied, and said my father was working late. Tom wasn't home. He was out with Rosie. Billy and Bobby were over in the park, Carol Jean and Jimmy sat in the living room watching television. Before we left the house, Joe handed me a small box. I opened it and inside was a 14k white-gold Benrus wristwatch with diamond chips on both sides.

It was a pleasant ride to the restaurant. Joe was a perfect gentleman, even opening the car door for me. The restaurant was elegant and delightfully quaint. The evening was magical with light and cheerful conversation. Joe even told some jokes.

"Did you know that I once dated a homeless girl? I liked her because after the date I could drop her off at any street corner," he chuckled, thinking his joke was funny.

When we got into the car and Joe started the engine, the sounds of jazz, Joe's favorite music, came from the radio. After pulling into the driveway at my house, Joe parked and insisted on walking me upstairs. Getting out of the car, he said, "Your father should be home from work. I'd like to meet him."

I was caught off guard. I hurried into the house ahead of Joe. Just as I feared, my father was home—drunk! I could hear him arguing with my mother. As I rushed up the stairs, Joe was one step behind me. I opened the door, just as me father gave my mother a shove. She fell backward over a kitchen chair, knocking the chair to the floor beside her. My father grabbed the chair and held it over his head, as if he were going to bring it down on her. "Daddy, stop it! Stop it!" I screamed, pulling him away from my mother, where she lay crumpled on the floor with her arms crossed over her head.

My father set the chair down. Turning, he looked at Joe and, in a drunken slur said, "What the hell are you looking at?"

"Please go, I have to take care of my parents. I'll talk to you later." I said, practically pushing Joe out the door. I was able to calm my father and get him into the playroom to his daybed. Then, I helped my mother into her bedroom.

Over the next several days, I couldn't stop worrying about what Joe must have thought. The following Thursday, when he came to drive me home from work, he didn't say anything about that night. I was surprised but pleased.

That fall, Joe drove me home every Thursday evening after work. After a goodnight kiss or two, I jumped out of the car and hurried into the back hall, waiting for Joe to leave; then, I went upstairs. On the Saturdays when we had dates, I kept watch out the playroom window and when Joe pulled into the driveway I ran down the stairs and hopped into his car.

Buffalo isn't very far from Niagara Falls, but I had never been to Canada or seen the falls until Joe drove me there. He also took me to see a movie at one of the theaters in the downtown theatre district. Joe was generous and he seemed to really care about me. Cautiously I began to let my heart trust him.

In November, Joe's mother invited me to Sunday dinner. This was to be the first time Joe would meet Tom and my father, not counting the brief moment when Joe and my father looked into each other's eyes on the night of my seventeenth birthday.

As I waited for Joe, Tom got his camera and took my picture. I was dressed in a beige suit, sitting in a dining room chair, with my back straight, hands in my lap and feet together, posed just like the portrait of Aunt Loretta that I saw on the wall in her dining room. I continued sitting at the dining room table, telling my parents about Joe and his family, what little I knew about them, when Joe knocked on the kitchen door.

Joe said he would be over to pick me up at noon and he was. Our house was warm and smelled of the chuck roast, potatoes, onions and carrots that were roasting in the oven. Billy, Bobby, Jimmy and Carol Jean were in the living room, watching television. Tom was on the phone talking to Rosie.

"Joe, you know my mother. Daddy, this is Joe," I said walking Joe into the dining room.

My father got up from his chair and walked over to shake hands with Joe. "My daughter tells me you're twenty-three years old. Aren't you too old for her?" My father didn't wait for an answer. He turned away and went back to where he sat at the table drinking a cup of coffee.

"Hi," Tom said to Joe, after he came into the dining room to get a look at Joe. Then, he went back to the kitchen where he continued his phone conversation with Rosie. That was it! Joe had met my family and he even seemed to like them.

We arrived at Joe's house where he parked on the street. Most of the houses in his neighborhood were built close together, without driveways. The house he lived in was a two-family "salt box" style, without a porch or overhang above the front door.

Joe's mother was a short, plump, gray-haired woman who was born in a small fishing village outside of Naples, Italy. She spoke in English with an Italian accent. I had the feeling that she was very warm-hearted. I liked her immediately. His brother, Sammy, said a quiet "Hello," then returned to his bedroom.

During my visit, Joe's mother told me that she had married Joe's Sicilian father after the death of his first wife. She also told me that Joe's father died when Joe was only twelve years old and soon after that, Joe's older brother died.

She had to work to support the family. Joe was left to the influences of the street corners. I guess you could say that without a father or an older brother to keep him in line, Joe did what he wanted to do. At age sixteen— after finishing eighth grade—Joe dropped out of school. He worked in the neighborhood at odd jobs including shining shoes. The same as Tommy had. Most Italian mothers treat their sons like royalty, but, in Joe's case, his mother doted excessively on him.

For dinner she served homemade tomato sauce and meatballs with pasta. It was the first solid food that I had since my tonsil operation a few weeks ago. At first I didn't think I could eat anything, but with her encouragement, I finished the dish of pasta she set in front of me. I even ate the cannoli she served for dessert.

Whenever I talked to Jeanie, she badgered me about dating Joe, "He's the only one you've ever dated. How are you going to know if he's the right one if you only date him? She and Joe didn't like each other from the moment they met. Joe made critical remarks about her weight and she said he was manipulating me. I had to make a choice. Foolishly, I made the choice to cut off contact with my only girlfriend! Our pact to always remain friends had been broken!

Even my family disapproved of my dating Joe. My father said, "Why do you see in that guy? Can't you find a boy your own age?"

My mother said, "Be careful, because a guy like Joe will take advantage of a girl like you."

Tom said, "He's a smooth talker, and I bet he's got only one thing on his mind." I knew Tom and my parents meant to give me good advice, but I didn't listen. After all, I was seventeen years old—I knew what I was doing!

Joe took me on another date. He told me it was to be a "special date." We were going to see *Cinderella on Ice* at the Buffalo Auditorium. I was excited that I was going to see one of my favorite stories, performed on ice.

I took a bubble bath and washed my hair; I went into my bedroom, closed the drape across the door and dropped the white chenille bathrobe to the floor. Wanting to be perfectly dressed for the occasion, I slipped my arms into my white brassiere, stepped into my white panties and pulled them up over the white garter belt, trimmed with black lace. From the vanity dresser I took a pair of nylon stockings and attached them to the clips at the ends of the garter belt, making sure the dark seams were straight. Stepping into my white half-slip, I was ready to dab the right spots with Chanel No. 5 before I put on my new aqua dress with the empire waistline.

Joe arrived on time. Before we left the house Tom said, "Let me take your picture." Snap! The photo was taken. I wonder, how many girls have a photo taken on the last day of their innocence?

After enjoying the fairy-tale magic of the Ice Capades, we left the Auditorium. Joe didn't drive me straight home. He drove to an area near the Niagara River. I wasn't familiar with that part of the city; I didn't know that the area was referred to as "Lover's Lane." Joe parked but didn't turn off the engine. We sat, talking about the ice show and listening to jazz. Joe moved closer and we began kissing. Suddenly, I sensed strong, passionate feelings stirring within Joe and abruptly I tried to pull away.

As I struggled, his mouth pressed harder on mine. He had unzipped his pants, and his hands were pushing up my dress and grabbing between my thighs, pulling my panties aside. I tried to pull his hands away. The harder I resisted, the more he leaned into me, pushing me down on the seat.

"No! Stop! Stop! Please stop! What are you doing?" The girl who looked at herself in the vanity dresser mirror and made a promise to stay a virgin until her wedding night was broken-hearted, as she straightened her clothes and sat up.

"What are you crying about?" Joe asked, as he zipped his pants and moved back behind the steering wheel.

"I trusted you, Joe!"

"You know you wanted it. You know I'm giving you an engagement ring for Christmas and I'm going to marry you next year, when you're eighteen, so stop crying."

"You say you're going to marry me and you never, even once, told me that you loved me!"

How could I have been such a fool? This was my own fault! Maybe Jeanie was right when she said that I was blinded by the glitter of a man with a car. I wished I had listened to my parents and Tom. In truth, I ignored my own feelings of danger, because I thought Joe loved me and wouldn't hurt me.

I was too ashamed to tell anyone what happened. I couldn't tell Jeanie or my mother or my father or Tom. That night changed me in a way I didn't like. I didn't feel clean anymore. I felt dirty. When I went places with Joe and his friends were there, I couldn't look at them, without thinking they knew I was a ruined girl. My treasure was gone, who would want me now? From then on, Joe having his way with me, whenever he wanted, was impossible to stop.

Joe kept his promise. When he came to my house on Christmas Day, he gave me a diamond engagement ring for a Christmas present. My parents weren't happy about the engagement, but didn't object to me accepting the ring.

When Joe and I were alone I asked him, "Is this the same ring you gave to Joanne, the other girl you were engaged to?" Joe had told me about Joanne, and how he snuck into her bedroom and took back the ring after he broke off the engagement.

"No, I gave that ring to my mother to pay her back for the trip we took to Italy a couple of years ago. My mother had that diamond set into the ring she wears. You can ask her." Being engaged didn't give me the joy that I expected.

On Monday, December 26, I began a new job as a medical secretary. The doctor's office was a one-girl office. My job was filing insurance forms, scheduling hospital procedures, billing and answering the phone. I also assisted the doctor in the treatment of his patients, handing him the instruments he requested, sterilizing the equipment and cleaning the tray for the next patient. If the phone rang while I was in the treatment room, I rushed to the reception room, answered it and hurried back. Oh yes, I also kept the ledgers current, cleaned the office, and made the bank deposits.

My salary was double what I had been getting as a salesclerk. I cleared fifty-seven dollars a week. I wore a nurse's uniform and it was an easy walk to the doctor's office. Best of all, I didn't have to let Joe drive me home from work every Thursday. I loved this job!

The second week in January, to my horror, I missed my period. I thought I might be pregnant, but I wasn't sure. I went to the Catholic Church, lit a votive candle and said a prayer. I felt helpless and the church was the only place I could go to.

When I told Joe I was pregnant, he was angry. He told me he would take me somewhere to have an abortion. I refused. Crying and pleading, I said, "You told me you wanted to marry me—what difference does it make if it's now or next October?" When Joe realized that I would never agree to an abortion, he agreed to marry me, but first he wanted to be sure I was pregnant.

A few days later, Joe took me to a doctor's office on Elmwood Avenue. The nurse stood by while the doctor examined me. He gave me a pelvic exam. That hurt! The doctor concluded that I was probably pregnant, but needed blood work to confirm it. According to the information I gave the doctor, the baby would be born the last week of September.

That night, I turned on the water in the bathtub, poured in some bubble bath salts, sat on the closed toilet seat and watched the bubbles form as the tub filled. The words, "I'm pregnant, I'm going to have a baby," repeated over and over in my head. When the tub was filled, I sank my body into the warm water and cried softly.

In my bedroom, I knelt by the bed and silently said the Lord's Prayer, as I usually did, followed by the prayers that Catholics said—the Hail Mary and the Act of Contrition. At the end, I added, "Please god, help me."

Joe came to my house the following Sunday and together we told my parents that I was pregnant. My father said, "You damn well better marry her!"

My mother gasped, "Oh no!" She was only thirty-seven years old and I was making her a grandmother. After everyone settled down, Joe and I walked across the street to the rectory, where I introduced Joe to Father Richard and told him about the situation.

Following that, I completed the religious instructions and was conditionally baptized, with Joe's oldest sister, Zina and her husband, Giacomo, as my godparents. I made my confirmation, with Joe's other married sister, Rina, as my sponsor and took Holy Communion. Now, I was officially a Catholic.

Joe was laid off from his construction job until the spring. We didn't have enough money to rent an apartment of our own. Arrangements were made for us to live with Joe's brother and his mother in her three-bedroom house. We moved all the things that I had bought during the past year to his mother's house: the china, the cookware, the towel sets, the sets of sheets and a wool blanket. We also moved my clothes, storing everything in Joe's bedroom. At the local furniture store, I put a box spring and mattress set on layaway, to be paid off and delivered when we had our own apartment.

I had to quit my job at the doctor's office in South Buffalo because Joe told me he was too busy to drive me to and from work. He should have said he had no intentions of giving up spending his days at his favorite coffee shop on the West Side.

A local bridal shop had a January clearance sale. I was able to get a good price on a white-lace bridal dress. It was tea-length with three-quarter length sleeves and a scooped neckline. For something blue, Nanny gave me one of her handkerchiefs with blue lace tatting around the edges, which I pinned to the crinoline slip. For something borrowed, Joe's sister, Zina, loaned me her wedding veil. With the new penny my mother gave me for good luck taped inside my shoe, I was ready for the wedding day.

"Nancy, it's time to get up. Today's your big day. Aunt Barb and Nanny will be here, soon," my mother called from the kitchen. My eyelids fluttered. Then, they opened wide. I got out of bed and looked out the window. There was a light wind in the bright morning light, blowing the dusting of new snow, promising the day would be cold, but sunny.

I had a strange sense of happiness but I was also plagued by a sense of sadness, as I walked down the hall to the bathroom. Carol Jean was just getting out of bed when I went back to the bedroom. She hurried down the hall to the bathroom before the boys awoke.

Off came my nightgown. Looking into the mirror, I saw a slim tummy that was hiding the reason why I must get married. Suddenly, I was aware of the chill in the air on this winter morning. Hurrying to get dressed, I put on my white bra, white garter belt, nylon stockings, white panties and the crinoline half-slip that I fastened at the waist. I was now ready for the white wedding dress.

Carol Jean came back just as I slipped it over my head. "Honey, will you zip me up?" I turned around. With her innocent, little-girl smile she pulled up the long zipper.

On February 11, 1956, six months to the day that I met Joe, with my parents' signature on the marriage license, my father walked me down the aisle of St John's Catholic Church. As I took my first steps, I saw Jeanie, sitting in the back of the church, her head covered with a silk-print kerchief tied under her chin. For one frozen second in time, our eyes met. I thought I saw a tear drop onto her cheek. That was the last time I saw Jeanie, my life-long friend!

Taking a deep breath, I looked away and focused ahead where my maid-of-honor, a girl Joe selected, walked ahead of me. Joe wouldn't let me ask Jeanie to be my maid-of-honor.

Father Richard asked, "Do you take this man, for better or worse, till death do you part?" It was a question that gave me no choice. Of course, I had to say, "Yes."

Nancy Lee, seventeen years old. With the new penny my mother gave me for good luck taped inside my shoe, I was ready for the wedding day, February 11, 1956.

PART II
ADULT YEARS

CHAPTER SEVEN
Thorns and Roses

"Every wife needs a good slap to keep her in her place."
"Barefoot and pregnant, that's the way to keep them."
"The man is Master of the house; the woman is the Slave."

IT WAS OBVIOUS THAT Joe was angry with me because I was pregnant and I wouldn't have an abortion, forcing him to marry me. We never went out together anymore. He spent his days at the coffee shop and on the weekends he went to the nightclubs. I stayed home with his mother and brother, Sammy.

I tried to pretend that my best friend, Jeanie, didn't exist. The truth was, I missed her and hoped she missed me. Joe wouldn't allow me to visit her or my parents. I accepted that reluctantly, thinking that I was married now and didn't need them anymore. I was wrong. I came to realize that leaving home didn't bring happiness. Just like Dorothy did in the movie, *The Wizard of Oz,* I often whispered to myself, "There's no place like home; there's no place like home."

Living with Joe's mother and brother, Sammy, wasn't easy for me. The bedroom we slept in was off the living room, where Sammy sat watching television. I was always embarrassed when Joe told me to go into the bedroom for one of his "quickies."

Another thing that made it difficult while living in his mother's house was attending Joe's neighborhood church. I remember the first Sunday we attended his church. After the service, Joe left the pew ahead of me and walked outside. I worked my way past the congregation, trying to keep up with him. When I got outside, I saw Joe smoking a cigarette and talking to a girl. She had beautiful, long, black hair. I walked over to them and stood, waiting for Joe to introduce me. He and the girl gave me a quick glance and continued talking. After a few minutes, she said goodbye to Joe and walked away. "What the hell is wrong with you? Are you ignorant? Can't you say hello to my friend?" Joe scowled behind a fake smile, as he flung his cigarette into the street, grabbed my elbow and pulled me along the sidewalk.

"Joe, I was waiting for you to introduce me. I didn't know who she was. I thought she might be your old girlfriend, Joanne, and you didn't want me to talk to her."

On another Sunday while in church, I got dizzy and almost fainted, making a "scene." That made Joe really angry. He went into a rage when we got to his house. Even his mother couldn't quiet him, as he stormed out the door and drove off.

I wondered whatever made me think Joe loved me, or whatever made me think I loved Joe. The only thing I was sure of was that I was pregnant and I had to be married. Over the next several months, my waist thickened and my clothes got tighter.

"Look at her—she's fat," Joe complained to his mother.

"Joe, she'sa no fat, that'sa you baby."

Joe didn't have to tell me I looked fat. I could see for myself that my body was changing. I didn't like the effects of pregnancy either. I especially didn't like the fact that the smell of coffee perking and spaghetti sauce simmering on the stove made me sick to my stomach. And, I craved my mother's fried potatoes.

Every Friday and Saturday night, Joe ate dinner, dressed up, splashed his face with Old Spice cologne and went out to his favorite nightclub, leaving me behind with his mother and brother. "You can'na stop Joe; he'sa always go'na out," his mother said.

She had told me that once she bolted the back hall door, locking Joe out to teach him a lesson about running around and staying out late. When Joe found the door locked, he banged and banged, but she wouldn't open it. After the banging stopped, she assumed Joe resigned himself to sleeping on the hall floor. The next morning, she got up, unlocked and opened the door. She found that Joe had ripped up all the linoleum from the back hall floor.

In the spring, Joe was back to work at the construction job and we were able to rent a small, four-room apartment on the West Side, not far from his mother's house. The front door opened into the living room where we put the red, fold-down sofa that we bought. It set across from the wingback chair and the mahogany pedestal table that Nanny and Grandpa gave us for a wedding present. Next to that was a black-and-white television set that Joe bought from his friend. In the bedroom off the living room was the bedroom set Joe's mother bought for us as a wedding present. I made the last payment on the layaway and the mattress and box spring were delivered the same day.

The little bedroom off the kitchen would be the baby's room. Tom brought over the wooden highchair, Jimmy's baby crib, and a gold colored, plastic cross, which I placed on the wall above the crib. We bought a used, wringer washing machine and put it in the bathroom. The back door opened into the kitchen where a red-and-gray, Formica top table with four, gray, plastic upholstered chairs was placed by the window. Also in the kitchen was the Singer cabinet sewing machine that Nanny gave me.

Now that we were in our own apartment, nothing had changed; Joe still went out every Friday and Saturday evening without me. I kept myself busy knitting, crocheting, sewing and making clothes for the baby. I didn't like Joe going out every weekend, but I couldn't stop him. "Joe, why do you always have to go out? Why can't you stay home and watch television with me?" I tried to get him to realize he was a married man, and that Johnny, Sonny and most of his friends were single men.

Joe came out of the bathroom combing back his black hair, putting the comb in the back pocket of his slacks. "Why should I stay home with you? Look at you and your fat belly." With a swagger, he turned and walked out the front door, letting the screen door slam behind him.

That night I stopped feeling sorry for myself and decided to take action. I had enough of his running around without me. Before I went to bed, I locked both the screen door and the front door. "I'll make him wait until I get out of bed to open the door, and I'll take my time about it," I told myself, as I got into bed.

A little after three o'clock in the morning, I heard the front door slam against the living room wall, and then another slam as the door was shut. Joe had forced the screen door open and unlocked the door. He charged into the bedroom, pulled me out of bed by my hair and threw me to the floor. "Don't you ever lock that door on me again," he ranted. "Look at you like a dog lying on the floor! Get up and get back in that bed!" He wasn't done with me yet.

The next morning, I packed Joe's lunch while he finished his coffee. After he left for work, I phoned Father Richard. "Father Richard, I don't want to be married anymore," I cried.

"You're emotional now because you're going to have a baby. Call me back after you have the baby. If you still feel the same, we'll talk about it then." I felt hopeless—and the priest wouldn't help me.

"Mama, I don't want to be married anymore. I want to come back home," I pleaded, when she answered my phone call.

"I can't help you. I have my own problems to deal with. We were just told that we have to move. Don't cause any trouble and he won't hit you." My mother had her hands full caring for my brothers and sister. Billy was now thirteen, Bobby was twelve, Carol Jean was ten and Jimmy was eight—my mother couldn't help me.

"Nanny, I don't want to be married any more. Can I come and live with you and Grandpa?" I pleaded over the phone. Nanny told me that Grandpa was in the hospital. I was sad to learn that Grandpa Meyer was very ill—Nanny couldn't help me.

Joe's mother already saw how he treated me, but she couldn't do anything about it. My parents had never hit me or insulted me. Joe did both. It seemed that he got mad at me whatever I said or did. There were no women's shelters in the 1950s. At least I didn't know of any. I had nowhere to turn. I had to stay married and make the best of it.

Someday I'll leave Joe, I promised myself. I fantasized about what my life would have been like had I stayed as Zack's girlfriend. 1956 was the year I would have graduated. I imagined what it would have been like to walk on the stage in the auditorium and receive a diploma, and to attend the Senior Prom. Would I have gone to the Prom with Zack?

Joe didn't want anything to do with my family, and he didn't want me to have anything to do with them, either. He called them drunks and trash. Not long after my desperate phone calls for help, my mother phoned to tell me that Grandpa had died. Joe wouldn't let me go to the funeral. He went into a rage when we got a card from Nanny, thanking us for the flowers. I didn't know that my mother had included Joe's and my name on the basket of flowers from the grandchildren.

A short time after Grandpa died, Tom and Rosie were married. Nanny went to live with them on Glen Avenue, in their second floor flat. My parents and younger siblings had already moved into the lower flat of the same house. Whether by coincidence or design, the house on Glen Avenue was next to the house that my father's parents and Uncle Harold rented. They, too, had to move when the Seneca Street house was sold.

September 20 was the due date for the baby. In August, I gave birth to a wrinkly, five-pound, eleven-ounce baby girl. She was perfect in every way. I was ecstatic with joy! I loved her with all my heart. God had heard my prayer; he gave me this child to love. My daughter—the words felt strange and wonderful. I would make sure she had a secure childhood. I vowed she would feel safe and loved.

The baby was born on a Wednesday morning. I left the hospital on Saturday morning. During those three days in the hospital, Joe hadn't come to see the baby or me, not even once. He was mad at me because the baby was a girl. "You know I wanted a boy. You can't even do that right," Joe said on the drive home.

Boy or girl, it didn't matter to me as long as the baby was healthy. And, she was! From babysitting and helping my mother with the younger children, I had learned how to care for my baby. I nursed her because I wanted to care for her the way I thought a good mother did.

One day, just before Joe came home from work, the baby woke and started crying. I picked her up from the bassinette, sat on the couch and began nursing her. She hadn't finished when Joe came home dirty with sweat from his construction work. He walked straight into the living room, demanding, "Put that baby down and get me my dinner!"

"The baby hasn't finished nursing. Your dinner is ready on the stove; you just have to put it on the plate."

Joe grabbed the baby from my breast and plunked her down in the bassinette. "There, she's done. Now, get me my dinner."

I did what Joe told me, with tears running down my cheeks, as I listened to my baby cry for her dinner. That was just one of the many times I had to cater to Joe's demands before I could tend to the baby. I was soon forced to give up breastfeeding.

Almost a year later on a Sunday summer afternoon, Joe hurt me really badly. The baby finished her bottle. I put her in the crib for a nap and busied myself cleaning up the kitchen after our noon meal. Joe was in the living room sitting on the couch watching television and eating a bowl of ice cream.

"Here!" he said, holding the empty bowl out in front of him.

"What does that mean? 'Here'."

"What? Are you stupid? It means get me some more ice cream! That's what it means!"

I walked into the living room and took the bowl. As I walked to the kitchen, I said, "You could have asked me in a nice way."

In a flash, Joe grabbed my hair from behind. I didn't think my remark was going to make him so mad. "I don't have to ask you for anything! You're my slave! You should know what I want!"

Then I made a big mistake and answered back, "My girlfriend told me to keep away from you. I wish I'd listened to her." Joe swung and hit me in the face with a hard blow. Suddenly, in horror, I realized what was happening. I flailed at him, trying to protect myself. He threw me to the floor, pinning me down with his knee on my swollen belly. I was breathless, crying, and gasping for air. Each time I attempted to move away, he slapped my face hard.

"Stop! Stop! Help me! Help me!" I screamed, hoping the neighbors would hear my cries. I screamed for my life and the life of the baby inside my swollen belly. Joe got off me. I managed to get to my feet. "You're crazy," I said, as I headed toward the bathroom. I just started to close the bathroom door when he pushed it open and continued slapping my face. My blood splattered the walls. I collapsed to the floor, crying and gasping for air.

I wasn't the only one crying. My eleven-month-old baby girl awoke from her nap and was crying out for me. Joe walked out of the bathroom and went back to the living room where his rage settled down to a quiet indifference. Slowly, I got up from the floor and went into the baby's room to comfort her.

When she quieted down, I put her back in her crib and stayed in her room until she fell asleep. Outside her bedroom door, I picked up the receiver of the phone that set on the cabinet sewing machine and called Joe's mother. "Joe hit me. I need your help," I said in a whisper so Joe wouldn't hear me from where he sat on the couch, watching television and sucking the corner of his shirt.

Joe's mother told me that her friend, Mr. Brasso, was at the house and he would drive her over. I sat at the kitchen table and waited for them. It wasn't long before she and Mr. Brasso knocked on the kitchen door. Her response, when she saw me with a split lip, swollen face and dried blood under my nose was to get Joe from the living room and push him into the kitchen, where I sat at the table.

"Kiss'a you wife. Tell'er you'a sorry," she said in mock anger. That's it! That was all she was going to do? Wasn't she or Mr. Brasso going to tell Joe he couldn't do that to me? I was seven months pregnant and she never even asked about my unborn baby. In a few minutes, they left and I was alone with Joe again. The rest of the day I stayed quiet. All through the night, I slept in terror as I lay next to Joe.

The next morning the alarm rang. I was sore all over and my eyes were almost swollen shut, but I knew I had better do what Joe expected of me. I didn't want to give him a reason to hit me again. I made his coffee and packed his lunch. Before leaving for work, he said, "I told you I was sorry, but I'm not. If I had to do it over again, I would!" He walked out and slammed the kitchen door shut.

I was shocked! I was scared! I was hurting! I was helpless! I had to get out of there, or he could hurt me again when he came back. Where could I go? I had seen my mother slapped by my father, but never like this. I thought she would know my fear and help me. I phoned her. "Mama, you've got to help me. Joe hit me again. I can't take care of my baby."

"Honey, I can't help you. You have to make the best of it," my mother said, thinking I was complaining about one of the slaps that Joe usually gave me.

"You have to come. Joe beat me. I'm going to die if you don't come!" I continued sobbing, crying, and begging in despair, "Mama, please, I can't stay here. Joe said he would beat me again!"

"Calm down. I don't know when I'll get there, but I'll get there. Stop crying and wait for me." I hung up the phone. When my baby girl awoke, I changed her diaper, warmed a bottle, sat her in the highchair and gave her a Graham cracker. I couldn't dress her. I hurt too much.

The knock on the kitchen door meant that my mother was there. I got up from the kitchen chair and opened the door. My mother gasped, "Oh, my God! What did he do to you?" She didn't ask any more questions. She just said, "Get your things. I'll get the baby's things." My mother took a bag from under the kitchen sink, handed it to me and hurried into the baby's room, saying to herself, "That son of a bitch, I'll kill him when I see him!"

I carried my bag and the diaper bag that my mother handed me. She took the baby out of the highchair and we went out the kitchen door and into the taxi waiting at the front of the house.

"Ok, let's go!" my mother told the driver.

The driver asked, "What happened? Did you get hit by a car?"

"Turn around and mind your own business; just take me back to my house," my mother answered. I breathed a sigh of relief. That was the first time since I married Joe that I felt safe. The cab driver dropped me off at the emergency room in Mercy Hospital. Then, he drove my mother and baby girl to her house.

The doctor in the emergency room tended to my split lip and packed my nose with gauze asking me, "How did this happen?" After I told him, he said, "A man should never hit a woman, not even with a rose." He told me I should file a police report. How could I file a police report? I was in South Buffalo and this happened on the West Side. I wasn't going back there to file a police report. Besides I didn't want to start trouble!

I stayed in the emergency room until the doctor determined that my unborn baby was not in danger of a premature delivery. When Tom and my father came home from work, they were shocked and angry when they learned what had happened. Tom drove my father to the hospital to get me and take me to their house. It was the first time I would see my parents' lower flat and the upper flat where Tom, Rosie and Nanny lived. I was glad to see my younger brothers and sister, but sorry that they had to see me in such a pitiful condition. I knew I didn't look like the big sister they had remembered.

Over the next five days I rested while my mother and sister took care of my baby girl. On Friday after work, my father came straight home, without stopping in the tavern and my mother didn't drink any wine while I was there. Tom and his friend, Ronny, wanted to go after Joe, but my father told them to stay out of it because they would only get themselves into deep trouble.

On Sunday, after we finished dinner, my younger brothers and sister were outside playing. I was in the living sitting on the couch with my mother and my baby girl on her lap. My father sat in his stuffed chair, reading the newspaper. The outside door to the front hall was open. We heard someone come into the hall and knock loudly on the door that opened into the living room.

My father got up to answer it. Giacomo, Joe's brother-in-law, was in the hall with Joe behind him. Giacomo, a big burly man, asked in a rough voice, "Is Nancy here?"

"Who the hell do you think you are coming to my door, asking for my daughter?" my father challenged.

"I'm her godfather, that's who I am," Giacomo answered.

"Well, who the hell cares? I'm her father!" It sounded like my father was getting ready to fight. I got up from the couch and pulled my father's arm, backing him into the living room. My father didn't know that Giacomo was a man you didn't argue with. He was a powerful patriarch in the family.

Giacomo turned and grabbed Joe by the back of the neck, pushed him into the living room. Without letting go of Joe, he said, "Look what you did to your wife! What man does that to a woman?" Joe stood there with a hurt, little-boy look, like he got caught with his hand in the cookie jar. He gave me a meek, helpless look, but he never said a word. Giacomo said, "Get your things together, Nancy, I'm taking you back to your house where you belong."

My father turned to me and asked, "Do you want to go back or do you want to stay? It's your choice, not what he says." I looked at my mother. She was still sitting on the couch with my baby girl on her lap. She pursed her lips tight, pulling them back into a smile, tilting her head, but she didn't say a word.

What choice did I have? I didn't want to go back, but I knew I couldn't live there and spend the rest of my days sleeping on the couch, while my baby girl slept in bed with my mother and sister. I had another baby on the way. I had to go back to Joe. I'm sure my father believed I would be okay, or he wouldn't have let me go.

Giacomo drove Joe, our baby and me back to our apartment and left after giving Joe a stern warning. "She's my godchild. You mess with her again—you mess with me."

The next morning, I awoke to the sound of the alarm clock and washed up in the bathroom where the blood splatters were still on the wall. I made Joe's coffee and packed his lunch. Joe left for work. I managed to take care of my baby girl the rest of the day and wash the blood off the bathroom wall. After I finished feeding her an early dinner, I sat her in the teeter-babe jumper. A little before Joe would be home from work, there was a knock on the kitchen door.

I opened it, and was surprised to see my mother standing there, still wearing her apron over her housedress. "Mama, how did you get here?"

"Oh, honey, I took a taxi. I just want to make sure you're okay, it being your first day back and all. Nanny came downstairs to look after your brothers and sister."

"Mama, why didn't you take off your apron before you left your house?" I asked, as I gave her a hug and a cheek kiss.

"I need it on if I'm going to help you make dinner," she answered, with a quick smile.

"You don't have to help me; I already made dinner. Sit down. It's so warm outside; you must be thirsty. I'll get you some Kool-Aid."

My mother pulled the teeter-babe jumper closer to her chair and sat down at the kitchen table. I put ice cubes in the two glasses and poured the Kool-Aid. While we sat at the table, talking and drinking our Kool-Aid, Joe opened the door and started to walk in. He froze in his tracks when he saw my mother.

My mother quickly stood up and rushed toward him, grabbing him at the neck by his shirt with her left hand. With her right hand she pulled a paring knife out of her apron pocket. Through clenched teeth she said, "You son of a bitch, if you ever touch my daughter again, I'll kill you!" Oh my God! What was she doing? Did she think her threat was going to stop his rages? At that moment, I loved her for being my voice and saying what I couldn't say, but didn't she realize I would have to live with him after she left?

"Now that we have an understanding, Joe, get yourself back in your car and drive me home," my mother said, as she let go of his shirt. Not saying a word, Joe turned and walked back out the door. He must have known it was the only way my mother was going to leave the house. "I'm going now, honey. You should be all right, as long as you don't make any more trouble for yourself," my mother said, giving me a hug and a cheek kiss.

My mother was a sensitive person by nature, but could be courageous when necessary. I don't know what she said on the ride if anything because, when Joe returned, we didn't talk to each other. I busied myself with the baby, getting her bathed and ready for bed while Joe ate his dinner and watched television. When it was time, we went into the bedroom without speaking. It was just wham-bam-no-thank-you-ma'am—but I was used to that!

In October, a little more than two months from the beating, I gave birth to a healthy baby boy. I thanked God that I had a boy. Now, Joe would be happy. My newborn son, whom I loved so much, brought some peace to the chaos in my life. This time Joe came to the hospital. He even brought me a dozen red roses. Twelve weeks later, I was pregnant again. The apartment would be too small for three babies. We needed to find a bigger place to live.

Saving for a down payment had been my number one priority from the beginning of our marriage. I was determined to own a house where my children would be secure and grow up together. The construction season lasted from spring through fall. To Joe's credit, he worked very hard to support us. I managed our finances, recording every cent spent and showing the ledger to Joe at the end of the month. We had many arguments about the thrifty meals that I made and the money he spent going out every weekend.

I was nineteen years old and into the seventh month of my third pregnancy when I had saved enough money for a down payment. In August 1958, we bought a big house in a desirable area outside the city, in a suburb that had an affluent feel. It was a quiet, safe neighborhood with tall elm trees standing guard at the front of the house and many more along the street and in the nearby park.

The center of town wasn't far away. It had all of the stores necessary for practical living: a post office, two banks, a drug store, a dentist, a hardware store, a flower shop, a jewelry store, several restaurants and churches of different denominations. Best of all, they were all within walking distance.

The back yard reminded me of the back yard on Duerstein Street, except this house had an apple tree, not a cherry tree. It, too, had rhubarb plants and a fence with hollyhocks. The big, turn-of-the-century house had two floors of living space with an attached office, a finished basement with a half-bath, and a third floor attic.

The first floor had a large living room with a bar, a formal dining room, a large kitchen and a lavatory. The second floor had four bedrooms and a full bathroom. A staircase led to the third floor attic. It was the house of my dreams!

In October, two months after we moved into the new house and three weeks after my twentieth birthday, I gave birth to another beautiful baby girl. Now, I had a two-year-old daughter, a one-year-old son and a newborn daughter. Fortunately—given all the many cotton diapers I had to change throughout the day—I had an automatic washing machine. That was the first major purchase we made after buying the house. In good weather I hung the diapers outside to dry; in bad weather, I hung them indoors, just as my mother had done for so many years.

When I was a foolish young girl, I blamed my mother for everything that went wrong in my life: I thought she should have made my father stop drinking; she should have gotten angry because he didn't make more money; she should have been emotionally stronger, not trying to drown her sorrows in wine. I thought she should have done this or done that. How could I have been so judgmental and unsympathetic to a woman's struggles?

On a Saturday night, in early spring, we were finishing our dinner when the kitchen phone rang. Joe was excited to hear that his friend, Tony, a Merchant Marine, was back in Buffalo. "Hey, Tony, how ya doing? Eight o'clock? That'll be good, okay!" After giving our address and directions, Joe hung up the phone, turned to me and said, "My friend, Tony, is coming over. I'm going out with him tonight." Joe was really happy about going out with Tony. He was in a good mood when he headed upstairs to get ready for the night out.

"Who's Tony?" I asked, knowing not to object to Joe's going out.

"He's a friend," was all Joe said, and I left it at that.

At eight o'clock, while I was still upstairs bathing the two oldest babies and getting them ready for bed, the doorbell rang. Joe answered it. With my son safely in the crib and my daughter in her bed with the guardrail, I walked down the stairs. A really good-looking guy stood in the living room. "Tony, that's my old lady" Joe said, pointing in my direction. I was only twenty years old. I wasn't an old lady, or was I?

I lowered my head to my chest, uneasy about Joe's remark and said a quiet "Hello," as I walked over to pick up the baby from the playpen to get her ready for bed. After they left the house, I filled the yellow, plastic tub with warm water and bathed her with castile soap, diapered and dressed her. She felt so soft, and smelled so sweet as I cradled her in my arms while she finished her bottle. Lifting her over my shoulder, gently patting her back, as I went up the stairs to put her in her crib.

In my bedroom, I stood in front of the dresser mirror and took a good look at myself. The sadness in my eyes was the same sadness I had often seen in my mother's eyes. What I saw made me cry. My hair, which I let grow again, was pulled back in a ponytail. My face was without make-up and I was dressed in a cotton housedress with ankle socks and loafers. I did look like an old lady!

Every Saturday evening, Tony rang the doorbell at eight o'clock, came into the living room to say hello to me and then take Joe out to wherever they went. On a Saturday in the early summer, Tony came to the house with two blondes. Because he was movie-star good-looking, I thought Tony was telling the truth when he called out to me, "Hey, Nancy meet my two lovely ladies."

From the kitchen, where I stood at the sink, pouring boiling water into the baby bottles to rinse them, I looked toward the living room, and couldn't help notice one blonde's bright red lipstick and full breasts under her taut black jersey. "Hello," I called from the kitchen. I stayed there because I was ashamed of how I looked compared to them. I later realized that one blonde was Tony's date and the other blonde was Joe's date.

I wanted Tony to leave Buffalo and never come back to our house again. Joe had almost stopped going out Friday and Saturday nights when we moved away from the West Side. He only went out occasionally, until Tony showed up. I didn't dare complain, though. My only recourse was to pray this prayer for nine consecutive days:

NOVENA TO SAINT JUDE
May the Sacred Heart of Jesus be adored,
Glorified, loved and preserved throughout
the world, now and forever. Sacred Heart
of Jesus, please pray for me. Saint Jude
worker of miracles, please pray for me.
Saint Jude helper of the hopeless; please
pray for me (Please make Tony leave
Buffalo). Thank you Sacred Heart of Jesus
for answering my prayer. Thank you Saint
Jude for interceding on my behalf (Thank
you for making Tony leave Buffalo). I will
encourage devotion to you, always.
Amen

The second Saturday after I finished the Novena, Joe wasn't getting dressed to go out. He sat in his brown leather chair in the living room, listening to jazz on his reel-to-reel tape recorder and playing his trumpet along with the music. "Aren't you going out with Tony, tonight?" I asked, as I started up the stairs to get the children ready for bed.

"Tony left. He went back to sea," Joe said sharply, bringing the trumpet back to his lips. I truly believe that my prayer to Saint Jude was heard and answered. That was the first of several times over the years that I turned to prayer for assistance. It has never failed.

Soon after that, some good things were coming my way. Joe was staying home on weekends and we started our own construction company. From the Bible, I chose a name for our new business and filed a DBA (Doing Business As) certificate.

We had a business phone installed in the home office. However, Joe wouldn't allow an answering machine for the phone. I had to personally answer the calls for the job estimates. I wasn't happy staying inside the house all day near the telephone, while my children played unattended in the back yard, but the business was profitable, allowing me to buy them whatever they needed.

During the weekdays, Joe was on the job site. In the evenings he went alone to measure the prospective jobs and brought the measurements home for me to figure the math. Then, he phoned the customer and discussed the price. Joe wasn't home much during the week and when he was, the children and I tried to stay out of his way. He had a quick temper!

Once a week, I left the house to do the grocery shopping. It was on one of those days in the early summer of 1961 when I met someone who would become a life-long friend. Dressed in a white and lilac, floral print sundress, I walked to the store with my four-year-old walking beside me and with my two youngest children in the baby carriage.

A lady with two little girls walked toward me. As she came closer, the attractive blonde with her short hair swept back, dressed in a white T-shirt, khaki slacks and white sneakers, gave me a friendly smile. We paused and introduced ourselves. "I'm Marge," she said, smiling a friendly smile. "I live on Main Street, across from the junior high school."

"I'm Nancy," I said, smiling back. "I live near the junior high school, too." We lived within view of each other's house for the past two years and had never met before that day. Even more of a surprise to me was learning that Marge was born and raised in South Buffalo, where she graduated from South Park High School in 1953. She told me that she also spent many summer days at the swimming pool in Cazenovia Park.

From the start, our personalities clicked. Marge and I talked, sometimes about Joe, but usually about our children and the way to keep weight off. It felt good to have a friend again. My sense of self-worth and my independent spirit were beginning to come back. But I wasn't totally independent. I still needed to learn how to drive a car.

Without a driver's license, I did most of the Christmas shopping through Sears & Roebuck, Montgomery Ward or JC Penny catalogues. They delivered items to the house. Our town also had a WT Grant store within walking distance. I wanted to look through the store to buy a few more things for the holiday.

After the children were bathed and snuggled in their beds, I tucked the covers closer around them and kissed them goodnight. Standing in the hall, I recited with them the prayer, "Now I lay me down to sleep…" Then, quietly, I walked down the stairs.

"Would it be okay if I went into town for a few more things?" I asked Joe who was sitting in his chair with his feet up on the ottoman, watching television.

"Don't be long." Joe answered, as he inhaled his cigarette. I threw on my coat and hurried down the street to the center of town. WT Grant's display window was decorated for the holidays with gift-wrapped packages under an aluminum Christmas tree. To the side of that, four Christmas stockings were hanging on a cardboard, red brick, fireplace. It was exciting to be out at night shopping. The store was open until nine o'clock. I had almost a full hour to shop.

I hurried through the first floor, then down to the toy department in the basement. There were signs marked "Discount," everywhere. I couldn't resist filling the shopping basket with all it could hold: Tinker toys, Lincoln logs, plastic army men and a little china tea set. A child-size, rocking chair, upholstered in red and gray plastic caught my eye. I thought the children would like it, so I grabbed it and hurried up the stairs to cash out. Everything fit into the paper bags except the rocking chair. I had to carry it as it was.

It was snowing when I left the store. The big flakes landed softly on the paper bags, making the bags wet. I struggled to protect them from breaking open while struggling to carry the rocking chair. As I hurried down the street, a car slowed as it drove past me. Then, it pulled to the curb and stopped. A man leaned across the seat and rolled down the window. "Can I give you a ride?"

"I don't take rides. Thank you, anyway." The man got out of the car and walked up to me. He was a big man and very tall, making me a little frightened. "I'll scream for the police if you don't leave me alone," I threatened.

"Don't you know who I am? I'm the chief of police."

"Show me your badge," I insisted.

"Now, can I help you?" he chuckled, showing me his badge.

"I'm sorry, I didn't know who you were, Yes, I would like a ride," I said, feeling foolish because of the way I acted.

"Where do you live?" he asked, taking the rocking chair from me and putting it into the back seat of the car. I told him my name and the address. "So, you're the contractor's wife."

"You know my husband?"

"I know everyone in this town."

When we reached my house, I asked, "Will you come in and tell Joe who you are?" As I exited the car, I added, "He might not believe me if he sees me getting out of your car."

"Yes, and I'll tell him the hard time you gave me accepting the ride," he said with another chuckle. Joe didn't like that I accepted a ride, even if it was from the chief of police. He agreed to teach me to drive. The following spring, I got my drivers license.

Not long after that, I was sitting behind the wheel of our car, waiting at the bank's drive-up window, when it was rear-ended. The driver of the other car stepped on the gas instead of the brake. I was thrown against the steering wheel.

Three days later, as I stood at the sink washing the lunch dishes, a hot wetness ran down my legs. I hurried into the bathroom—it was blood! I was four months pregnant and losing my baby. I didn't know what to do. I grabbed the phone and called Marge. "Marge, I'm hemorrhaging. What'll I do? I cried into the phone in a low voice, trying not to alarm my children.

"Lie down and put your feet up. I'll be right over." Marge came immediately, put me and my three children into her car, dropped the children off at her house for her husband to watch, and rushed me to the hospital. I miscarried the baby!

It was Saturday and Joe was out with one of his friends. At dinnertime he came home and read the note I left on the kitchen counter. He came to the hospital and brought me home. Then, he changed his clothes and went out for the evening.

Besides being depressed over the miscarriage, I learned that I was anemic. The doctor told me I was stressing my body and suggested that I shouldn't get pregnant for a few years.

"I have no control over getting pregnant or not getting pregnant," was my hopeless reply.

"Yes you do; I can prescribe oral contraceptives." What a welcome surprise! For the first time since I met Joe, I would have some control over my body. Now, I had a choice and my choice was to not to have any more children with Joe!

The birth-control pills must have awakened my libido, because I felt the urge to explore my body. Soon I discovered ways to pleasure myself. The first time I had an orgasm I had mixed emotions. I was both delighted and ashamed. The church taught that it was a sin to pleasure oneself. I tried to restrain and keep my thoughts pure, but some shows on television stimulated my desires.

"Bless me, Father, for I have sinned," I told the priest in the confessional.

"What is your sin, my child?"

"I pleasured myself," I answered in a whisper, hoping he heard me and I wouldn't have to repeat it.

"You mean, you masturbate?"

"I pleasured myself," I whispered again, not understanding what he meant. I didn't know what I did had a name.

"Put ten dollars in the poor box and say ten Hail Marys. Now, make an act of contrition while I give you absolution."

That was it? I wasn't going to hell! I could do it again. I could have *la petit mort*, the French word for orgasm, and all I would have to do is pay ten dollars and say prayers? Pleasing myself brought relief to my body, but it couldn't satisfy my soul. It couldn't take away my longing for intimacy and my longing to be loved.

Joe continued going out on weekends. One Friday he didn't come home at three o'clock in the morning, as he usually did. He came home the next day around noon. He walked quietly into the house and into the kitchen where I stood at the stove heating the children's lunch. They were now ages six, five and four years old. I didn't stop what I was doing. I didn't even turn to look at him. Something inside me had changed. I stopped caring what Joe did!

"I couldn't make it home last night. Something came up," he said, with a satisfied grin. Joe knew that I knew what he meant. Was "something came up," supposed to be funny?

"I don't care what you do anymore, Joe," I said without emotion. Calmly, I added, "Someday, I'm going to leave you."

"You'll never leave me. Where would you go? Back to the street where I found you?" Joe was right in one sense—I had nowhere to go. If I left Joe what would happen to my children? Would they have to be taken care of by strangers, while I worked? Would they be separated from each other? I must wait until they're grown, safely out of the house and on their own. Then I'll go, I promised myself!

During the early years of my marriage, my higher sensory perception wasn't very active. But, with the death of Joe's mother, I began to experience spirit communication again. A mystery that I have yet to solve occurred the night of her funeral in 1964. I loved Joe's mother and I felt that she loved me. She taught me to crochet and knit and gave me all her secret recipes. I was devastated when she had a stroke and died.

Following the funeral service and the burial at the cemetery, the customary refreshments were served at my house. It was a small gathering of family members, including Joe's two sisters, Zina and Rina, their husbands, and Joe's brother, Sammy. The gathering lasted until early evening.

Shortly after everyone left and my children were in bed asleep, Joe went upstairs to bed. I sat in the living room, crying softly. In my mind, I talked to Joe's mother, telling her how much I missed her. Joe called down the stairs for me to come to bed. I left the dirty dishes on the kitchen counter and went upstairs to bed. I awoke around four o'clock in the morning and couldn't fall back to sleep. I was restless and didn't want my tossing and turning to wake Joe. I got up quietly and went downstairs.

In the kitchen, I filled the sink with hot, soapy water to wash the dishes. I stood at the sink, longing for Joe's mother to still be alive. "I miss you. I'm sorry you died. I love you. Where are you?" I whispered to her, as I sobbed softly and continued to wash and rinse the dishes.

Something strange happened—the first awareness I had was that I was very cold—freezing cold! I opened my eyes and looked down into the sink. My hands were resting in the cold dishwater. I took notice of my legs. They were stiff and very cold with my knees locked. Slowly, I began to relax and leaned forward, resting my forearms on the edge of the sink. Looking toward the kitchen clock, I saw it was six o'clock—almost two hours had passed!

Joe came down the stairs and asked, "Why didn't you shut off the alarm clock before you came down?"

"I think I fell asleep standing at the sink," I told Joe, puzzled about what happened to me.

"You're nuts, that couldn't happen," he said. To this day, I wonder what happened? How did I lose almost two hours of time? Did my mind leave my body, and, if so, where did I go?

Almost a year later, I had my first vivid dream of Joe's mother. She was all white and fuzzy, but I recognized her, "How can I see you? You're dead." I asked her, in my dream. She didn't answer. She just gave me a loving look; her face reflecting a calm peace.

The next morning, I told Joe, "Your mother came to me last night in my dreams. She was happy and peaceful." Joe gave me a look that indicated he thought I was crazy.

The visions of Joe's mother occurred several times over the next few years. Each time she seemed a little farther away from me. One night, when she came to me in my dream, Joe's intellectually challenged brother, Sammy, stood beside her. He was smiling. In my dream, I asked her, "Why is Sammy with you?"

She answered, "~*Sammy is coming soon*~." Then, she moved away and disappeared.

The next morning, I said to Joe, "Your mother came to me, again, last night. She said that Sammy is going to be with her soon." Joe didn't say anything; he just gave me a side-glance and walked away. Sammy wasn't even sick!

The following Saturday when Joe answered the phone, his sister, Rina, gave him the sad news. "Sammy is dead."

Joe turned and looked at me with a puzzled expression and said to his sister, "Nancy told me he was going to die."

"How could she know," Rina asked? He had a heart attack only this morning." That experience has led me to believe that on a super-conscious level, children, the intellectually challenged, and many of us are made aware of our crossing over shortly before it occurs. There is always a loved one who already passed over, or a loving spirit with a desire to assist and welcome us to the other side.

As the years passed, with my friend, Marge, as my confidante and emotional supporter, my marriage to Joe became more bearable. Even though I mentally disconnected myself from Joe, I tried to be the perfect wife. I kept my weight down and my appearance up. The house was always shiny-clean, like Nanny kept her house. I managed the business end of our company and the checkbooks balanced. I was always available whenever Joe wanted me. On Sunday mornings I prepared the meatballs that went into the sauce, setting it on to simmer before I left for church with the children.

My daughters wore white cotton gloves and pretty bonnets. My son dressed in a navy-blue suit with a proper hat that he took off when he went into the church. I tried to give my children the childhood that I had wanted. As they got older, I made costumes for the girls' dance recitals and took an active role in the Boy Scouts of America to help my son learn the true virtues of manhood.

However, their childhood wasn't perfect. When they got older, Joe insisted that I ride with him when he went on estimates. I was forced to leave the children home alone. They were twelve, eleven and ten years old—too young to be left alone. They needed me to be in the home to help them with their homework and I wasn't there. They needed me to be in the home to give them a sense of security and I wasn't there. I didn't have the courage to protest.

Joe's friends didn't argue with him either. One of his friends, Rick, a tall, light-haired Irishman with a strong desire to be Italian, was married to an Italian girl named Rosa. Joe called his friend "Crazy Rick," but not to his face, of course. Joe liked to tell the story about when Rick took a baseball bat with him to collect a debt for Joe. Rick threatened to "break the guy's kneecaps," if he didn't pay up—the debt was paid.

Joe and Rick sometimes went out together on the weekends. On a Friday in the summer, Rick showed up at the front door. Joe was late coming home that day. I let Rick into the house and poured a cup of coffee for him, leaving him at the kitchen table, to drink his coffee while he waited for Joe.

I went back up the stairs to the bedrooms to finish what I was doing. When I heard Joe come into the house, I started down the stairs, stopping at the landing when I heard the tone in his voice asking Rick, "What are you doing here?"

"I'm waiting for you. We're going out tonight, aren't we?"

"No, Rick, not tonight. Call me tomorrow." Joe answered, walking toward the front door, indicating for Rick to leave. Rick walked past the staircase and out the door. Joe closed and locked it. His face was red with anger, as he backed me against the wall and yelled, "Don't you ever let him or any man into this house when I'm not home! Do you understand? Never!" he said, jabbing his finger into my chest.

Joe believed the world was a dangerous place. Maybe he was right. In January 1968, the United States' involvement in the Vietnam War peaked with the Tet Offensive, a series of surprise attacks by the Vietcong on South Vietnam. In April, Martin Luther King Jr. was shot and killed at the Lorraine Motel in Memphis, Tennessee. In June, Bobby Kennedy was assassinated at the Ambassador Hotel in Los Angeles, California. It was a tragic year for the United States.

Adding to the tragic times, my father was one of the many men who were out of work, due to the closing of the Bethlehem-Lackawanna Steel Plant. My parents were back on welfare. Billy, still a bachelor, continued living with my parents who had moved from their flat into a housing project on the north side of the city. A few years earlier, Bobby had married and was on his own, and shortly after that, Carol Jean had married and moved away.

On the bright side, in November 1968, my brother, Jimmy, was married. Soon after that, my mother stopped drinking and my father only drank occasionally. My mother made an effort to fix herself up and she seemed full of life, again. I was thirty-one and my mother was fifty-one years old when we first talked to each other, woman-to-woman.

I needed a new cocktail dress for a political fund-raising dinner. On Thursday, I got into my Mercedes and drove to the housing project to get my mother and take her to the Mall. When I finished looking through a few stores and found the right dress, we stopped at a nearby restaurant for lunch. After ordering, my mother looked at me with misty eyes. "Honey, I want you to know that I'm sorry I wasn't always there for you." Reaching for my hand and giving it a tender squeeze, she added, "I have a lot of regrets. I failed you and I'll never forgive myself for that."

"Mama, that's all in the past. I was angry with you for the longest time, but now I know how hard it must have been for you." She took a tissue from her purse and dabbed her tears. My mother needed me to say, "I forgive you," and I did.

In 1969, the idea of self-empowerment was sweeping the nation and the "flower children" were gearing up for a gathering in Bethel, New York at the Woodstock Music Festival. I wasn't part of that generation of music; I was on the cusp of the generation that loved rock-and-roll music, the sounds of the big bands and jazz music that the nightclubs in Chicago provided.

Chicago is a fabulous city, seemingly a city where the people of various backgrounds live in harmony. On several occasions, through the years, Joe had personal business to attend to in Chicago. We flew there together, while my mother stayed at our house, taking care of our children. We were in Chicago on a St. Patrick's Day when both the Chicago River and the beer ran green. On another trip, we went to the Blue Note nightclub where we heard the soulful music of Maurice White. But, the memory of Chicago that stands out the most is of an event that happened at Tad's Steak House.

As we walked along the street, the aroma of steak grilling on an open flame was too much for Joe to resist. We entered, took a tray from the stack and walked along the line, gathering the porterhouse steak, baked potato, tossed salad and a roll with butter. After paying the cashier, we headed down the stairs to the basement dining room. It was a busy place, with businessmen and shoppers sitting at the little square tables, eating their lunch. Suddenly, I noticed a large, white man with a stubby beard, wearing a long heavy coat walking from table to table, eating scraps from the plates left behind by diners who had finished eating.

"Joe, look at that man. He's hungry."

"He's a bum. He shouldn't be here," Joe said, after a quick glance at the man stuffing his coat pockets with rolls left on the trays.

I couldn't take my eyes from the hungry man who gnawed the meat from the bones left on the plates. A black man came down the stairs with his tray of food, looking for a place to sit. When he saw the hungry man, without hesitation he walked over to him, set his tray of food on the table and indicated to the man to sit down and eat. The man did and he relished the meal.

Never have I been ashamed of being white, but on that day I came close. Of all of the people in the dining room, only the black man understood the message, "Whatever you do unto the least of them, you do unto me."

When we were ready to leave, Joe asked the worker who was clearing and wiping the tables, "Why do you let that bum in here?"

The worker turned to look at the white man with the stubby beard and said, "He's not a bum; he was a great boxer. He's just down on his luck now." That incident left a very powerful impression on my thinking about the way we are often too quick to judge people. Now, when I see a homeless person or someone down on his luck, I look beyond the external and see someone who at one time may have been admired. My awareness of other peoples' suffering was not limited to their emotional and spiritual needs. I was also becoming aware of their physical pain.

One morning, I awoke with a stabbing pain in my side. The pain came for no reason. It was sharp and constant. I got out of bed and put on a robe. I told Joe to take me to the hospital that something was terribly wrong with me. On the way down the stairs, the phone rang. "Wait here, I'll be right back," Joe said. He went down the stairs to the kitchen to answer the phone. I steadied myself, holding onto the staircase railing.

Joe came back saying, "That was my sister, Rina. She's taking Charlie to the hospital. He's having pains and she thinks it's his appendix." As soon as Joe said that, the pain left me, the same way it began—immediately.

That was the first time I experienced another person's pain as if it were my own. Years later, I learned to recognize and control my physical sensitivity to other peoples' pain. However, once in awhile, I have to ask, "Is your back hurting or is that my back hurting?"

Another spirit communication occurred when Giacomo, my godfather and Joe's brother-in-law, died unexpectedly of a heart attack. A short time after he died, Joe's sister, Zina, misplaced her diamond ring. "I've looked everywhere and I can't find it," she told Joe when she phoned to tell him how upset she was.

A few nights later, I had a dream in which Giacomo told me the ring was behind the backsplash of the kitchen sink. The next morning I phoned Zina. She looked where I told her the ring would be. "How did you know it was there?" she asked, crying with joy.

"I just guessed," I answered, not wanting to spook her by saying that Giacomo had told me.

Back to the "real world." In 1972 our family went on a trip to Italy. The children were now ages fifteen, fourteen, and thirteen years old and on spring break. While in Rome, we saw all the usual tourist attractions, including the Coliseum, the Spanish Steps and Trevi Fountain. We took a horse-and-carriage ride through the city. We even took a taxi ride around the Circus Maximus where horses and chariots raced in ancient times. The taxi driver was breaking the law. But, as Joe always said: "Everybody has his price."

On Easter Sunday, we walked from the hotel, passed Castle St. Angelo, and crossed over the Elio Bridge leading into the Vatican City. In St. Peter's Square, we joined the many people waiting for the address and blessing of Pope Paul VI. Before returning to the hotel we visited the Vatican gift shop, where I purchased a 14k gold cross. Walking back to the hotel, I noticed a sign in a shop window that advertised side-trips. After reviewing what was offered, we decided on seeing southern Italy. The all-inclusive travel package would take us to Naples, Capri, Amalfi, Pompei and Sorrento.

Back at the hotel, we washed and changed for dinner. The menu was in Italian. The children and I didn't know what to order. Joe pointed to items, one after the other. "This, this, this, this, this," he told the waiter. The waiter rolled his eyes and walked away with a smile. "Buon appetito," he said, when he returned with his arms full of serving plates. I was embarrassed because of the many plates of food that he brought to the table. Of course, we couldn't eat it all.

The first stop on our tour was Naples. After we settled the luggage into our rooms, we strolled down to the Bay of Naples and watched the fishing boats come in to unload their catches of the day.

The next morning, we boarded the tour bus and left Naples. As we rode along, Joe said, "I have a daughter somewhere near here." What was he saying? Could this be true or just a lie to hurt me? "Yah, when I came here with my mother, her half-sister had a daughter who wanted to come to America. She was easy. She thought I was going to bring her back and marry her. Didn't my mother tell you about it?"

"How do you know she had a baby?" I asked quietly, so my children sitting behind us couldn't hear.

"Oh, she had a baby all right, a girl. My mother gave me hell, because I brought shame to her. Yah, she was my kid all right."

I remembered that Joe's mother had sent clothes to Italy. "Who are the little girl clothes for?" I asked, when I saw Joe's mother packing them. "This'sa for my sister, Caroline. Her daughter has'sa baby girl." As we rode along the seacoast I couldn't stop thinking about the girl who would now be a little older than my firstborn.

We continued on to Anacapri where we ascended Mount Solaro to view the Island of Capri. At the station for the twelve-minute chairlift ride, I began to get nervous. I disliked the idea of the children sitting in an open chairlift, riding high above the ground, with nothing but a movable bar to hold them in. "It's safe, cut the act. I'll take the first chair, the kids next and you last," Joe said, making his way in line.

I watched vigilantly, as everyone quickly plopped into the chairs as they swung by and the attendant snapped the bar closed across their lap. I plopped into the seat and we began the ride up the mountain. When out of sight of the ticket booth, Joe turned to look back. "Hey! This is fun," he yelled, and held his arms up.

"Don't you dare do that," I shouted to the children, "Keep the bar down and hold on!" During the whole time we rode to the top, I was in a state of intense fear. Only when we reached the ground safely did I begin to breathe. "What's wrong with you?" I yelled at Joe, "Why would you do that?"

"Knock it off. You're making a scene," Joe said under his breath, with a false grin.

The next stop on our tour was the village of Amalfi, where we would eat a late lunch. The bus traveled northward up the mountain along the narrow, twisting Amalfi Drive. There were hardly any guardrails to keep the bus from plunging down onto the craggy sea boulders, far below on the rocky shoreline. The tour guide suggested, "When we stop for lunch, have a Lemoncello. It will steady your nerves."

Back into the bus, we rode the thirty miles through the Sorrento Hills to our next overnight stay at a hotel atop the hillside of Sorrento. I was in awe of the beauty of this little seaside town. Pots filled with brightly colored flowers, red bougainvillea bushes planted along the walls, and hanging gardens of lavender-colored wisteria were everywhere.

After dinner, the children walked back down the winding road to the city. Joe and I went outside to the hotel balcony where there was a breathtaking view of Naples and the nearby islands. The air was sweet smelling with a floral fragrance as the warm breeze swept across the balcony. I looked out across the little city below and into the blue waters of the sea in the distance, and I said to Joe, "This is romantic, Joe, isn't it?" Thinking he might feel the same, I added, "Tell me you love me."

He didn't say it. As many times as I asked over the years, Joe would never tell me he loved me. "Come on, let's go to the room. We've got some time before the kids get back," was his only response.

The next morning, after breakfast, we were on our way to Pompeii. We saw the house of Vettii. In the atrium was a fresco of Priapus, the god of fertility, whose symbol is an enormous phallus. Joe nudged me and jokingly asked, "Look familiar?" We returned to Rome, where we spent a few more days seeing the sights. Then, we boarded the plane for the flight back to the United States.

After we returned, I told Joe, "Someday I'm going to leave you." I was angry with him for the way he treated us during the trip.

"Everything you know I taught you! I made you! I own you! You can never leave me!" That night, I got out of bed, refusing to let Joe use me for his sexual pleasure. "Who the hell do you think you are, the queen of Sheba?" he yelled, getting out of bed after me.

He spun me around and continued to yell. His hand swung across my head and struck the side of my face with a hard blow. With the pain of the slap, I heard a sharp ringing in my right ear. Joe raged out of the bedroom. "Everyone up!" he ordered, charging into the children's bedrooms flipping on the lights. "I don't sleep, you don't sleep!"

My oldest daughter ran into my bedroom. She saw me with my hand to my ear and asked, "Are you okay, Mom?"

"Everything is all right. Go back to your room and go to sleep," I told her, knowing that Joe had gone downstairs and was probably sitting in his chair, sucking on the collar band of his T-shirt, as he often did after one of his rages.

The children knew their father would slap me or throw something at me, if I made him mad. They saw him throw his shoe at me and they saw him throw a plate of food at me, cutting me on the forehead. Usually when he yelled, they just shut down and closed off. That was all they could do.

The next day, I went to the doctor to find out why I couldn't hear from my right ear. As I suspected, the doctor confirmed I had a ruptured eardrum. "Joe, you ruptured my eardrum," I told him when he returned from work.

"That'll teach you. Don't ever say no to me again!"

Only my doctors and girlfriend, Marge, knew how badly Joe treated me. His business associates and friends didn't see what went on inside the house. They only saw how well Joe treated me. I wore designer clothes, fur coats and expensive jewelry. I drove a Mercedes and lived in a beautiful house.

Joe would never say he was sorry. Again, I thought of leaving. This time, however, I could take the children and just walk away because they were older and could care for themselves as I worked to support us.

The following Saturday, I told the children that I had something important to tell them. We went into the living room. The three children sat on the sofa, and I sat in a chair near them. "I'm thinking of leaving your father. How do you feel about that?"

"Where will we live? Where will we go to school?"

"What about my friends? Would I see them again?"

"Won't Dad be mad at you?"

The questions seemed to be nonstop, questions I didn't have answers for. "I don't know what's going to happen. I just need you to pack some of your things into your suitcase and we'll go to a hotel for tonight. I'll work it all out later."

"Mom, it won't work," my oldest daughter said, with tears welling in her eyes. "We can't go. Dad will make us come back, and he'll really be mad, then."

My youngest daughter didn't say anything. She just sat quietly as tears filled her eyes. "I wish you weren't my parents. I wish somebody would adopt me," my son said, getting up and going upstairs to his bedroom. I was shocked! I didn't know my son felt that way!

It was useless, my oldest daughter was right. I hadn't thought it through. I put the thoughts of leaving into the recesses of my mind for a time when the children wouldn't be involved. I couldn't add more misery to what they were already experiencing.

"Don't worry, I'm not going to leave your father!" I called out after the girls, who were walking up the stairs with tears in their eyes. "And, don't tell him anything about this talk," I said in quiet resignation.

CHAPTER EIGHT
Beginning To Be

Jewels, furs, expensive cars and fabulous vacations—I had them all. Emotional support, warm caresses and intimate nights—I had none.

IN THE SPRING, the county advertised for a bid on the work they would need done during the coming year. A twenty-five dollar deposit was required for the plans and specifications of the bid, refundable only after the bid was submitted. I drove downtown and paid the twenty-five dollars.

When Joe saw the massive amount of pages that had to be filled out and the technical language of the specifications, he wasn't interested in the job. I didn't want to lose the twenty-five dollars. I filled out the paper work and bid the job high, thinking other bids would be lower and we wouldn't get the contract. As it turned out, the bid I submitted was the only bid the county received. We were awarded the contract.

For three years in a row, I submitted a bid and we were awarded the contract. That's how we could afford anything we wanted. The loans for the vehicles and construction equipment were paid off. I was also able to pay off the mortgage on the house and on the half-acre property, with the construction garage. We were completely debt free and had money in the bank.

Our business was doing well enough that Joe even let me get an answering service. He treated me much better now, except for his occasional rages. Joe had the florist deliver a dozen long-stem roses every anniversary. He bought me a ten-carat sapphire ring for a birthday present and a mink jacket for a Christmas present. He even bought a new Mercedes for me to drive.

I had several paranormal experiences during those years; one occurred in our neighborhood on a Saturday afternoon. A police car passed our house with sirens blaring. I was alarmed because my daughter was down the street playing with her friend. I ran to the front of the house to see what was happening. My daughter came running home to tell me that a little boy had gone missing.

While everyone was frantically running around, calling his name and looking for him, I knew the best way I could help was to use my mind to try to find him. In my vision, I saw dark, calm water. I knew he was in water. The Niagara River was near, but that was flowing water, so I knew he wasn't there. The only other standing water that I knew of was a pond, nearby.

Quickly, I got into my car and drove the couple of blocks away. I parked and studied the calm water. As I gazed over the surface of the pond, I knew the young boy wasn't in that water. I didn't know where else to look. I didn't know about the in-ground pool that one of the neighbors had. Later in the afternoon, the sad news came that the young boy was found dead. He had wandered to the neighbor's backyard, slipped under the cover of the pool and drowned.

Soon after that incident, Joe's friend, Rick, was dying from kidney disease. I held his hand when we visited him in the hospital and I thought he smiled at me. Two nights later I was startled awake. I opened my eyes but saw nothing in the darkened room. I closed my eyes again and tried to go back to sleep. "~*Nancy~*" I heard Rick's voice. Startled again, I opened my eyes. Of course, Rick wasn't in the bedroom. I must have imagined it, I thought. I closed my eyes and again tried to sleep. "*Nancy~ tell Rosa goodbye ~ take care of the baby.*" I heard Rick's voice as plain as if he were standing in the room. I knew I wasn't dreaming because I wasn't asleep.

I opened my eyes and woke Joe saying, "I'm getting up. Rick won't leave me alone." I went downstairs at around four o'clock in the morning and sat in the living room. I was about to doze off when the phone rang. I hurried to answer it, looking up at the clock. Who would be calling me at five-thirty in the morning?

It was Rosa saying, "Nancy, the hospital called. Rick is dying. I have to hurry to the hospital. Can you come over to keep an eye on my children?"

I told Rosa that Rick was already in the spirit world and gave her the message from Rick. She was one of the few that knew I could communicate with spirits. "Rosa, be careful driving to the hospital. Rick is gone; there is no reason for you to hurry."

At another time, I received a spirit message from a total stranger. While I was in the hair salon, I overheard a woman saying that she was getting her hair done for her mother's funeral, which was the next day.

As I listened to the woman talk, I saw an image of very tiny scissors, with a goose or duck's head at the hole where the thumb would be placed. I had a strong urge to tell the woman, "Give the scissors to your sister," so I told her.

"What did you say?" she asked in a surprised voice, adding as she turned to face me, "How do you know about the scissors?"

"I don't know. I just had to tell you that." Then, I described the scissors. She took the tiny scissors out of her purse, telling me that just that morning, she and her sister had an argument over who should have their mother's scissors. "Your mother wants your sister to have them," I told her, in a gentle voice.

"Can you still see my mother?" she asked quietly, as she put the scissors back in her purse. I explained that I didn't actually see her mother, but I felt her presence next to her. The woman reached out and gave me a hug, thanking me for the message. "My mother never liked to see my sister and me fighting. My sister is all I have now; I'll give her the scissors, if that's what my mother wants."

That was the first time I gave a message to a stranger. I tried to ignore my inner feelings of knowing things but there were a lot of times when my mind manifested thoughts about what was going to happen or already had. I knew insignificant things, such as knowing a woman in the supermarket fought with her husband that morning.

Sometimes, when Joe and I went out to dinner, I could feel the presence of spirits around people. I had the feeling that, if I focused, I would be able to give them messages that the spirits were trying to send. But, that would make Joe angry, so I didn't.

In the fall of 1973, Marge, my unpretentious friend, who knew I had unusual experiences, told me that a psychic was giving a talk on the paranormal at the local YWCA. The two-hour presentation was from seven to nine o'clock that evening. For a long time, I wanted to understand what was going on with my strange experiences. I was very interested in hearing what the psychic had to say and asked Marge to pick me up after dinner so I could go with her.

I knew that with Marge already in the house, expecting me to go with her, Joe would be less likely to object. Marge came to the house as planned and said, "Come on, Nancy, it starts at seven, we don't want to be late."

Joe was sitting in the living room watching television. I casually said, "I'm going with Marge to the YWCA."

"First, get me some coffee," he said, not objecting to my leaving—just as I had planned! I gave Marge a satisfied smile, brought Joe a cup of coffee, put on my leather jacket and we walked out the door.

"Why do you let Joe treat you like that? Why don't you stand up to him?" Marge asked, zipping her navy-blue windbreaker as we walked to her car.

"If I did, Marge, I'd pay for it later. It's not worth it. But, someday I'm going to leave him."

The psychic's talk included an explanation for the experience I had with the green, velvet dress when I was a young girl. "Psychometry" is what she termed it, explaining that by coming in contact with an object, facts concerning the object or the owner of the object could be known. Marge's invitation to the YWCA that night was the beginning of the many years that I would spend in researching and investigating the world of the paranormal. My journey began by attending every class, every seminar and every workshop the psychic offered.

That's how I met Angie who assisted the psychic in her classes and workshops. "You're a rosebud about to blossom," Angie said when she noticed that I had unusual abilities. She soon became my friend and one of my mentors. Angie exuded a quiet self-confidence. Although she was female, she always dressed in slacks or a pantsuit and wore sensible shoes. She didn't have use for a purse. Whatever she needed, she carried in her pockets. I never knew a female who sometimes thought like a man. She was very good at dealing with problems and working with groups of people.

Angie told me that I was being over-protective of my children, who were now seventeen, sixteen and fifteen years old. "They need to learn to make decisions for themselves and figure things out for themselves," she told me. Maybe she was right. Maybe I was using my children to fill my need to feel loved! Joe and I went out to dinner and social gatherings, with our Italian friends, occasionally. I was his dance partner and his bed partner. At which times we didn't have conversations. Our conversations were limited to the business or what he disliked about the children and me. So naturally, I devoted my life to the children.

When Angie came to my home and met Joe, I was surprised how well they got along. Maybe it was because she was Italian, or maybe it was because of her friendly, non-threatening, self-confidence. Joe never argued with her the way he did with me.

Almost on a daily basis, Angie and I met and had "reading sessions." She showed me how to use a visualization technique that started me on my way to refining my sensitivities. This one-on-one with her allowed me to develop and channel my natural energies. My ability to perceive future events increased through the almost daily practices. I sat quietly, closed my eyes and took a few moments to relax. When I reached a level of total peace, Angie asked questions and I gave answers, which she recorded in a notebook. While doing these practices, my spirit felt so light that I actually felt as if I was rising a few inches from where I sat.

Angie was going on a one-week trip to Florida, where she planned to visit some friends including a psychic-medium, who had an office in Orlando. She invited me to go with her. I knew Joe would say "no" if I asked. I told Angie that she would have to ask Joe if I could go. When Joe came in the house, she asked him.

"Joe, I want Nancy to come to Florida with me to meet an important psychic that I know."

"I don't want her to get carried away with this psychic stuff," Joe told Angie, as he lit a cigarette.

"She's old enough to make up her own mind what she wants. Right, Joe?" Angie stood her ground, adding, "Besides, she'll be with me."

In February 1974, Angie and I boarded a plane at the airport in snowy Buffalo, New York and landed at the airport, in sunny Pensacola, Florida. We rented a car and drove down the coast, hugging the shoreline of the Gulf of Mexico.

In St. Petersburg, we visited with Jane, a woman Angie knew. She lived in an apartment building that had red bougainvillea, orange birds-of-paradise, white gardenia, pink azalea, and blue plumbago plants everywhere. How refreshing to see this beauty in contrast to the cold north. I felt like I was in the Garden of Eden.

Jane, wearing a polyester pantsuit and sensible shoes, was quite attractive as a middle-age woman. She invited us to dinner, after which we had a friendly conversation. We discussed Jane's interest and research in color therapy.

Angie told her that we were heading to Orlando to visit a psychic-medium. She also told Jane that I was developing my sensitivity and suggested that I do a reading for Jane. I felt a little self-conscious, but Aggie convinced me that it was only for fun, so I agreed to do it. I took a comfortable position, closed my eyes and relaxed. I don't know why, but I automatically place my right hand palm up and my left hand palm down when I do a reading. Angie placed a ring in my right palm and I closed my fingers, making a fist to hold the ring.

My first visual image was a quick flash of a Catholic nun's face. When images start to form, I'm ready for questions. It's necessary for Angie to ask me questions, because in the state of focused awareness, I have a sense of detachment from everything around me, including whatever object I was holding in my hand.

Angie began by asking me, "Who owned the ring before Jane? Where did she get it?" I told her that I envisioned a cobblestone street and two people in a horse-drawn carriage, "The man gives a woman the ring."

"Where are they? Where are you now?" Angie asked.

"I don't understand. The ring belongs to that woman, but I see Napoleon Bonaparte. The woman is dying. She's in a hospital. A nun picks up her clothes. The ring falls to the floor. The nun picks it up and puts it in her pocket. The nun takes it to a church. War! People running! Fighting! The church! I see smoke and looting of the church. Now, I'm on a ship. Two men, mean, dirty, one looking at the ring. He's holding the ring. The other man has a knife! He stabs him and takes the ring!"

The vision of the two men and the stabbing upset me. Angie told me to move away from the scene and go back to the man and woman in the carriage. Angie asked, "What are they doing in the carriage?"

"They're talking. The man gives her the ring as a token of love, but she can't wear it, because it has to be a secret. His brother has something to do with the secret."

"Who is his brother?" Angie asked.

"Napoleon Bonaparte." I answered, without hesitation. I continued telling her what I envisioned, "The ship. I hear 'Liberty–Justice for all.' I think of the Liberty Bell in Philadelphia and the New England colonies. (In my mind, I saw a huge white mansion, similar to a southern mansion. I felt this was also a home of the same family who lived in the New England colonies).

My visions were so strong that I felt as if I were there; I was part of what I was seeing. It wasn't like watching it play out on a movie screen. I was there. But, I couldn't alter anything or interact. From the time that I first envisioned the knife attack, I began shaking and couldn't stop. For that reason, Angie decided to end the reading.

I opened my eyes and looked at the ring. I was astonished to see that it contained a design of the *fleur-de*-lis. Jane and Angie didn't say a word. They just looked at each other and smiled.

"What a great story," I said when Angie read the notes back.

"It might not be a story. What you said might be true. I bought the ring from a reputable jeweler, who was handling it as part of an estate sale. He told me the ring was originally owned by a Bonaparte, but he didn't know how it got to America," Jane said, with a pleased smile.

That reading was an "aha moment" for me. I began to understand that the unusual experiences I had since childhood were of a psychic or spiritual nature. I understood that life isn't three-dimensional. It has more dimensions not discernable by the naked eye; dimensions that can be tapped into by use of a higher consciousness. I also realized that being alone as I often was, while growing up, caused me to turn my thoughts within, which is similar to meditation.

We left Jane's apartment and found a motel for the night. The next day, we planned to drive to Orlando to visit Anne Gehman, the psychic-medium that Angie knew. Before we left the motel, Angie asked me to do my thing, as she called it. I closed my eyes and after a few minutes I was ready. "What are we going to see in Anne's office?" Angie asked, as she lit her brown cigarette.

"I see Beatrice Lilly. Now, I see Arabs. I can't see her office." I saw a large building on a busy highway, but I didn't tell Angie that. Then, I gave up trying to see anymore. "I'm way off on this one," I said, opening my eyes and standing up.

"Arabs!" Angie laughed. We both laughed. We were in Florida and I was seeing Arabs. How ridiculous that was!

We had a pleasant drive to the city of Orlando where we found Anne Gehman's office. It was in a large building on the main highway. Angie parked the car and we walked into the building. As we walked down the hall towards Anne's office, two men with dark complexions, dressed in tailored business suits walked toward us. As they passed, Angie and I looked at each other, "Are those Arabs? Why would Arabs be here?" Angie asked with a puzzled look. We reached Anne's office. Angie opened the door and we walked into a reception area. It was a very impressive office, the kind of office successful business people have. A lady dressed in soft pink and impeccably chic came out of the inner office and greeted us with a genuinely warm smile.

"Angie, how nice to see you," the attractive brunette said, in a soft voice. Angie introduced me to Anne and we chatted briefly about our visit to Florida.

"Nancy said that we would see Arabs in your office. Were those Arabs we just saw in the hall?" Angie asked, still puzzled why Arabs would be in the building.

Anne explained that the men were from Saudi Arabia. They had come to consult with her on matters involving their country. "What else did you see?" Anne asked, with a kindness in her hazel eyes.

"Nothing else. I only saw the Arabs and Beatrice Lilly."

"Do you know what my name is?" Anne asked.

"Yes, It's Anne Gehman."

"Beatrice is my first name, but I don't use it." I was just as surprised as Angie! We ended our visit with Reverend B. Anne Gehman inviting us to stay in the guesthouse at the Spiritual Research Society in Winter Park, where she was the founder and pastor. Angie and I rode over to the guesthouse, settled in, and then went to a restaurant for an evening meal.

The next day, we took in the sights around the town, did some shopping and had dinner. We returned to the guesthouse shortly before the evening church services. "Do your thing and tell me what you see at the church this evening," Angie said, picking up her notebook to record what I would say.

"I see the initials H and S. You will be asked to speak after the service." I opened my eyes and saw that Angie was flustered.

"I'm going to speak? What would I speak about? You must be wrong, and H. S. doesn't make any sense."

We left the guesthouse and walked across the lawn to the entrance of the church. Inside, near the entrance, was a poster with the picture of a white-haired man. The poster announced that Harold Sherman, a world-renowned psychic researcher, was going to be a guest speaker.

Following the church services and the speech by Harold Sherman, Angie was asked to come up to the platform and say a few words. We ended the evening with the opportunity to spend time with Harold Sherman and ask him questions about the experiments that he had conducted with Dr. J. B. Rhine of Duke University and astronaut Edgar Mitchell. I also purchased some books he had previously published, including *You Can Communicate With The Unseen World*, featuring Reverend B. Anne Gehman. And, Harold Sherman graciously added a personal note to me, along with his autograph. After a few more days enjoying the Florida sunshine, Angie and I boarded a plane and flew back to Buffalo.

Since that Florida visit, I have visited Anne at the Spiritualist Camp in Lily Dale, New York and at her home in Virginia, where I was invited for a New Year's Day lunch. However, my fondest memory is of the time Anne had a speaking engagement in Buffalo. Her new shoes bothered her, so I switched shoes with her before she went on the stage. "You don't really know a person until you walk in her shoes," I said, jokingly.

With Anne as my mentor in spiritualism, I learned these things: A medium does not call up the dead. The spirits come with the clients and hopefully they leave with them. There is a difference between visions in meditation, in dreams, and in spirit contact. The hardest thing to learn is how to open and close the level of contact at will; a spirit guide is necessary for that. A good medium must be free from a strong ego or a desire for self-promotion. Mediums are not open to spirit contact twenty-four hours a day and symbolism is the root of spiritual development.

I am fortunate to have kept Anne's friendship over these many years. I still treasure the letter she sent to me following our first meeting in which she said, "Dear Nancy, Wishing you the very best in your search for truth and spiritual unfoldment. I only wish we lived closer together so that I could be of greater assistance to you. I feel you have a great potential toward mediumship and psychic ability and your awareness of the needs people have in this world for spiritual guidance can direct your life in a meaningful way. Sincerely, Anne"

The Florida trip made me more aware of my sensitivity. Also, I was beginning to think differently. Watching my children grow allowed me to see the world through their eyes. Life was full of things that I never noticed before. Gradually, as they grew more independent and self-confident, I became more independent and self-confident. It was as if I had been trapped in a time warp until Angie came along. I awoke to discover I was thirty-six years old.

I wanted to stretch my wings and fly. I wanted to explore the world that my teenagers were living in. They were in high school; they had many friends; they had jobs outside the home; they did volunteer work; and, they could go wherever they wanted as long as they were home before their eleven o'clock curfew.

My teenagers helped me recover my lost years, allowing me to grow with them. That is probably why, to this day, my oldest daughter claims that she raised me, and still teases me about it.

I know I wasn't always there for my children when they wanted me. I know I should have had the courage to stand between them and their father's rages. I know I should have insisted they be helped through college. I know I made a lot of mistakes that they have forgiven me for. I also know they never doubted my love for them.

With the new self-confidence that I gained during my time spent with Angie, I became more assertive in establishing a solid relationship with my parents. Once a month, I drove them to the supermarket and often took them to the shopping mall where they sat in the corridor smoking a cigarette and watching the people pass by while I shopped.

My mother and I also went to Hengerer's Tea Room where we enjoyed the cucumber sandwiches, raisin scones with clotted cream, petits-fours and assorted miniature chocolates. There, my mother spoke of her lost opportunities and crushed hopes. "Honey, my life has been like a rose, in the beginning, it was beautiful, but with the passing of time, the petals began to fall."

We went to the Hengerer's Tea Room many times where our conversations were filled with laughter and tears as we discussed the past. My mother told me how she met my father and fell in love with him at first sight.

"I was pregnant when I married your father," she said, lifting a finger to her lips in a shushing motion and looking me directly in the eyes, as if she were telling me a secret.

"Mama, I knew that. It wasn't hard to do the math. Your wedding anniversary is in July and Tom was born the following February."

She told me about the day of the accident when she fell and cut her hand. She told me about the dream she had shortly before I was born. She told me about baby Anna Belle and how she died. She told me about her adoption and how her birth mother died.

"Mama, your sister Barbara visited you. Why didn't your other sisters or your brother ever visit you?"

"It's different when you don't grow up together. There's no real closeness. I didn't know I had three sisters and a brother while I was growing up. Nanny didn't tell me I was adopted until I needed my birth certificate for my marriage license."

"Tell me why you and Daddy didn't sleep together?" I asked, knowing that was going to be a hard question for her to answer.

"I had a feeling that something was going on between your father and my girlfriend, Ellen Thom. When I asked her, she admitted that she and your father cheated on me. I was going to divorce your father after I heard that, but for the sake of you children we stayed married with the condition that we wouldn't sleep together anymore. Your father agreed. He thought that, after awhile, I'd give in, but it didn't work out that way. We had many fights over it through the years. Now, no more questions. Drink your tea."

My mother confided in me that she felt she wasn't a good enough daughter. She told me that while growing up, Nanny was never satisfied with the way she did things. She also told me that she had dreams that sometimes came true. She was my mother, but now I had a sense of closeness with her that I never had before. Now, she was also my friend, as she shared the details of her life with me. Having a close relationship with my mother and some female friends to emotionally support me, my life was becoming more enjoyable. There is much to be praised about women supporting women.

My two oldest teenagers were now in college and the youngest was a senior in high school. I planned a tour of Mexico for their spring break, with an inner knowing that it would be our last family vacation.

On the first night in Mexico City, we dined in an expensive restaurant, among the other well-dressed tourists. The maitre d' directed us to a large round table, with a white linen tablecloth, linen napkins and pewter chargers. The food was delicious and the service was excellent. "Dad, the smoke is going in my face," one of my teenagers complained, as Joe smoked a cigarette and drank his coffee while we finished our dessert.

"You mean like this," Joe said, picking up his cigarette, inhaling deeply and deliberately blowing the smoke in the same direction as the one who complained. I couldn't finish my dessert because tears choked in my throat. I couldn't speak up because that would make things worse. Before walking back to the hotel, we meandered through the shops. I bought a black, pigskin handbag for three hundred dollars. Whenever I felt badly, shopping momentarily took away the hurt—I did a lot of shopping!

The next day of our guided tour we were taken to the Floating Gardens of Xochimilco. There we boarded a colorful Trajineras (boat) that took us through a portion of the canals. We sat on the benches that lined both sides of the arched gondola that was trimmed with brightly colored paper flowers, and listened to the two mariachi bands on board providing delightful music for our enjoyment.

A few people were dancing to the music. The tour guide reached for my hand and pulled me up to the center of the gondola. Putting his arm around my waist, he tried to dance with me. I glanced back at Joe. The look on his face told me he was angry.

"I have to sit down, please," I told the guide as I pulled away from his grip and hurried back to sit next to Joe. The tour guide got the message in Joe's unspoken expression that said, "You can look, but don't touch." The gondola ride wasn't fun anymore.

When we arrived at our hotel in Acapulco, we ate dinner in one of the three hotel restaurants. There were real orchids on the table. I was served a delicious red snapper, fresh from the sea as I watched the sun drop into Acapulco Bay.

The next morning we took a taxi to the shopping district, where the song *"La Cucaracha"* was sung in Spanish, leaving no doubt that we were in Mexico. After another few days, the vacation ended and we rode a taxi to the Acapulco airport. With our luggage checked, we boarded the plane and returned to the States.

In March, almost as soon as we returned from Mexico, my nineteen-year-old daughter left home, She moved to California with her fiancé to finish her college education. My eighteen-year-old son was told to leave the house! He had nowhere to go, so he joined the Navy. The only joy in the house was my seventeen-year-old daughter. But, she busied herself with her senior year at school, a part-time job, and her social life. Most of the time she wasn't home. Sadly, now, the house of my dreams was empty!

That year, 1976, was an emotionally difficult year for me. Except for the one night a week when Joe and I went out to dinner, we went our separate ways. Joe resumed spending his nights out, usually going to Toronto with his bachelor friends.

I got my GED (General Equivalency Diploma) and took the usual required college courses at the university and consulted with Professor Clarence Dye regarding my research into trance states and hypnotic regression. One night a week I had a few girlfriends over to the house for discussions about the paranormal.

Summer was passing quickly. In early August, my mother saw her gynecologist. She had been experiencing pressure in her lower abdomen. The doctor's examination didn't find any cause for her discomfort. She and I both passed it off as something she ate. I put it out of my mind, returning to my busy schedule.

My daughter and her fiancé returned from California to prepare for their wedding. When she called the major hotels, she learned that all the ballrooms had been booked a year in advance. She resigned herself to having a small, simple wedding. I wouldn't hear of it; I was determined that my daughter would have a grand wedding. I phoned the Sheraton Hotel and was told. "I just hung up the phone from a cancellation. You must be psychic."

There were almost three hundred guests at the wedding. My mother and I were extremely pleased that my daughter had a beautiful September wedding, the kind of wedding that we would have wanted for ourselves.

In the early part of October, after my daughter and her husband returned to California, I resumed my weekly visits with my mother. Thursday, after having my hair done, I drove to my mother's house to pick her up for lunch. I knocked on her door and walked in. She was sitting at the kitchen table with an agitated look on her face. "Is everything all right?" I asked, with an uneasy feeling.

"Yes," she answered quickly. Grabbing her coat from the back of the chair. She slipped her arms into the sleeves and we left. Not satisfied with the way she said "yes," I asked her to tell me what was bothering her.

"Wait till we get there. I'll tell you about it then. I have to think on it a little longer," she said, in a distant low voice. I didn't pressure her any further. I could see she was lost in thought as I drove to Hengerer's Tea Room. I parked the car and we rode the elevator to the second floor. The hostess seated us at a table in the corner and brought the tea service, pouring hot tea into the cups.

"Honey, I had a terrible dream last night, and I'm frightened," my mother said, setting the teacup back down in the saucer and looking at me with a serious expression.

"What do you mean, you're frightened? Tell me about it."

She took a deep breath and said, "I was in a room, alone, and several men dressed in white came into the room and kept jabbing me with needles. Then, I saw Nanny and followed her. When we came to a hill, she disappeared. I climbed the hill. When I got to the top, ahead of me was a field of flowers. I saw Nanny in the field with a lot of other people. She was calling to me to follow her."

Lifting the cup to her lips to mask the dread in her voice, my mother added, "You know that sometimes I dream things that come true. Do you think the dream means what I think it does?"

I didn't have the courage to tell my mother what I thought, so I said, "I know you've missed Nanny during these past thirteen years that she's been gone. The wedding probably brought back memories and a longing for her." I didn't want to confirm or believe what seemed obvious to both of us.

A few weeks later, on Friday, October 29, I drove my parents to the hospital, where my mother admitted herself for observation to determine the cause of her discomfort. The hospital observation on admission stated: Abdominal pain. Rule out ovarian problem. Plan to admit to observe and to do a barium enema.

After she was settled in, I told her I would be back to visit her on Monday. While driving my father home, he asked me, "Do you think your mother is going to be okay?"

"She'll be fine. Don't worry," I answered hesitantly.

Instead of our usual Thursday night out, Joe and I went to dinner on Sunday, Halloween night, and dined at an Italian restaurant in Niagara Falls, Canada.

After dinner we walked to our car parked near the Clifton Hill strip of tourist attractions. Passing the Harry Houdini Museum, I noticed a man standing outside the entrance to the museum. I recognized him. He was Allen Spraggett, a famous paranormal researcher and author of many books. I had met him at one of the seminars that I attended.

Allen told us the museum was closed to the public that night. He asked if I would like to join the group inside and participate in the 50th anniversary séance. I was honored. Of course, I knew of Harry Houdini, but I didn't know much about him. As Allen Spraggett, Joe, and I entered the museum we walked past the display cases housing the Harry Houdini collection of assorted magic paraphernalia. We entered a room where the other invited quests and the news media gathered. Joe took a seat among the media.

I was introduced to Walter B. Gibson, Sidney Radner, and Milbourne Christopher. Allen directed me to a seat at the huge round table, on which were placed items once owned and used by Harry Houdini, including handcuffs and shackles. "Nancy, meet Mrs. Dunninger," Allen said, introducing me to the gray-haired lady sitting to my right.

"Hello, Mrs. Dunninger," I said, taking her hand, as we joined in the circle of hands around the table. The lights were dimmed and the room was hushed. I closed my eyes and went into my relaxed state. After a few moments of silence, the woman with blonde hair and bright red lipstick began the séance. "Harry, if you are here give us a sign," she said. There was silence and no sign.

After a few more moments of silence she continued the séance saying things about Harry Houdini and answering questions about him from those around the table. She told us that she couldn't receive any messages from him, the reason being that he may not be in spirit anymore; he may have already reincarnated.

I became very agitated and angry, but didn't understand why. I was only there to observe and to lend my energy to the séance. I hadn't planned on making contact with Harry Houdini. It shouldn't have bothered me when she said he had reincarnated.

"*Lies~ lies~ lies~ France~ élan~ tell Joe.*" These words from the spirit world repeated in my head. With my eyes still closed, the astrological sign for Aries followed by the sign for Taurus flashed before me.

"What's the matter, Nancy, what do you see?" Allen Spraggett or someone asked.

"I don't know. I'm feeling very angry. I see zodiac symbols and I'm supposed to tell Joe something. But, I don't understand any of it. The séance ended and the lights were turned back up.

"Do you know my husband's name?" Mrs. Dunninger, the woman on my right asked, as I started to leave the table. "His name was Joe. He and Harry had a special friendship."

"Oh, I didn't know that." I told her, with an embarrassed smile, because I didn't understand what the message was about.

Insight Productions Company Ltd. of Toronto filmed the event that evening. I signed a release for the filming company, was paid the customary five dollars and said goodbye to Allen Spraggett.

Joe and I returned to the States. But, I couldn't get the séance and the symbols out of my mind. Why did I see the zodiac symbols? What did the coded message mean? I wrote, Aries, Taurus, élan and tell Joe on a sheet of paper, intending to contact Allen Spraggett later. For now, though, I was occupied with thoughts of my mother.

On Monday morning, I got into my car and rode to Mercy Hospital in South Buffalo. My mother was resting comfortably in a semi-private room, not far from the visitor's waiting room. "How are you doing, Mama?" I asked, walking over to where she was lying between the white sheets. My mother, a heavy-set woman with her hair streaked gray and wearing no make-up, looked much older than her fifty-eight years.

"Not too bad, but they haven't found out why I get all this pressure," she said, circling her hand over her lower belly. Reaching up to touch my hair, as I leaned over to give her a kiss on the cheek, she added, "I like your hair that length, and it hasn't any gray."

"Mama, I get it colored at the salon, that's why. I probably have more gray than you," I said trying to make her smile. We visited awhile and I assured her that I would look in on my father and Billy. "Don't worry about them, you'll be home soon," I told her, refusing to believe what my higher sensitivity told me.

After examining the results of the tests, her gynecologist and her general physician determined that she had a metastasized carcinoma in the abdomen. Every day, I arrived at the hospital at six o'clock in the morning and stayed until the night shift came on at eleven o'clock. I felt that I should stand guard to make sure everything possible was being done to make her comfortable.

The nurses told me that she could take nothing by mouth, not even a drop of water. When they couldn't see what I was doing, I wet her lips with the corner of a wet washcloth, sometimes making it really wet and letting her suck on it. I stroked my mother's hair and powdered her with talc. In a small way, I was becoming her mother.

One afternoon, when my father walked into my mother's hospital room, he was carrying a glass vase with a long-stem, red rose. There was a haunting sadness in his eyes as he placed the vase with the red rose on the bedside table. My father stood looking into my mother's moistened eyes, not saying a word. In those few, intimate moments, I could feel the love they still had for each other.

All the hurt and anger that had passed between them over the years didn't seem to matter anymore. But, it was too late to make a difference in their lives or the lives of their children. Although no words were spoken, I'm sure a lifetime of memories flashed in their minds. Memories and thoughts of what could have been: if only my father hadn't committed adultery with Miss Thom; if only my mother had forgiven my father. As I stood looking at my parents, I realized the life-changing power of forgiving. It can bring joy or sorrow to both those directly involved and those in the sidelines.

When visiting hours were over, my father gave my mother a light kiss on the lips and walked out of the room. Billy drove him home, as he had done every day. The message that he loved her and he always would was conveyed when he brought a rose for my mother.

In her final days, the morphine drip made her drift in and out of consciousness. When I came back to her room after talking with Billy, who was in the waiting room, my father was standing by my mother's bedside, gently holding her hand while tears were rolling down his cheeks. I began to cry with him and slowly walked him out of the room. Billy met us in the hall. I walked them to the elevator, said goodbye and returned to my mother's room.

Not once had Joe accompanied me to the hospital. He even complained that I went. "You don't have to go to the hospital again," he said, one morning, as I came out of the shower. "Stay here and take care of the house!"

"The house doesn't need me! You don't need me! My mother's dying— she needs me!" Before I could finish dressing, Joe took my car and drove off, knowing that I couldn't drive his standard-shift pick-up truck. I had to rent a car to drive to the hospital. That was December 2, less than forty-eight hours before my mother's death.

In those last few hours, knowing the end was near, I spoke to her, hoping she could hear me. "Mama, remember your dream. Climb up the hill. Climb up the hill, Mama. Look on the other side. Nanny is there, waiting for you. See her, Mama, feel her love. Move closer to her." It wasn't easy saying that, as the tears flowed from my eyes, but my mother needed me to tell her it was all right for her to go.

I let go of her hand and sat in the chair by her bedside. As I closed my eyes, I felt goose bumps and a strange sensation on the nape of my neck. I opened my eyes and thought I saw a soft glow in the upper corner of the room. It made me think it was the spirit presence of Nanny, smiling at me.

I stood up, gave my mother a cheek kiss and said, "Good bye Nanny, good bye Mama."

I left the hospital in deep despair. I was exhausted and distraught with the sorrow of losing my mother. Slowly, I got into my car and began to drive home. "Oh God," I prayed, "Why does my mother have to suffer so much pain?" That is a question, I'm sure many people would like to have answered when their loved one is suffering. I don't know what answer they might get, but I got the answer I needed to hear.

An inner awareness exploded within my spirit. Instantly, I just knew that each and every one of us is accountable for all that we have done and all that we should have done. That awareness didn't come in the form of a voice in my head or even a few seconds of rational thinking; it was an epiphany, an instant knowing.

To redeem ourselves—thus purifying our spirit—we are given a choice as to the manner of our atonement. The suffering of pain while in the physical body is one of our choices. The suffering of spiritual pain is another choice. That involves knowing that the love of God is the greatest joy imaginable, yet not being able to obtain that joy.

I was made aware that my mother's super-conscious mind chose to purify her spirit with the fire of physical pain. That was the choice she made. At her passing, she would be free of atonement and she would be able to feel the full joy of God's love. With that awareness, I stopped sobbing and was at peace for the rest of the drive home.

The next day, on December 4, a nurse walked into my mother's room, and found her without vital signs. A little after four o'clock in the morning she was pronounced dead. As I was waking up, the phone rang, "This is Mercy Hospital. I'm sorry to tell you that your mother has passed away." My mother had died.

During the funeral service, my father tried hard not to fall apart, but tears rolled down his cheeks, as my tears did on mine. I bought a double plot so my father could be laid to rest beside my mother, when his time came. I knew that the day would come when I would have to say my final goodbye to him, too. Until then, Billy and my father would live together, taking care of each other.

My mother died twenty days before Christmas. There was a light dusting of snow on the frozen ground the day she was buried, making her final resting place seem so cold. Sometimes, when I visit her grave, I imagine the scent of perfume she wore. I still have her cobalt-blue bottle of Evening in Paris perfume in my dresser drawer, along with the last greeting card my father gave her, in which he wrote, "Happy 40th Anniversary, Love Ralph."

Another anniversary was about to get my attention. In the spring, while cleaning out my desk, I came across the paper with the coded messages from the Harry Houdini séance. The messages still puzzled me. So, I consulted with my astrologer friend, Judy.

She told me that the astrological symbols have descriptive phrases; she went on to tell me: "The phrase for Aries is—I am. The phrase for Taurus is—I believe." I knew *élan is* the French word for spirit. The coded messages that I received from Harry Houdini the night of the séance were, "I am—I believe—spirit." So there you have it!

I looked further into the identity of the people who attended the séance. I discovered that Joseph Dunninger was a magician, escapologist and mentalist. He was also a good friend to many notables in the magic community, including Harry Houdini.

Walter B. Gibson was the creator of *The Shadow* radio program. Walter was also Harry Houdini's ghostwriter. How very ironic, to have met the creator of Tom's favorite radio program. Milbourn Christopher was the chairman of the Occult Investigation Committee of the Society of American Magicians.

I have often wondered what would have happened if I had boldly proclaimed, "Lies, lies, lies," the night of the séance when the medium declared Harry Houdini had already reincarnated? Why had I received that coded message? Why did Harry Houdini's spirit give me the message to "Tell Joe"? Why wasn't Harry Houdini aware that Joe had passed over to the other side?

There was another famous Harry that I had a moment with. When Joe and I went to nightclubs together, I gradually learned to dance. At one of the nightclubs, I met Harry James, the famous trumpet player who had been married to Betty Grable. She was the original pin-up girl. With a request that sounded more like an order, Joe asked Harry James to play the song "*Crazy Rhythm.*" He did and Joe and I danced to the swing music. After the dance, Harry James smiled at me as I left the dance floor. Carmine, the husband of the other couple we were with, said, "Nancy, stand next to Harry James, and I'll take your picture." Harry James kindly agreed to the photo.

When Joe and I traveled—from Palm Springs to Chicago, from Miami to Montreal, from San Diego to San Francisco—we had VIP treatment. Whenever we went to Las Vegas shows or New York nightclubs, we didn't wait behind the velvet ropes and we always had first class seating. Frankly, I was living in luxury, but something was missing. I still felt empty inside.

In December 1978, using business profits and other investment profits, we bought a brick, twelve-unit apartment building. Each apartment had two bedrooms, a living room, a kitchen and a bath. In June, 1979, my youngest daughter moved out of the house and into an apartment of our building to help me manage it.

Now, I was totally alone in our house, both night and day. I wasn't happy there! The only time I spent in the house was in the home-office where I did the bookwork for our two construction companies. I took an apartment on the first floor of our building, using the living room as a classroom, where I gave instructions in the development of higher sensory perception. The two bedrooms were used as office space for Psychical Research Awareness.

In my class programs, I emphasized the importance of knowing who you are and why you believe what you believe. For example, I asked students to think about what formed their religious views and their political views. Also, to question the nature of their social prejudices? Have they blindly accepted their views because they were the views of their parents or others they may have looked up to? I asked them to begin to really think about how and why they have programmed such information into their minds.

Although my grandmother had strong views about religion, I was fortunate that my parents didn't. My parents' neglect of providing me with a solid religious structure allowed me to explore other religions and make my own choice.

I am very specific when I tell my students, "Do not blindly accept what I say to you. The information I give is from information I have gathered and how I have interrupted it." I am very specific when I tell my students that empirical knowledge can be easily obtained by developing higher sensory perception through purposeful practice.

On Saturdays and on some evenings, I attended the State University of New York at Buffalo where the courses I took included the study of Knowledge & Reality, General Psychology and the study of Death & Dying. Also, I completed a distance-learning program from the University of Metaphysics, in California.

I wrote my first book, which included information on how to develop higher sensory perception. The primary message in my first book is to begin to be aware of how truly wonderful we are. It is important that we love and value who we are, now at this moment in time, before we begin to awaken our own natural higher awareness. We must know and believe that we are worth the time and energy it takes to develop higher sensory perception. We must realize HSP is meant to be a tool for spiritual growth.

The second message is for us to begin to be all that we can be by developing our own higher sensory perception. Pay attention to our thoughts and feelings. Record our dreams and meditate upon them to understand the messages our sub-conscious mind is trying to give us. Make conscious choices that are in alignment with our higher purpose. Stay in tune with our inner guidance. Take inspired action in our daily life.

Joe supported me financially in getting my book published, but he never took the time to talk to me about what I wrote. Know Thyself was a chapter that addressed negative behavior and encouraged people to identify that behavior and make positive changes. I am sure my book inspired many people to take a good look at who they were and how they acted, but the one I wanted most to inspire—Joe—wouldn't pay any attention to me or what I had to say.

We were growing farther and farther apart. We spent time together only on Thursday evenings when we went out to dinner, or on some Sundays when we went out to brunch. The remainder of the days and nights we went our separate ways. Joe went to his favorite coffee shop to hang out during the day, and every Friday and Saturday nights he went out with "the boys." Sometimes they drove to Toronto to listen to jazz, not coming home until three or four o'clock in the morning. I appeased my aloneness by delving deeper into paranormal research.

In the fall, a psychic in the Buffalo area asked if I would like to witness her investigation of a haunted house. As a paranormal investigator, I welcomed the opportunity to witness that psychic at her work. I wasn't familiar with her method of an all-night session, in which she would enter in and out of a trance. The date set for the investigation was on September 8, 1979.

At eight o'clock in the evening, I drove my car down the long, dark, country road and parked in front of the little house that was claimed to be haunted. Mary, the owner of the house, opened the door. I was surprised to see so many people when I walked into the living room. The psychic's husband, who worked at the same place as the owner of the house; two of the psychic's assistants, two of the psychic's friends, a news reporter and a photographer were all crowded into the living room.

The psychic, dressed in a sleeping gown, was stretched out on a recliner-chair and covered with a satin quilt. The psychic's husband began the session by talking her into a "trance." Soon, the psychic said she was ready to begin. Her husband asked me if I wanted to question her. As the psychic went in and out of a trance, she mentioned names, dates, and incidents, claiming they were associated with spirits who were in the house.

When the morning came, the psychic said, "I have concluded my investigation." It disturbed me that she would leave the owner with thoughts that spirits were roaming through her house. This wasn't my investigation, so I said nothing at the time. I had to respect the owner's choice to contact that psychic and not my own organization, Psychical Research Awareness Association.

Monday's *Courier Express* newspaper carried the story that I assisted in putting the psychic into a trance. I hadn't done that. I merely asked her questions. The newspaper also stated that I was a field reporter for Duke University's Psychical Research Foundation. I was a field reporter for Dr. William Roll, director of the Psychical Research Foundation, which had a mailing address at Duke Station, North Carolina, but it was not part of Duke University. Unfortunately, misinformation does get printed in newspapers.

A few weeks later, Mary, the owner of the house, phoned my office. She told me that the psychic wasn't interested in the case any longer. Mary told me that the psychic suggested she contact me if she wanted a more intense investigation into why her house was haunted. I agreed to take on the case.

From the Philosophy of Parapsychology course I had taken at the university, I learned that I could be easily influenced by what I heard during the psychic's "trance" state. True or false, it didn't matter; I couldn't trust myself to be objective. I would need assistance from another researcher on the follow-up investigation. Mary agreed to let me invite another investigator to work with me.

I am fortunate to have been acquainted with Professor Paul Kurtz, who at the time was the founder and chairman of the Committee to Scientifically Investigate Claims of Paranormal (CSICOP). I explained the situation to him, adding that the house was well known and open to the public on selected days for guided tours. He welcomed the invitation to lend his assistance. "Two fellows from the Secular Society are visiting here. Do you mind if I bring them along?" Professor Kurtz asked.

"I don't see a problem. I'm sure the owner won't object." A visit to the house was scheduled for the following Tuesday, September 25, 1979. Professor Kurtz and the two gentlemen met me at a nearby restaurant and followed in their car as I drove to the house in a suburb of Buffalo. We parked our cars and walked to the front porch.

Mary opened the door before I had a chance to knock. She welcomed us in with a big smile. Professor Kurtz initiated the investigation by walking through the house with the two men from the Secular Society. I turned on my tape recorder and followed them.

When our on-site investigation was over we left and headed back to the city. At my office, I compared the transcripts from the night of the psychic's session with the recording of the interview that Professor Kurtz conducted.

Mary denied that she had an interest in the paranormal. However, her first contact with the psychic was when the psychic gave her a reading at a friend's house. Also, Mary had talked about having the book, *The Amityville Horror.* There were many contradictions. The psychic who gave Mary the information that her house was indeed haunted was only one of many psychics whom I had been requested to follow up on.

Another incident occurred when I was asked to speak with a young man to reassure him that the things a psychic had told him were not true predictions.

The nineteen-year-old was depressed because his girlfriend had broken up with him. Being depressed he missed work too many times and was fired. Searching for future happiness, he went to a psychic for a reading. Halfway through the session, after not hitting upon anything that the young man could relate to, the psychic asked, "Do you have any questions?"

"My girlfriend broke up with me; are we going to get back together?"

"No, I don't see another girl in your life for two more years."

"I lost my job; will I be getting another one soon?"

"No, I can't see any job."

The young man paid the psychic, went home and took an overdose of pills, trying to commit suicide. Fortunately, his sister found him unconscious, lying on his bedroom floor. He was rushed to the hospital where his stomach was pumped, saving his life.

Until I pointed it out, the young man hadn't realized that it was he who told the psychic about breaking up with his girlfriend and losing his job. I reminded him reassuringly that if the psychic didn't know that, how could she know what would happen in his future?

Through the years, I have tried very hard to inform people that higher sensory perception is something that may be developed by anyone. I believe that higher sensory perception is a valuable tool and may be useful in helping others when it is used properly.

Also, I believe that people—who call themselves psychics—have a right to be compensated for their work in helping others. However, I do not believe that this work should be depended on as a means to making a living. When that happens, the psychic may be tempted to place more emphasis on the money than on helping the client.

Returning to the investigation at Mary's house, even if a haunting had been taking place in her house, she, for a number of reasons, may have exaggerated the accounts of the alleged phenomenon. So far, in my research and investigations of the paranormal, I was finding more hallucination and fraud than I was finding answers and truth. I was becoming even more ashamed that I might be considered a psychic.

Although I believe in the ability to develop higher sensory perception, I don't believe that ability should be used haphazardly. In October 1979, a reporter agreed to interview me for a follow-up story of the case, giving me a chance to set the record straight.

[The following is from the article printed in the *Buffalo News*]
Whether participation in a seemingly harmless séance, or the trip to a psychic reader, with hopes for answers, many are experimenting with something they know little or nothing about. Some who claim to be psychics don't know what they are doing, and they often hurt people by giving negative readings or false information. Even true psychics are not "on" all the time. Often, they, too, may generalize about health, wealth and love.

One of my ongoing research projects concerns an area house that the owner claimed was haunted. Not all the activities in the house were related to spiritual energies. Professor Paul Kurtz and I believe it may have all resulted from the owner reading *The Amityville horror.*

As my research continued and my world expanded, I became more independent and emotionally stronger. I began to defend myself against Joe's temper. Maybe as a better way of saying it, I was finally growing up. What a joy it was to learn that I wasn't too old to learn and what a joy it was to have friends to share my joy.

I stayed in touch with my Italian girlfriends. We met for lunch once a month. We always lunched at an elegant restaurant, eating and talking for hours. They spoke of how they would stay forever young and beautiful, and they had.

These women were born in Florence, Rome, Sicily, or in the Calabria region of Italy. Our conversations were peppered with Italian words punctuated with hand gestures. I admired how they could shift so easily from Italian to English when they realized I didn't understand what they said.

My good friend, Maria, was beautiful and exuded a glow of quiet elegance. Rose was attractive with olive skin, dark eyes and short, black, wavy hair. She had five sisters. Each one was Hollywood-glamorous. My friend, Lila, had beautiful, long, black hair. There was something striking about Lila's physical appearance; she had everyone's attention as soon as she entered a room.

Carrie had red hair and always dressed in a skirt and blouse with sensible pumps, the traditional outfit of a successful real estate agent. My friend, Mary, had a distinct gentility that led you to believe she had been raised a lady who was meant for the finer things in life. Rita was a warm, petite, attractive woman with a bright smile. Josephine and Carmilina were sisters-in-law and both were the epitome of Italian high style. Also, there was my friend, Bessie, who had the face of a de Vinci woman.

My Italian girlfriends were the wives of wealthy men; the jewels and designer clothes they wore and the cars they drove left no doubt of that. Some of us were also members of the Buffalo Chapter of Women Interested in Cystic Health (WIICH), a fundraising organization that lunched at various Country Clubs and fine restaurants once a month. Although some of their husbands knew Joe, none of them was one of "the boys" that Joe went out with.

I no longer live the lifestyle of my Italian friends, but that doesn't matter to them. They've remained true and loyal friends through all these years, just as Marge has.

Nancy Lee with Harry James (1977). At one of the nightclubs, I met Harry James, the famous trumpet player who had been married to Betty Grable, the original pin-up girl.

Nancy Lee at a book signing (1979). I wrote my first book, which included information on how to develop higher sensory perception. The primary message in my first book is to begin to be aware of how truly wonderful we are.

The Basement at the Leroy Investigation (1980). Breathing the air in the basement was like breathing terror itself, but I wouldn't allow myself to panic.

CHAPTER NINE
Good Against Evil

Of course, not everything that goes bump in the night is a ghost.
Some experiences can be easily explained—and some can't!

MY DAUGHTER AND HER husband left California, returning to Buffalo where they bought a house. My son finished his three years of active duty in the Navy and was living on his own, going back to college while serving three more years in the Naval Reserves. My younger daughter, still living in and managing our apartment building was happily involved in a serious relationship. Joe continued his lifestyle and I continued mine.

Except for the vacations to Acapulco every year, Joe and I didn't spend time together. Even then, we went our separate ways. Joe liked to stay where it was air-conditioned and I liked to lounge in the sun by the pool. Not wanting to spend the thousands of dollars every year in Mexico anymore, I thought it would be better to buy a vacation home in the United States. After a quick trip to Florida to select the style of the house we wanted built, Joe and I returned to Buffalo where I continued my research.

As founder and director of the Psychical Research Awareness Association, I was asked to investigate a claimed haunting in a turn-of-the-century building in Leroy, New York. I contacted Brenda, my assistant, and Grace, A psychic medium, to work with me on the case.

They met me at my office on April 25, 1980. We got into my Mercedes and I drove along the Interstate Highway and through the streets of the town, arriving about an hour later at the unoccupied, two-story stone building.

The owner and her daughter were inside waiting for us. I told the owner that if there were any spirits present, Grace would try to make contact. Brenda, as usual would record the session and lend her energy, and I would take photographs and be the observing investigator.

The owner told us that most of the strange activity occurred in the basement. We walked through the first floor to the back of the building and went down the narrow staircase into the basement.

The walls were all of original stone. The approximate height from the dirt floor to the hand-hewn support beams overhead was a little over five feet. There were no windows. The only light in the basement was from the bulb that dangled from the center of the ceiling, casting a harsh light on the damp walls.

The following is taken from the transcripts. I asked the questions while Grace attempts to uncover the mystery of what is causing the paranormal activities.

"Grace, are you feeling anything?"

"Yes, something straight up and down. I see chains as if it's something binding. It's a symbol of these people or spirits. They're bound to this place"

"What do you feel is present right now? (Grace begins to gasp for air. In a short time she regained control). What are you getting, Grace?"

"I feel sick. (Grace almost cries). Something traumatic happened here. There were two partners, but one didn't want the other. They argued about the split. I feel that one departed very suddenly. I feel the coldness on the side of my face again. There's something untold. I can't get to it; something that they want someone to know; murder! You will find something that will lead to it. It happened many, many years ago. I keep hearing many, many. Traces are almost gone. There was a murder here. Body isn't here. They say this person stumbled and fell and at that time it didn't go to an investigation. The man didn't stumble and fall. They're telling me he was murdered.

Something is present. I can smell it. I feel totally iced as if I'm in a cooler. The smell is there, terrible, like rotting flesh; a body was here. I want to say it was moved but I can't be positive. I'm iced! I'm at a point of saying it was here. I keep hearing, 'It was here,' over and over again."

"The body that you say was here—was it male or female?"

"It was male. I don't feel anything too strong here; I feel it stronger over there. (Grace indicates the front of the basement). I think I'm going to be sick." (Grace heads for the stairs).

We three agreed about feeling a strong energy force at the far end of the basement. Not taking my eyes from the far corner of the basement, I said, "Brenda, go with her, make sure she's all right. I'll be okay until you get back." I knew if I looked away, something terrible would happen—but I didn't know what!

Breathing the air in the basement was like breathing terror itself, but I wouldn't allow myself to panic. I remembered what my father once told me: "You're only afraid if you think you're afraid." I reached for the gold cross on the chain I wore around my neck. It was the cross that I bought in the Vatican gift shop, blessed by the Pope. I always wore it—it made me feel safe.

As Brenda headed up the stairs a blue, glowing, iridescent orb began to form in the far corner of the basement. The orb just hung in the air. I thought I could keep it from moving toward me as long as I kept my eyes on it. Soon, it became a battle of good against evil.

The bulb that dangled from the center of the basement went out. I was in total darkness. I tried to remain calm while I kept my eyes on the blue orb that seemed to be glowing brighter. A strange feeling at the nape of my neck gave me goose bumps.

"Brenda! Turn the lights back on!" I yelled.

"I didn't turn them off!" Brenda yelled back.

The blue orb became larger and brighter as it came toward me. I felt a deep jolt in my stomach and a trembling in my legs. It whizzed past my ear with a cold rush of air and the harsh guttural whisper *"One ~ Not~ Three."* It was a message that it wanted only one of us! Which one did it want?

I couldn't remain calm any longer. I panicked at the threat, turned and ran toward the stairs, hitting my forehead on one of the overhead beams. As I felt the pain of the impact, the lone bulb, hanging from the basement ceiling, came back on.

"Nancy, are you okay?" Brenda asked as she started down the basement stairs.

"I hit my head and Grace is sick. We better end this and come back another time," I answered, taking a last look behind me as I walked up the basement stairs.

I told the owner, who waited in the front of the building with her daughter, that we couldn't do any further investigation because Grace felt ill. I told her that I would contact her at a later date. We gathered our things and left.

While on the thruway driving back to Buffalo, I was in the right lane when suddenly the steering wheel jerked from my hands. It made a sharp turn to the left, taking the car into the left lane toward the center island of grass that separated us from the oncoming traffic. As hard as I tried, the steering wheel wouldn't turn back! It was locked in place! I tried with all my strength to free it and make it turn to the right, but it wouldn't move. "Oh God! Oh God! Help me!" I cried out. Suddenly, the steering wheel unlocked and jerked to the far right. I held on tight and brought the car under control, pulling it to a stop at the side of the thruway.

All three of us were badly shaken as we got out of the car. "We need to cleanse our aura and create a shield of protection, before we go any further," I said, feeling that an evil entity had attached itself to us, causing the car to go out of control. Brenda, Grace and I held hands, forming a circle and recited the Lord's Prayer, followed with me leading us into a visualization of the protective white light of God and His goodness.

We returned to the car and continued on, thanking God that we made it back safely. Immediately, I phoned the owner and told her that she needed to contact a Catholic priest. I told Joe what had happened and he drove the Mercedes to the Great Lakes Motor Company on Main Street where we bought the car. They couldn't find any reason for the steering wheel locking up like it did. When Joe came back, he said, "What in hell are you doing all this shit for? There's nothing wrong with your car. If you don't know how to drive, stay home!"

I'll never forget the terror I experienced when the cold whisper came past my ear, and the danger we were in when the evil power took control of the steering wheel. Those in the spirit world, wanting to get messages to their loved ones, do not come through to me in that manner. That's why I believe it was an evil energy, something that I will not deal with.

A few weeks later, a homicide detective, whom I had worked with several times in the past, contacted me regarding a murder he was investigating. He took a shirt from a plastic bag marked, "evidence" and handed it to me. "What do you get from this?" he asked.

I held the long-sleeve plaid shirt with the bullet hole and told the detective, "I see him standing in a doorway talking to another man. He knows the man. The man shoots him. The man runs from the porch." Then, I gave the detective a description of the man with the gun. He put the shirt back in the bag, thanked me and left. I made a few quick notes about my impressions to be typed later. I usually kept a file on the work that I did, hoping the information would be validated at a later date.

On a Sunday afternoon when Joe and I returned from brunch, I went into our home office to type the notes for my files. Joe came into the office to see what I was doing. "What's that? Is that a contract for another job?"

"No, it's a homicide case that I'm helping with."

"They're stupid if they believe all that shit you tell them, and you're stupid if you believe there's a devil. There's no devil. Here I'll prove it." Joe dropped his pants and bent over, "Here, Beelzebub; come on Beelzebub. Ha! Now, what do you think?" Joe taunted as he pulled up his pants.

"Joe, you're a fool to tempt evil," I said, getting up from the desk. I walked out of the office.

The next morning, Joe awoke with a swollen tongue and red bumps across his face and chest. He surely didn't expect this to happen, but I wasn't surprised. "What is this? What are these bumps?" Joe asked when he came out of the bathroom.

"You asked for it, yesterday, when you called Beelzebub."

"Oh, you're not going to start with that shit again. It's probably the berries I ate."

"It's not because of berries. I warned you," I said, with dread in my voice. I felt an eerie presence in the air. Joe dressed and went downstairs where he phoned the doctor for an appointment that morning. Do you want me to go with you?" Joe didn't answer. He just walked out the door.

The doctor told him that it looked like an allergic reaction. He prescribed some pills for Joe. I prayed and Joe took the pills. The red bumps went away. The next day, trying to prove to me that his swollen tongue and the red bumps had a physical cause, Joe came home from the construction job in the early afternoon and taunted me again. He dropped his pants, chanting for Beelzebub!

"You're a fool," I said in disgust and turned back to the work logs to prepare the payroll. This time, Joe didn't have to wait; the red bumps began to appear as he was pulling up his pants. "Joe! Your face! Look at your face!" Joe hurried into the bathroom. I followed behind. Joe looked in the mirror with a shocked expression, as more red bumps appeared. "Ask God to help you!" I pleaded.

"Beelzebub! Get out! God, get Beelzebub out of me!" The red bumps began to disappear.

I have no explanation for how this happened to Joe, other than it may have been some form of negative energy at work. That incident took place more than thirty years ago. It left Joe with such a lasting impression that, even to this day, he tells the story.

After Joe had that bad experience with unseen energies, he still objected to my research and helping law enforcement agencies with the cases they were working on, but he let me do it anyway. One unsolved case that still troubles me is a homicide where a young woman was stabbed more than one hundred times.

On a sunny afternoon, I met several detectives at a site where the young woman's body was found. After a few minutes of focused awareness, I was able to envision flashes of the murder scene while it was happening. The murder took place in the late hours of the evening, close to midnight. The stabbing occurred in a different spot from where the detectives indicated the body was found.

I was drawn to an open field, nearby. One of the detectives followed me there. I told him that I envisioned a small group of young people, sitting on the ground and standing around, drinking and smoking. The victim was one of them. She and a young man were arguing about something. She got up and started to run away. The young man and another young man chased after her. One man pulled a knife from his boot and began stabbing her.

Then, I envisioned the young man, still holding the knife in his hand, fleeing the scene. As he passed the small group in the field he yelled, "Let's get out of here!" The group scattered. He hurried away running along railroad tracks, hiding the knife under one of the rails, as he headed home. I knew that the victim's jaw had been broken, something that was not told to the family or reported in the news. I gave a first name and a description of the young man and the weapon to the detectives.

Not long after that, I was asked to go to the police station where I was shown some photos. One of the young men in the photos matched the description of the young man that I envisioned, right down to the distinctive belt buckle he was known to wear. His name was one letter off from the name I had given.

I was surprised to learn there were railroad tracks not far from the murder scene. Unfortunately, by the time the area was searched, the railroad tracks had been torn up and replaced. The weapon was never found. The case remains unsolved. For that reason, among others, I don't like to talk about the work I have done with law enforcement agencies. It isn't safe!

In August 1980 we were informed that the builder had finished our new house. It was a typical Florida-style house, with kitchen, living room, dining room, three bedrooms and two bathrooms. Joe and I flew down to inspect the new house. We stayed in Florida for one week, while we purchased the basic furniture and appliances necessary for a vacation home.

A few days after we returned to Buffalo, my assistant arrived at my office to find me lying unconscious on the floor. I was taken to my doctor's office where my blood pressure registered extremely low. At only one hundred and twelve pounds, five pounds less than when I married Joe, I was both physically and mentally exhausted.

The following day, Joe brought home two of his bachelor friends. He wanted me to cook dinner for them. After they finished eating, Joe and his two friends left for the evening to listen to jazz at some nightclub. I was hurt that he wasn't concerned about me.

I had warned Joe many times that someday I was going to leave him. Now, I was ready. However, I didn't know how to get a divorce. I needed legal advice. Our lawyer, Bill, was also our friend. I wanted Bill, as a friend, to give me advice on how to get a divorce.

On Monday morning, September 29, after another lonely weekend and one day before I turned forty-one years old, I showered, dressed in a silver-gray blouse with a dark blue skirt and matching heels and headed out the door. I didn't call and make an appointment. I just drove downtown and parked in the lot across from the building where Bill had his office. I hoped to be able to catch Bill before his lunch break.

As I waited for the elevator to take me up to his office, the elevator doors opened and Bill stepped out carrying on a friendly conversation with another man. We were both surprised to meet at that exact moment.

"Nancy! Hello. You know Jack Kemp, don't you?"

"Hello, Mr. Kemp," I said reaching my hand out to shake his.

"What are you doing in the hotel?" Bill asked.

"I was hoping to talk to you, Bill"

"Have you had lunch?"

"No, not yet."

"Good, have lunch with me. I'll be just a minute." Bill and Jack Kemp, the famous Buffalo Bills quarterback and U.S. Congressman, walked away. Jack Kemp started for the steps leading down to the front door. Bill shook his hand, turned and came back to where I was waiting. He took my arm and walked me to the hotel luncheon room where we had a friendly conversation while we ate.

"Now, let me tell you why I came to see you," I said, while we drank our coffee. "I want to divorce Joe and I don't know how to do it. I don't even know how to tell him that our marriage is over."

"Let's go up to my office where we can talk," Bill said, with a surprised look. Not another word was said until we took the elevator to the eleventh floor. Bill put the key in and unlocked the door. His secretary wasn't at her desk as we passed it. She was still at lunch. We walked into Bill's private office and he closed the door. Bill took a seat in the leather chair behind his huge mahogany desk and I sat down in one of the two, black, leather chairs in front of his desk. "Tell me, why do you want to divorce Joe?"

How could I explain why I wanted a divorce? The past five years of our marriage weren't really bad. Joe let me buy anything I wanted. He didn't hit me anymore, and I had a lot of time by myself to do whatever I wanted to do. Nobody would understand why I wanted a divorce because they only saw what Joe or I allowed them to see. They didn't know that I felt like I was living in a loveless marriage. They didn't know that I thought of sex with Joe as his act of power over me, not an act of love. True or not, that's how I felt.

I wasn't just divorcing Joe the way he was now. I was divorcing Joe because of the man he had been during the first twenty years of the marriage; the Joe who broke my heart a thousand times, the one who made me cry a thousand tears.

I opened my mouth to explain. I wanted to tell the whole story, from why I had to marry Joe, to the beating when I was pregnant and the ruptured eardrum when Joe hit me following the trip to Italy. Joe was the reason that my children moved out of the house at such an early age. But, no words came out. I tried to hold back the tears, but I couldn't. They rolled down my cheeks, as I said, "I'm tired of being lonely. I want to be loved. I want to be wanted, not needed."

"Why don't you stay with Joe and have an affair for awhile, until you get over this?" Bill didn't understand that I was serious about wanting a divorce. "Look, Joe treats you well. Are you sure you want a divorce?" he quickly added, handing me a box of tissues. Bill didn't believe that I was determined to end this charade of a marriage.

"Bill, all I want is for you to tell me what I have to do. Do I have to stay married because I can't prove adultery?"

"The divorce laws in New York State are different now. You can file a separation agreement; after one year of living apart either spouse can file for a divorce, with neither judged to be at fault.

"Bill, I'm going to go through with this," I said, knowing that the divorce wasn't going to be easy. "Will you tell Joe that I saw you and that I'm going to divorce him? I don't think he will believe me." Bill agreed to phone Joe the next day. I thanked him and walked out of his office, sad but happy that I had taken the first step.

The next night, the phone rang and I walked into the kitchen to answer it. Bill called, as he promised. "Thank you for calling. No, I hadn't changed my mind," I told him when he asked.

"Joe, Bill wants to tell you something." When Joe walked into the kitchen, I handed him the phone and went back into the living room. From where I sat on the gold-colored, velvet sectional in the living room, I couldn't see the expression on Joe's face when Bill told him. I didn't want to see it. I needed to close off any feelings that I might have. The phone conversation lasted about five minutes.

"So, you want a divorce? You want to break up this empire that we got?" Joe said, when he came back into the living room.

"I told you many times that someday I would leave you. You wouldn't believe me. When the construction business ends for the season and I close the books for the year, I'm going to leave. I'll drive down to Florida and stay in the new house. I need to get away to have time to think this through."

"Remember this, a million for defense, not one cent for tribute!" Joe smirked.

"What is that supposed to mean?"

"It means that I won't give you one red cent if you leave me. That's what it means!"

All through October, November and December, neither Joe nor I talked about what I intended to do. I carried on, inviting the children to the house for the holiday dinners as usual, but I think they knew what was coming.

On January 11, 1981, with my luggage in the trunk of the red Mercedes, Joe and I walked out the door for the two-day drive to Florida. He wouldn't let me drive down alone. He insisted that I take the Mercedes not the Dodge hatchback that I had bought a few months ago for the trip. I didn't like it that Joe still had control over what I did, but because he agreed to a celibate relationship following Bill's phone call, I didn't object.

There were no problems during the trip down or during the few days that Joe stayed at the new house. Amazingly, not once did he pressure me for sex. When I was settling in, we drove to the Sarasota Airport where Joe boarded the plane to return to Buffalo.

I hoped that having a comfortable new home along with the Florida sunshine and warm gulf breezes, would give me a chance to rest and think clearly. With my head full of confusing thoughts, I walked along the beach, under a sky colored red by the sunset. I thought about how it would be if I divorced and how it would be if I continued to stay in the marriage.

My thoughts never were clear about what I would actually do. I needed to make a decision that not only would affect Joe and me, but would affect my adult children as well. A divorce doesn't just involve the husband and wife. It involves the whole family. There will be holidays, celebrations and other family events and I didn't want my children to have to choose between their parents.

I stayed in Florida alone for another few months. The beach was not a place for a woman alone to enjoy the sun or swim. Whenever I tried to relax and enjoy the day, some man would approach me and start a conversation. Luckily, Warm Mineral Springs, a natural, outdoor spa wasn't far from the house. Some say the underground springs is the spot that Ponce de Leon called the "Fountain of Youth." It was the perfect place for a woman alone.

Every morning when I awoke I put on my bikini and cover-up. Then, I packed an apple, a bottle of tonic water and crackers into my straw beach bag, along with a towel, a Mexican serape and a book. That was it; I was set for the day. By nine o'clock in the morning, I was at the entrance of the spa, waiting for it to open. Being the first one to enter gave me the chance to get a lounge chair in my favorite spot, near the far side away from the entrance.

When the Spa closed at five o'clock, I packed my beach bag and drove back to the house. I took a quick shower, blow-dried my hair, put on my make-up and dressed for dinner. That was my daily routine. There was no mail and no phone calls to answer. I liked my new freedom.

The only thing that I didn't like was how I stood out as a woman alone. This was an era where it was frowned upon for a woman to leave her marriage. "How many, please?" asked the hostess, when I walked into a restaurant.

"One," I said, with a guilty smile. I was embarrassed that I was alone. The hostess seated me at a small table, apart from the other diners, making my aloneness feel even more pronounced. It didn't take me long to figure out how to be seated at a table where I blended in with the other diners. "How many, please?"

"Two, my friend is joining me later," I lied. When the waiter came with the wine list, I told him that I was ready to order. "My friend is only joining me for coffee," I lied again.

I'd been in Florida almost a month when Joe phoned me for the first time. He asked if he could fly down so we could celebrate our 25th wedding anniversary together in the Bahamas. "Yes, that would be okay, on one condition—no sex." He agreed.

I had an unusual feeling when I saw Joe walk through the gate at the Sarasota airport. It reminded me of the first time I saw him, when he swaggered into the store where I worked. We got into the Mercedes—Joe behind the wheel with me next to him. He would never let me drive when he was in the car. That wouldn't be macho!

Early the next morning, we boarded the plane for Freeport. We planned on a five-day trip. We were like strangers, plopped down in the middle of a romantic place. This trip was just like all the others we took together— except for the ban on sex. Nothing was ever going to be different. I was sure of that now.

The trip was cut short when my daughter phoned to tell us that there had been a fire in one of the apartments of our building and the tenant died of smoke inhalation. We left on the next flight off the island and Joe returned to Buffalo.

As the days passed, I realized how alone and lonesome I really was. I missed my children, my family and my girlfriends. I thought I could make a new life for myself in Florida, but I wasn't happy being so far away from all the people I loved. I phoned Joe and told him that I was going to drive back to Buffalo to give us another chance. He seemed pleased and asked when I was coming. "I'm leaving tomorrow. I should be there late Saturday night."

I cleaned out the refrigerator, which was practically empty anyway. I put my luggage in the trunk of the Mercedes, locked the door, and began the drive back. For hours, I drove north, listening to the songs of country music by Loretta Lynn and Willie Nelson. The station occasionally broke up with static, but the music remained the same. The tunes were all about broken hearts and lost love.

Continuing my journey north, I was no longer sure of what state I was in. Was it Florida, Georgia or South Carolina? It was as if they were all the same southern landscape. The sun was setting and I decided to stay the night at a Ramada Inn. According to the highway billboard, it was at the next thruway exit. When I checked in, the girl at the desk informed me that I was in South Carolina, just over the border from Georgia.

Early the next morning I continued to drive north. The driving was uneventful until I reached Pennsylvania. In early March the roads in Pennsylvania were slick in some spots. I was crossing over a long bridge, when the driver in the car directly ahead of me slammed on the brakes, causing me to hit my brakes.

The Mercedes had steel-belted, radial tires. When the breaks were applied hard, the tires become like steel blades on ice. My car skidded, hitting the concrete barrier on one side of the bridge, then the concrete barrier on the other side of the bridge. Because this was a bridge on the thruway, the oncoming traffic was separated by a wide grassy median. My car came to a stop on the incline at the end of the bridge. Needless to say, I was quite shaken.

An overland trucker from Consolidated Truck Lines pulled off the road and came to my aid. My car was perched on a slant at the top of the incline. I was pressed against the door on the driver's side, afraid to move. The truck driver carefully opened the door, helping me out. He helped me walk up to the edge of the thruway. Then, went back to my car and carefully, but very slowly, drove it off the incline parking it at the side of the thruway. There, he made sure the dented fenders were clear of the tires in the wheel wells.

I thanked him and assured him that I was okay and able to drive. "Take it easy, little lady. The roads are slippery in these parts." A few deep breaths of the fresh crisp air helped to clear my mind. I got into the car and continued on, arriving in Buffalo around three o'clock in the afternoon.

It was Saturday, of the first week of March, when I unlocked the door and walked into the house. The house was a mess. Newspapers, cardboard take-out coffee cups, and dirty ashtrays littered the living room. Clothes were strewn about the bedroom, and I think the rumpled sheets on the unmade bed were the same sheets I had put on the bed when I left. The house smelled of stale cigarette smoke.

I opened some windows to let the fresh cool air blow through the house. I changed the linens on the bed, threw a load of clothes into the washing machine and got busy washing the kitchen floor, cleaning the bathrooms, vacuuming and dusting as fast as I could. I wanted to surprise Joe with a clean house.

I closed the windows, turned the heat back on, showered and dressed, thinking that Joe and I would go out to dinner when he came home from wherever he was. In the living room, I turned on the radio and listened to relaxing music while I waited. Around seven o'clock, Joe came in the front door. "What happened to the Mercedes?" were the first words out of his mouth.

"I had an accident on an icy bridge in Pennsylvania," I said, continuing to tell him how it happened.

"Good thing you had the Mercedes. If you took the Dodge it would've been smashed." How foolish I was. What made me think Joe would be happy to see me? He didn't even mention how clean the house looked or how nice I looked. "I didn't expect you until late tonight. I've got plans with the boys. I only came home to change my shirt," Joe said, with his innocent little-boy look and a sly smile, adding, "I hope you don't mind?"

Nothing had changed. It was going to be another night when I would be left alone, even after rushing home to be there for him. Did I mind? You bet I did. Did I tell him? No. What would be the use? He wasn't really asking.

After he left the house, I took a book from the walnut secretary in the living room, and sat on the sofa. In a short while, the words blurred. I tried to keep awake, but my eyes began to close and I gave in to the fatigue, dozing off to sleep where I sat.

It was too late to start what had been missing those twenty-five years we were married. I didn't have the feelings a woman should have for her husband. I didn't trust or respect Joe. I didn't love him and I didn't hate him. I had no feelings for him either way. At best, we were just business partners; our conversations were limited to the business. We never talked about current events, my interest in parapsychology, or my dreams for the children's future. I didn't want to continue to live in a marriage where a wrong word became a trap and a false step brought criticism. I felt like I had to be constantly on guard.

Besides, Joe would never tell me the things that I longed to hear. He never told me that he loved me, or that he liked the way I kept the house, or that I was a good cook, or that I did a good job helping him establish and manage the two construction companies. This loveless marriage was dead and I knew it.

"Joe, this marriage isn't working. I don't want to be in this house with you anymore," I said, after a few weeks of the same old routine. "I'm not going back to Florida, I'm going to move into the apartment that I use for my office."

I was surprised that Joe didn't give me a hard time about my decision to move out of the house.

I put my office furniture into storage. Over the next several days, with the help of my daughters and the use of my son's car, which had a hitch, I rented a trailer and moved a twin bedroom set, my walnut secretary and my personal things from the house. I bought a new living room set and what was necessary for me to live in the apartment for the required one-year separation period.

When I put the key in the door, turned the lock and pushed the door open, it was a time of new beginnings for me. The greater part of my life had been defined by my relationship with Joe and my role as a mother. Now, I would be able to freely express my thoughts and opinions. I would be able to set goals for myself.

Joe hired Bill as his lawyer and I used a lawyer who didn't know either Joe or me. I had to do some bargaining with Joe before he would agree to sign the separation papers. I listed all our assets and Joe marked off the ones that I would have to turn over to him and the ones I could keep. His list included the two construction companies, the half-acre construction yard with concrete block building and all the construction equipment. Also, he kept the money from the accounts receivable, the investments we had in the stock market, the twelve-unit apartment building, the Mercedes and anything he wanted from the house.

My list included the family home, the new home in Florida, the Dodge and the cash in the bank. "Who gets the electric can opener?" Joe joked, as he signed the agreement. Joe wanted to stay in the house that he signed over to me until he could have a new house built for him self. He told me that I could stay, rent-free, in the apartment building. I wasn't happy about that, but I didn't have a choice.

A few months passed and I was beginning to adjust to this new way of living, when Joe phoned and asked me to come to the house. I didn't mind if he wanted to talk with me. I wasn't heartless. I wasn't ending the marriage because I was in love with someone else. I just didn't want to be married anymore. On the drive to the house, I rehearsed my little speech, asking Joe to tell me he loved me. I wanted to get it out before I fumbled it.

When I walked into the house. Joe was sitting in his brown leather chair with his feet up on the ottoman and his trumpet in his lap, as he usually did on Sunday afternoon. I sat on the couch and looked directly into his eyes, as I spoke. "Joe, first, let me tell you what I have to say. You know you beat me when I was pregnant and you know you ruptured my eardrum. I need to hear the words that say you're sorry. And, you never said the words "I love you." I need to hear the words that say you love me. If you say it, I'll come back and we won't get divorced," I said softly, holding back the tears.

Joe lowered his head and looked down at his trumpet. There was a few minutes of silence. I thought that Joe was thinking how to tell me what I needed to hear. Then he looked at me and said quietly, "Come on, let's go upstairs." I was speechless. I know it had been a long time since we had sex, but I couldn't believe he could be so insensitive. I was asking him to do his part in saving the marriage and all he wanted from me was sex. No, that couldn't be it. Maybe I was wrong. Maybe he wanted to tell me romantically upstairs in the bedroom.

I gave him the benefit of my doubt and followed him up the stairs. Joe hurriedly undressed and got into bed. I slowly unzipped my sleeveless pink sundress, letting it fall to the floor. I stepped out of my pink panties and unhooked my pink bra. I stood for a moment, letting Joe fill his eyes with my naked body, which was tanned everywhere but in the places that the bikini had covered.

Joe lying on his back, smiled at me. I waited for him to say the words that would tell me he loved me. There was just silence. I slowly moved into the bed, with my knees on either side of Joe's naked body. With my back straight, I raised my arms and lifted my long auburn hair, holding it in an upsweep. Our bodies not yet touching, I smiled, saying softly, "Tell me you love me."

"You have a beautiful body," Joe said, reaching up and cupping my breasts in his hands.

"Is that all you have to say?" I said seductively. Joe just grinned. "Take a good look, because this is the last time you'll ever see it." I got off the bed and put my clothes back on, as Joe watched without saying a word. I walked down the stairs and out the door. It was clear that I really needed to go through with the divorce. Taking a deep breath, I drove away and didn't look back, as I wiped a tear from my eye.

CHAPTER TEN
Romance vs. Research

The hollow sounding beat of a lonely heart echoes a sad rhythm as it mourns for love—a love that doesn't have to ask, "Do I have to give up me to love you?"

I TOLD MYSELF THAT I was strong and didn't need a man. I told myself that I was independent and my own woman. The separation and divorce wasn't easy; it was a hard, emotionally draining process. I often stayed awake at night feeling hungry, but it wasn't a hunger for food. It was a hunger for love, both physical and emotional. I wanted a warm body and a warm heart to lie next to me in bed. Someone I could love and give myself to. I longed for love. I wanted to experience sex as meaning something. I wanted to experience it as an act of love.

I was forty-three and he was fifty-five years old when our eyes first met. It was on a Saturday in July, at a hotel in Toronto, Canada. We were just two of the many people enjoying the late afternoon sun as we reclined in a poolside chaise. I was in a black bikini that I bought when I vacationed on Catalina Island one summer. He was wearing Speedo swim trunks. In the air was the scent of masculinity, a magnetism that drew my attention toward him.

He was gorgeous. His tanned skin almost glowed. He was slim and fit, with a body that looked well exercised. His blond hair with gray at the temples added sophistication to his manly appearance. He glanced my way and noticed that I was looking at him. When I smiled, he got up from his lounge chair and walked over to me. As he came closer, I felt the power in his self-confidence. I knew this meeting was going to lead to a fabulous romance.

"May I sit here, or are you reserving it for someone?" he asked, pointing to the empty chaise next to me.

"No, I'm alone. I don't think we've met. I'm Nancy," I said, reaching out my hand.

"Allow me to introduce myself, then; my name is James," he said, turning my hand and gently touching his lips to the back, not shaking it as I thought he would.

"May I ask why a beautiful woman like you is sitting here alone without a man to fend off a bachelor playboy like me?"

"I'm in Toronto on business. I come here on weekends and will be leaving tomorrow for my home in Buffalo." I replied quickly.

"Yes, darling, but why are you alone? Where is your man?"

"My agent doesn't stay at the hotel with me; he just makes the arrangements for me to stay here on weekends while he drives me around to the appointments he made. I consult with and advise various business people in the Toronto area.

"Your agent? You're not married, then?"

"No, I don't want to be married!" I replied in a matter-of-fact tone. After a brief moment of silence, I returned to my quieter self and said, "I'm sorry, I didn't mean to be so sharp with you."

"What businesses do you consult for?" James asked, changing the subject because he could tell the word "marriage" upset me.

"Owners of horses at the Woodbine Racetrack, the La Bastille Restaurant in Mississauga, a restaurant in Oakfield and other places although I have no idea of their location. I don't usually know where I'm going until I get there. I haven't any appointments for today, but I'm staying here anyway because my room has already been paid for. Why are you staying at the hotel, James?"

"My home is north of Toronto. It's more convenient for me to stay in the city when I have business with my lawyers." Seeing that I was interested in his conversation, he added, "I own fifty thousand acres of land boarding the northern shores of Lake Ontario. I lease it to two mining companies. Unfortunately, they haven't restored some of the land, in accordance with our contract."

The conversation continued with the normal pleasantries about the beautiful weather, the hotel service and the food in the dining room, becoming more personal as we talked. I told him that I was divorced and had a married daughter and another daughter and son who lived on their own. Anyone could see that we were attracted to each other. I was instantly charmed by James, but tried to keep my feelings hidden.

"If you're not dining with anyone this evening, perhaps you would like to join me for dinner. Shall we say, about eight? I'll meet you in the lounge, my darling." He reached for my hand and, again, touched his lips to the back and walked away, leaving me sitting there like some dumbstruck schoolgirl.

"Yes, I would like that," I said slowly, even though he was out of hearing range.

That evening, after a refreshing shower, I dressed in a black evening dress and black-strapped heels. I put my hair in a French twist and applied just enough cosmetics to give me color and sensuality, but a natural look. I dabbed my wrists with Chanel No. 5 and took the elevator to the first floor lounge, where James was sitting at the bar, dressed in a cream- colored suit with a fresh white shirt opened at the collar with no tie. He was sipping a glass of Lillet with an orange twist. He stood up and smiled when he saw me.

Reaching for my hand, he kissed it and held the back of the barstool, as I took a seat. He nodded to the bartender and the bartender set a glass of the Lillet aperitif on a paper coaster in front of me. "Darling, you look like a princess."

"Thank you," was all I could bring myself to say. Calling me darling again and now princess, I felt like a dumbstruck schoolgirl.

In the elegant dining room, the waiter opened a bottle of wine and we dined to the sounds of soft piano music while we enjoyed dinner conversation, getting to know more about each other. James told me that he and his sister had come to Canada after World War II, adding that he made his fortune in real estate and the stock market. "Women were always available to me, so I thought it would be easy to find a good woman when I was ready to settle down. I focused on hard work and making my fortune Now, I find that a good woman is not so easy to find."

"Are you saying that you haven't known many women?"

"Oh, my darling—no—I am not saying that. I have known many, many woman, perhaps hundreds. That is why I am called a playboy. What I am saying is that I am no longer focusing on making my fortune. I am content to be with only one woman." He reached across the table for my hand, smiled and said, "That's everything about me. Now, tell me about yourself."

James seemed genuinely interested when he learned that I used my higher sensory perception in my business consultations and that I was a paranormal researcher. I told him about some of my experience, including what happened that past spring, when my agent and I attended the kick-off luncheon for the Canadian March of Dimes at Butterfield's Restaurant in Toronto.

"A young man with his lower leg in a cast, walked up to the microphone with the aid of crutches. With a deep Canadian accent, he gave a pep talk. I assumed he was one of the young people the organization had helped. When he finished the talk, he sat down at the round table next to me where I sat next to a woman from the press. I gave him a smile and continued my conversation.

After the lunch, we listened to the closing talk and were told that each person attending the luncheon was welcome to take one of the hockey safety helmets that had been placed on the tables.

The news reporter, sitting next to me, asked if the young man would sign her helmet. He did and then he picked up my helmet and signed it. He stood up, put his crutch under his arm and walked away. 'You forgot your helmet,' the news reporter said when I got up to walk away.

I told her that I don't want it; she could take it. After all, she was the reason the young man wrote his name on it, ruining it. Later, I found out that the young man was Wayne Gretzky, the world-famous hockey player."

When I finished telling my story, James said, "Darling, you are like a little lamb who is lost in the woods. You need a shepherd to look after you."

After dinner we rode the elevator up to my floor and James invited me to visit him at his home, handing me a calling card with his address. I agreed to see him again on the following Sunday after my consultations. I tucked the card with his address into my black clutch-purse. The elevator stopped and we got off. With my arm in his, he walked me to my door. Before putting the key in, I looked at James and wondered if he expected me to invite him into the room Spoken words weren't necessary; his thoughts were communicated through his eyes and his smile. The erotic thoughts that were projected into my mind told me what would happen if I let it. "Good night, James, and thank you for a lovely dinner."

With a tilt of his head and a smile, he took the clue that our dinner date had ended outside in the hall. "Good night, Nancy, darling." Taking my hand, he did more than just touch his lips to the back of it. He turned my hand palm up and kissed it with a tickle of his tongue on my palm. This made me flustered and I could feel my face blush, as he raised his head and smiled seductively.

I had no control over my expression. I smiled back, put the key in the lock, opened the door and hurried inside, closing it quickly, before I lost any more control, or gave in to the passion I felt rising within me. Everything about the evening was like a fairy tale. I was a princess and he was prince charming. The night was filled with dreams of being held in his arms while we made love.

Sunday morning, I awoke from a blissful sleep, but I didn't feel rested; I felt giddy and excited. I hurried about, packing up and when I left the hotel I felt like I was floating on air. The long drive back to Buffalo didn't seem as long as it usually did. All through the following week, I went about my usual activities, but I couldn't stop thinking about James and the past Saturday evening.

The following Sunday morning, following my weekend work in Toronto, instead of heading back to Buffalo, I left the hotel and drove to a town north of Toronto. After an hour of searching for the address on the card James gave me, I gave up and drove back to a little strip of shops that I had passed. Handing the card to one of the shopkeepers, I asked if he could help me find James' house.

"Yes, I know the house. Go back to the town of Kleinburg, stay on the main road and you can't miss it."

"I already traveled the length of the main road, but I didn't see a house," I said, in frustration

"Look for two brick pillars, turn into the driveway, go to the end and you'll find the house."

I followed the shopkeeper's directions. They led me to a huge red brick house. It was more than just a house. It was quite impressive with beautifully landscaped grounds and a pond near the entrance. A fountain, spilling water into a concrete shell was at the end of the long driveway. A row of fir trees lined one side of the brick house; beautiful gardens with flowering shrubs and a variety of roses were on the other side.

James was expecting me because I phoned him from the shop before I left. He was standing outside on the steps. I pulled up to the front of the house and parked. He walked over and opened the car door. How charming! His attitude was easy and carefree, and his smiling eyes awoke something in me that made my breasts swell under my white, silk blouse.

"This isn't what I would call a house; it looks like a mansion!" I said, glancing around, noticing a cluster of tiny purple grapes on the arbor along the far side of the house.

"You're impressed?" he asked, adding, "Let me show you around. I have thirty-six acres here, but of course you won't see all of that." Under the bright blue sky with a scattering of fluffy, white clouds, we walked the grounds for a few minutes. Noticing that my high heels were sinking into the grass, James suggested we return to the pavement and go into the house, where I could "freshen up," as he put it.

He opened the door and we entered into a large area with steps leading down to a wine cellar and a few steps leading up to another door. He opened that door and we were in a hallway with an antique, full-length, mirrored bench coat rack. Indicating the room to the left, James said, "My office, darling." In his office were a large desk, a brown leather chair and a matching sofa. Next to that stood a green, yellow-and-brown-plaid, wingback chair. The room had a distinct masculine look. Another room off the hallway entrance was a lavatory. The sink had a gold-plated faucet in the shape of a swan. James left me while I freshened up.

The kitchen was the third room off the hallway. It was a large, sunny room with a round, oak table and chairs that sat by a bay window, overlooking a lawn of mowed grass that seemed to go on forever. Off the kitchen was a dining room with a black walnut, china cabinet with matching table and chairs. The chairs were upholstered in white and gold brocade. The chandelier of Baccarat crystal hung low over the table, giving the room a touch of elegance.

The dining room opened to the living room, where ivory-colored drapes hung from the ceiling on each side of the sheers that spread across the center half of the room, shielding the room from the afternoon sun. A large urn filled with fresh flowers stood on a white, marble pillar near the staircase leading up to the second floor. Across from the wall of windows there was a large hall and the front entrance. I thought the door we entered was the main entrance, but obviously I was wrong. The living room had two Duncan sofas, upholstered in an old-world design of gold-and-brown brocade on a beige background, almost the same shade of beige as the carpets in the office, dining room and living room. I couldn't help noticing the large brass lamps with the silk bell-shaped lampshades.

James pulled out one of the dining room chairs and I sat down. On the table was a plate of Brie and Camembert cheese; another plate held assorted crackers. "I prefer St. Gabriel Liebfraumilch, but if you'd rather have Chardonnay I can get that for you."

"Really, no thank you I wouldn't know the difference. I usually drink red wine—Chianti or Cabernet Sauvignon."

"Then this will be a new experience for you," James said, as he poured the Liebfraumilch into the ruby-and-gold crystal goblets. As I saw a woman do in a movie once, I slowly ran my finger around the wine glass before I took a sip. Leaning back into the chair, I crossed my legs and took another sip. We talked and flirted, enjoying the cheese and wine. There were sparkles in his eyes, radiance in his smile, and warmth in his laughter. I was delighted just being with him.

Without having eaten any breakfast that morning, the wine affected me rather quickly. I wanted James to take me in his arms and make love to me the way I dreamed he would. I knew I had to leave without finishing the second glass, or I would cave in to his charm. "Thank you for a delightful time. I have to leave now, I have a lot of things to do back in Buffalo," I said, getting up to leave.

"We must do this again, darling." Calling me darling again made me smile in a silly way. I gave out a little sigh, as I walked ahead of him through the kitchen and large hall, and down the few steps to the outside.

After a few deep breaths of the fresh air, I began to come to my senses. "What am I doing here? I don't want to get involved with a man," I told myself. "Yes you do," I answered back. What a surprise! I was having a mental conversation with myself, as I walked to the car.

Before I realized it, the scent of his cologne invaded my senses, as his blond hair streaked with gray came inches from my face and his warm breath blew by my ear. I reached up and put my arms around his neck and welcomed his sweet kiss, gentle but with a passion that set us both on fire.

"Let me make love to you, darling; let me caress you, ravish you, delight you as you've never been before," he whispered in my ear, and I felt the hardening between his loins. My legs were losing their strength and I was about to crumble to the ground right there by the open door of my car.

A car's horn, honking loud and fast, broke the spell. It was coming from a silver-colored convertible coming down the driveway. "Hello James," a pretty blonde called out as she pulled up beside us.

"Jenina!" James said, with surprise. "What are you doing here?"

"I thought I would stop by to say hello, but I see you're busy. Maybe another time," she said, spinning the wheels of the car as she drove off in a huff.

"I'm sorry, darling; Jenina is a woman who doesn't know when it's over."

"Are you sure it's over? She doesn't seem to think so."

"Darling, believe me the last time we were together was over a year ago. She just won't go away. Don't let her bother you. She means nothing to me."

"I'm not bothered. I have no claims on you."

"Please, darling, you seem upset, but don't be." With that said, James kissed the back of my hand and I got into my car.

"James, I have to leave now, I'll be in Toronto next weekend, I'll come back then for another visit, if that's all right with you.

"I'll be waiting for you, darling."

I blew him a kiss as I pulled away and drove through the brick pillars, turning left onto the main road.

When I got back to Buffalo, I immediately phoned my agent and told him not to make any appointments for me because I had other matters to take care of. All of that week, I couldn't stop thinking about James and his continental ways.

I was tired of being a "pure spirit." With complete abandonment of my personality, I delighted in my thoughts. I couldn't stop thinking of how close I came to giving myself to him. I knew the next time we were together I would let him make love to me.

When Saturday morning came, I drove across the Peace Bridge into Canada for the drive to Toronto, then to the little strip of shops near Kleinburg, where I phoned James. "Hello, James, this is Nancy. May I come to your house this morning?" I asked boldly, without a tinge of guilt for what I was willing to do.

"Of course, darling, you can come anytime. Where are you? Are you in Toronto?"

"No, I'm in Kleinburg, nearby."

"Come, come, I'll be waiting for you."

When I pulled into the driveway, James was standing on the steps waiting for me. He opened my car door, just as he had the week before and I handed him my overnight bag, saying, "Just in case you invite me to stay the night, I had come prepared."

"Can this be my princess talking? What happened to the little lamb who was lost in the woods?" He laughed, delighted that I suggested I would stay overnight.

"You told me you had five bedrooms upstairs, and I was welcome to stay in your house instead of the hotel. I decided I would accept your offer. By the way, I'm not working this weekend so I don't have to leave until Sunday afternoon. Is that all right with you?" I asked as we headed into the house.

"Of course, darling, go upstairs and choose the bedroom you want to sleep in. I'll tell my sister that you'll be staying. Maria and her husband, Phillip, live in the other wing. She looks after the house and buys the groceries. I know you don't eat red meat. I'll have her get a nice salmon for you. I remember how much you enjoyed the salmon at the restaurant." James handed me my overnight bag. I carried it up the stairs, which were carpeted in the same light beige carpet that covered the second floor.

Only three of the five rooms were furnished as bedrooms. An assortment of rifles and hunting equipment lay about in the fourth room and the fifth room was completely empty. The master bedroom, I reasoned, was where James slept. The windows had white sheers with floor-to-ceiling red velvet drapes aside the sheers. The king-size bed, with a black-leather padded headboard was covered with a red, velvet spread that matched the drapes. On either side of the bed, the night tables matched the dark wood of the dresser and chest of drawers that stood next to the mirrored, sliding doors of the closet. The walls of the bedroom were covered in silk white wallpaper and the bathroom walls off the bedroom were covered in wallpaper that had a red-velvet-flocked design. This was definitely a playboy's bedroom!

In the second bedroom, I set my overnight bag on the maple bench at the foot of the double-size bed, covered with a floral print coverlet with matching bed skirt. The windows were covered with white sheers and a second set of ruffled sheers pulled to the side with white, twisted-satin drawbacks. On the maple dresser that matched the headboard and night tables, was a silver-plated, hand mirror, brush and comb set. This bedroom was very feminine compared to the other. I wondered who slept in this bed. Letting my imagination run wild, I envisioned the faces of many pretty women. I even had flashes of them lying naked on the sheets with James lying naked next to them.

With my overnight bag in hand, I walked down the hall to the bedroom with twin-size beds. Each bed had a navy-blue down comforter and feather pillow. I decided to sleep in that room. Taking my sundry bag from my overnight bag, I went into the hall bathroom, and put them on the dressing table near the sink then, went downstairs to the kitchen where James stood by the sink, opening a bottle of wine.

"Did you find a bedroom you like? Let me assure you darling, I'm not a wolf. Anything that happens between us will happen because you are willing. I have no reason to force myself on a woman."

After enjoying a cold glass of Liebfraumilch and a few minutes conversation about Canada, we got into James' Buick and rode around the back roads of the Canadian countryside. We stopped at a quaint little restaurant for a light lunch and then James drove us to a museum where he bought a black soapstone figurine that was hand-carved by the people of the north. He wanted me to have a souvenir of our first full day together. Back at his house, I sipped another glass of Liebfraumuilch while James prepared our dinner.

Maybe it was because I yearned to be affirmed as a desirable woman. Maybe it was because I hadn't slept with a man since my divorce, in what seemed like a lifetime ago. Maybe it was James with his sophisticated, charming, continental ways. Maybe it was the Liebfraumilch wine that James served with the broiled salmon dinner. Whatever it was I didn't care. I was ready for romance.

While James put the dishes in the dishwasher, I went upstairs to change into my lavender nightgown and negligee. James came up the stairs and went into his bedroom, as I was leaving the bathroom.

Although, I was willing, I was still a little nervous when I walked into the master bedroom. James was sitting on the edge of the bed, wearing only his briefs. It surprised me to discover that a sexually aware woman could still have the state of mind of a virgin. The feelings of the young, shy girl that I had been were still with me.

"Darling, you look a little apprehensive. Let me relax you." James reached into the bedside table and brought out a blue, bottle of Nivea body lotion. He laid it on the bed, stood up and slid the negligee off my shoulders, letting it fall to the floor. Then, he slid the spaghetti straps of my nightgown and let it fall around my ankles in a pile of lavender softness. In the light of the full moon shining through the sheers, James threw back the red velvet spread.

I got into his bed where I lay face down on the smooth white sheet. The touch of his hands on my bare skin made me tingle from the top of my head down to my toes. I knew he sensed what I was feeling, as his hands moved down to my lower back and then onto my thighs.

Gently, he turned me over. I was lying on my back when he put his finger to my lips, slightly parting them, I looked into his eyes as his mouth came down sweetly on mine and he put his tongue in my mouth. I had never been kissed like that before! He took his time as he kissed my nipples, then my belly and my thighs. Our bodies were no longer limited to the outside touch. He gently put himself inside me. I could never have imagined such a feeling.

When I lost my shyness, James took great delight in my responsiveness to him. My heart was pounding, I was gasping and moaning and then my whole body exploded. With sweet surrender, I was taken to ecstasy and rapture. Did other people do this? Did other women feel this way when they made love? I was delightfully in awe of the way I felt. Could he do this to me again? The answer was, "Yes"—and he did!

We lay in bed until late Sunday morning, my face still flushed with the passion of the blissful evening. After showering and dressing into a skirt and blouse, I swept my hair to one side, holding it back with a mother-of-pearl hairclip.

We took our cups of coffee and walked outside to the front of the estate, sat on the bench and watched the ducks swim about in the clear water.

Returning to the house, James made us a breakfast of crepes with fresh strawberries. We ate on the round, oak table near the kitchen window, set with white linen napkins, china plates and the best silver. "Why don't you stay?" he asked, brushing back the hair that had fallen free from the clip. His deep masculine voice was so appealing. But, I had to return to my house in Buffalo.

I told my agent that I wouldn't be working in Canada any more. He wasn't pleased, but he had to accept my decision. My time was now one hundred percent mine to do with as I wished and I spent most of the remaining summer days with James.

On a Saturday, I arrived at his estate early in the morning because we were going to spend the weekend on James' private island on a lake in the Muskoka area of Canada. I drove down the long driveway and parked my car. After a hello kiss, we got into James' Buick, which had been packed with provisions for the trip north. "You will enjoy the island, darling, I have a little house there; at night, the stars are so close, you can almost touch them.

When we arrived at the marina where his boat was docked, James took the bags of provisions from his car and put them on the boat. I carried our travel bags and waited for James to take them from me and help me aboard. Foolishly, I wore a skirt and high heel shoes—not the right mode of dress for boarding a boat.

James put the key in and started the engine. As we left the pier and headed into the calm water of the lake, I told myself, "This can't be true; it's like a scene from a movie." Huge pines and white birch trees lined most of the shores. There were only a few houses scattered on the hills among the trees.

As we came closer to his island, I could see a little bit of his house peeking from behind the branches of the fir trees. On the backside of the island were a dock, a boathouse and a helicopter pad. James slowed the boat and glided it into the dock next to the boathouse. He shut off the engine and we got out. James carried the provisions and I carried the travel bags up the path to the house.

When James told me he had a house on the island, I thought it was a cottage or a cabin, not a ranch-style house with a porch deck running across the front. We walked up the few steps at the end of the deck and James unlocked the door. "After you, my darling," he said, pushing the door open.

"James, this is beautiful." I walked in finding a stone fireplace reaching to the ceiling, built into the corner of the room. This room was the dining room. In the other corner, near the door, were curved bench seats upholstered in green leather, circling a round table. A long row of windows along the backs of the seats gave a panoramic view of the lake.

To the left was a room with an entertainment unit that held a record player and records. The unit also had a bottle of cognac and four brandy snifters, set on a round tray. Across from the unit was a sofa, upholstered in the same plaid as the wingback chair in James' office. The two rooms were one big space, without a dividing wall. Near the corner fireplace, a door led to the master bedroom. Off the other room, two doors, one on either side of the entertainment unit led into two more bedrooms.

On the left at the far end of the house, were a bathroom and a kitchen. The kitchen also had green leather upholstered seats circling a round table. Above the back of the seats was a row of windows, just like in the room at the other end of the ranch house. The house had running water that came from a pipe placed deep in the lake

There were other islands on the lake, but this was one of the few that had a sandy beach. I didn't bring my bikini, but that didn't matter because people couldn't see me, unless they were in a boat—there were no boats on the lake that afternoon. I undressed, wrapped myself in a towel and we walked down to the beach. I put my foot in to test the water. "It's so cold, I don't think I can swim in it," I said, running back to where James stood with a towel wrapped around the waist of his naked body.

"It's cold, darling, because the lake is fed by an underground stream." Dropping his towel, he grabbed my hand and pulled me after him. I let go of my towel and we both rushed into the cold water. He grabbed me and gave me a quick kiss, then took my hand again and pulled me back to shore.

The sun was still overhead as we dried off, spread our towels on the sand and lay side by side enjoying the warm breeze blowing over our naked bodies. James had told me there was a little town on the far side of the lake. I looked across the lake, where dark green fir trees circled the shore, but I couldn't see anything. There was nothing in the world except us, and that moment.

I can't blame it on the wine, because we didn't have any with our lunch. I can't say we were in love, because we didn't really know much about each other. I have to admit, it was pure sexual desire that made me want him. We lay there, naked on the sandy shore, kissing and enjoying each other's body. The new pleasures combined with warm breezes made me fall into a slumber as I relaxed in the safety of his strong arms.

The summer was so romantic. I felt as if we were the only two people on the earth. With James, I felt vibrant and alive, radiating with the pleasure of just being with him. On the warm summer nights we drank wine on the porch deck in the glow of the moonlight and listened to the water lap at the rocks along the shore.

We made love by the candlelight that glowed inside the glass globes, sitting on the night tables at the sides of the bed. I was lost in the moments of pleasure as my back arched and the flash of lightening rushed through my body. Totally spent of all energy, I drifted off to sleep in James' arms as I gazed out the bedroom window. With the moon high in the sky, it gave the room a soft romantic glow.

As summer came to an end, we spent our last day on the island. A gentle rain kept up through the day. James and I didn't mind the soft raindrops on our naked body, as we lay together on the beach one last time. It was very sensual, until the air turned cold.

Back inside the ranch house, James and I put on our warm clothes. That summer I added slacks and deck shoes to my wardrobe and now I was glad that I had. James poured us a snifter of cognac then, put some logs into the fireplace and lit a fire. We watched the leaping flames of the burning logs as we let the cognac warm us. The house had electricity, but that night we dined by candlelight and the glow of the logs in the fireplace.

My family and friends all knew that I was in a relationship with a man who lived in Canada. How could they not know? I was up there most of the time that fall and winter. Besides being a great lover, James was a great dancer and we dined in some of the best restaurants in Toronto. Most importantly, he made me laugh. James never asked me any questions about my childhood. He didn't pressure me about the circumstances of the divorce from Joe. The only comment he ever made was, "Joe was a fool to let you go, darling. He will see it isn't easy to find a good woman."

In the spring, my oldest daughter wanted to meet James. She rode up to Toronto with me. While my daughter, James and I walked the grounds, to my surprise, James told my daughter, "I'm in love with your mother." I was relieved when my daughter didn't respond. I didn't want James to think I would consider being married again.

Throughout most of the summer, James was kept busy with legal matters. I focused my attention on researching the paranormal. I leased two rooms in an office building in a suburb of Buffalo. One room I used as an office and the other I used as a classroom. I traveled, giving and attending lectures. One lecture I attended was by Dr. Gina Cermimara, an American author in the field of parapsychology. After her lecture, I introduced myself and she joined me for lunch, where among other topics, we discussed Electronic Voice Phenomena (EVP). I was interested in recording a spirit voice on the recorder that I used during my investigations.

In the fall of 1982, while James was hunting moose on his land on the northern shores of lake Ontario, I investigated haunted houses, made guest appearances on radio and television and was interviewed by the media

A newspaper article regarding my work as a psychic investigator appeared in the *Buffalo News* .It caught the attention of a faculty member at the State University of New York at Buffalo. He phoned my office on a Monday and asked if I would like to be interviewed on *Spotlight on Progress,* his radio show. I agreed, asking when and where? He told me the show would be taped on a Thursday night and aired on a Sunday morning.

He phoned back the next day, asking some questions about my research. I answered and we ended the conversation. The next day, he phoned again. "Why do you keep calling me?" I asked.

"I want to be sure that you're not microphone-shy, and I would like you to 'psych in' and give me some information about my personal life, if you can."

"Don't worry, I'm more than capable of doing a half-hour program, and I'll write down a few things about your very personal life and bring it to the station tomorrow."

Thursday evening, I dressed in a lavender knit dress and drove to the Rand Building in Lafayette Square. I was signing in when a man entered the building and the security guard said, "Hi, Dr. Canfield." I looked up and saw a muscular man with a strong face and kind eyes. He was handsome in a rugged sort of way. He reminded me of my father when he was younger. "Hello, I'm Allan Canfield, and you must be Nancy," he said, recognizing me from my photo in a *Buffalo News* article that had been recently published.

"Yes, I am," I answered, reaching my hand out to shake his. We rode the elevator to the recording studio on the seventeenth floor. In the studio, I sat back in the chair, crossed my legs and we began the interview. Dr. Canfield introduced me to the listeners and then he asked me the first question. My answer was more like an educational lecture. I went on and on talking, because I thought he wanted me to talk. After all, he did phone my office three times, saying he wanted to be sure I could talk.

"Excuse me, but I forgot what the question was that I asked you," he finally interrupted. "Before the show Nancy gave me some information about my private life. The information she gave me turned out to be extremely accurate. She is a psychic-sensitive and I think an authentic one." With that said, Dr. Canfield ended the show.

Taking my black Calvin Klein coat from where I placed it on the hall coat-rack, he held it for me, while I slipped my arms into the sleeves. Turning around, I pulled the belt tight around my waist and looked up at where he was standing in front of me. I was caught off guard as Dr. Canfield's eyes looked into mine for a brief second. The mutual attraction was undeniable. His gentleness and manly strength accounted for my immediate deep attraction. We rode the elevator down to the lobby and he walked me to my car.

The second time I saw Dr. Canfield was a few weeks later. He was at the television studio, where I was being interviewed on *Open Rap,* a Sunday morning program. My inner knowing told me that he was a man I could fall in love with and I didn't want to. I was happy with my new freedom and enjoyed the drives to visit with James whenever I chose.

Soon after I turned my attention back to researching the paranormal, I noticed that James began to do a lot of talking about our future together. "I know how attached you are to your dining room set. We can bring it up here and store it in one of the outer buildings," and, "Of course, darling, I will pay the bills; you will only have to pay for your lipstick. Your family and friends can come here to visit. They may enjoy Canada Wonderland."

On a Saturday when I was with James, he said, "You're still a little lamb, lost in the woods. Be mine, marry me and let me take care of you." He led me into the dining room. On the table was a glass bowl with green moss-covered-sand that the florist made up for the occasion. A little, plastic lamb stood among several tiny trees. Around the lamb's neck was hung a diamond ring. Looking at the ring, I thought about his proposal and how marriage to him and living in Canada would change my life. Although James had attributes, which I admired and respected—attributes that allowed me to surrender myself to him—I had to refuse his proposal. "It's a beautiful ring, but I can't accept it. I told you, I never want to be married again."

James reached in, took the ring out of the bowl and put it in my hand. "You can't refuse me twice in one day, darling. Keep the ring. I had it made for you." Giving me a gentle kiss on the forehead, he turned and walked away.

"James, are you angry with me?"

"No, darling, I shouldn't have surprised you like that. Come, have some lunch and wine; we will talk later."

My Italian girlfriend, Lila, didn't understand why I would refuse his proposal. She knew James could provide for my social, sexual, and financial needs. However, I hadn't told her about the strings attached to the proposal. James was fluent in German and three Slavic languages but I wasn't—I only spoke a little French and Italian. Every year, James traveled back to Europe, staying for several weeks in the town where his mother was still living. I would have to travel there with him. "Darling, you don't have to go with me, but if you don't, I can't promise that I won't be with another woman."

Leaving the United States and living in Canada also bothered me. I would be far from my family, friends and work. I had waited twenty-five years to be my own woman. I enjoyed my freedom and didn't want to give it up. After a few more months of seeing James, I began to worry that I might reconsider and agree to marry him. With that thought always on my mind, I gradually ended the relationship. I had the key to both his house and his heart. In the early spring I kissed James goodbye and gave back the key to his house.

I continued my studies at the University, taking courses in Sociology, Psychology, Cultural Anthropology, Interpersonal Communication, Women in Contemporary Society, Issues in Nutrition, Creative Writing and Public Speaking. These studies would aid me in researching the world of the paranormal.

I also discovered other methods and aids in researching claims of haunted houses. I used three questionnaires. The first was a Subjective Paranormal Experience Questionnaire (SPEQ). It was a fifteen-page questionnaire regarding any and all paranormal experiences, asking to explain what, when, where and how many times the subjects claimed to have experienced paranormal events.

The second was the Inventory of Childhood Memories and Imaginings (ICMI). It followed the guidelines of S.C. Wilson, PhD. and T.X. Barber, PhD. This inventory gave me insight about correlations between their childhood imaginings, and their paranormal claims. The third was a twenty-four page Neuropsychological Questionnaire.

Periodically, I appeared as a guest on *Night Call,* a three-hour talk show. John Otto hosted the radio program. One night in October, he broadcast the show live from a house that was claimed to be haunted. My two assistants, Linda, a tall, attractive blonde and Brenda, a tall, attractive brunette, came with me. We three were often referred to as *"Charlie's Angels"*.

Brenda recorded the sessions on a standard battery-operated tape recorder, to be transcribed at a later date. Linda took the photographs. She used a 35mm camera with a 400 speed, black and white, infrared film. I won't go into details of that case, but I will tell you that John Otto was surprised to receive a greeting from his Aunt Elizabeth, who was among the spirits that came through and—the camera captured ghost-like white forms.

Another time, when I was at the station doing John Otto's radio show, one of the callers to the program was a woman I'll call Laura. She related a story of strange things happening in her home on the West Side. Laura had a priest bless the house with holy water, hoping to put an end to the disturbances, but they continued. "Would you please help me?" she asked. I could tell by the sound of her voice that she was really troubled. I told her to call my office for an appointment and I would try to help her. She phoned the next day and we set the date for the investigation.

At five o'clock the following Friday, I locked the office door and headed home to prepare for the evening investigation. Fieldwork required a different manor of dress from my usual skirt and high-heels—the Leroy Case taught me that!

Before leaving to meet my assistants, I showered and dressed in black slacks, a white blouse, put on my white tennis shoes and took twenty minutes to meditate, asking for guidance and protection.

I drove to the West Side and parked the car across from the cape-cod-style house. I turned off the engine and waited for Brenda and Linda. It was a little before seven o'clock. The sun had already set and a cold rain was falling, but it was still warm for late November. As I waited, with the car window down a crack, I listened for any noises in the neighborhood. There weren't any. It was absolutely still outside, except for the faint sound of the falling rain.

When Brenda and Linda arrived, they parked behind me. We took our equipment and walked up the steps to the front door and rang the doorbell. A small, gray-haired woman, whom I presumed to be Laura, opened the door. Beside her stood her husband, Bob, a gray-haired medium-build man who later proudly stated that he was an ex-Marine. They were the only people living in the house. In the living room, Brenda turned on the tape recorder and Linda snapped some photographs. I opened my briefcase, took out a pen and a questioner and began the interview. All questions referred to periods during which they were not under the influence of alcohol, nonprescription drugs, or an anesthetic. In a short while, I came to the conclusion that these two people didn't seem to be craving attention or publicity. They had good relationships with friends and relatives and were both happily employed.

[The following is taken from my transcripts of the investigation]
Laura's Report For three or four months my husband and I experienced a horrible odor like old blood, ammonia and urine. It came at night, in our bedroom and down the hall, and stayed for an hour to most of the night. It would go from one side of the room to the other or just hover

from the ceiling halfway down to the floor. Nothing could discourage it from moving. We fanned it, walked through it and pleaded with it, but to no avail. I could smell it, I could taste it and I knew the odor was coming. It tasted just the way it smelled. It was old blood, ammonia and urine. It came every night for nearly four months without fail.Before the attempt was made to rid our house of the odor, I was standing on the other side of our bedroom while others in the room were away from me. The flesh on my face drew down as if by suction. The hair at the back of my neck bristled and my arms became leaden. At the same time, I turned ice cold and started to taste the odor. I stayed cold until the odor was gone, along with the spirits; then, and only then, did I feel warm again. The air in our room became sweet and clear again.

Bob's Report I've had the experience or feeling of having someone in bed with me. I could feel them bump up against me, and yet when I was able to turn around and see, there was nobody there. Also, I too, could smell the odor of old blood, ammonia and urine for nearly four months.

Following the initial interview, I took the flashlight from my briefcase and did a walk-through around the basement and the first floor kitchen, dining room, living room and bathroom, looking for any physical reasons that may have been the cause of the unnatural disturbances, such as banging pipes, dangling wires, small birds or animals that may have gotten into the walls and so on.

We all proceeded to the second floor where there were two bedrooms and a bathroom. Laura reported that most of the activities had taken place in the bedroom where she and Bob slept. Their first attempt to get relief was to seek the assistance of the Catholic Church. The evidence to support this was on the ceiling and walls of their bedroom. They were stained with the watermarks of holy water the priest used during the blessing of the house.

Linda stood behind the camera she placed on a tripod. Brenda put a fresh tape in the recorder and sat on the floor, forming a circle with Laura and me. Bob sat on the edge of the bed.

"Close your eyes, and take a slow, even, deep breath and tell yourself to relax," I said softly to Laura and Brenda, repeating this several times, until I felt that we three were relaxed. I said a prayer, asking for protection and guidance, as was my usual custom before I begin a session. Following that I asked, "If you are here, why are you here and what do you want?"

The air in the bedroom became cold, heavy and damp, making it difficult to take a deep breath. There was a light rain falling outside and the bedroom window was open slightly, but the atmosphere in the room wasn't light, fresh air. I began to envision images of faces so I described them. Sometimes, I heard names and repeated them. Bob identified one name as a fellow Marine that was killed in action. Laura also identified some of the names that I heard or the people that I envisioned.

After the messages and visions ended, I closed the session with a prayer and added, "You must follow the light and go to God and goodness. You are not welcome here." The air became light and it was easier to breath. We all noticed the change in the air and even commented on it.

I told Laura that subconsciously she had caused these things to happen by her desire to see or be with others who had passed over and that she must not wish in her heart for their presence. Laura and Bob expressed their gratitude and felt relieved that we made contact and helped the spirits advance toward the light. Brenda, Linda and I packed up, said a goodbye and drove back to our homes.

It was almost midnight when I unlocked the door and walked into my house. I was very tired. It took all the energy I had left just to brush my teeth, wash my face and fall into bed. I fell into a deep sleep, almost immediately. *"Nancy~ Nancy,"* someone calling my name brought me wide-awake.

"What? What's wrong?" I said, as I sat up and looked around the bedroom. Nobody was there! I turned on the lights and walked around the house, checking all the rooms and making sure the doors were locked. I was now fully awake and decided to sit in the living room, thinking that I may as well listen to the tape recording of the evening session. I cuddled up on the sofa, turned on the tape. Soon, I began to doze off. *"Nancy ~ I can't see ~ I can't see where to go."* It was a high-pitched female voice coming from the tape recording. It was a voice that I was hearing for the first time.

I could accept receiving messages directly from spirits, but the voice coming from the tape startled me. I hadn't heard it during the session. The voice came at the end of the tape, as I was closing the door to the spirit world with a prayer. Quickly, I picked up the phone and called Brenda. "Brenda, did you use a new tape or did you tape over something?" I asked when she answered.

"Nancy, do you know what time it is? It's the middle of the night. Can't this wait until morning?" she asked, trying to clear her head while she came awake. I hadn't considered the time, that's how startled I was by the voice on the tape.

"Sorry Brenda, but, the tape recorded a voice that appears to be a spirit's voice."

"Go back to sleep, there's nothing we can do about it now. Call me tomorrow."

Brenda was right. It was foolish of me to expect her to be as concerned as I was. She hadn't heard the desperation in the voice. Before I returned to bed, I closed my eyes, quieted my mind and focused on a vision of a radiating white sun. I imagined the sun growing larger and larger, until it filled the room. The energy of the white light surrounded me and radiated through me. Turning my thoughts back to Laura's house and in a soft voice, I said, "See the beam of light, follow the light of the sun; go to God." I opened my eyes and returned to bed. That was all I could do to help.

A few days later, when the film was developed, I matched the photos to the clicks of the camera that were on the recorded tape. The clicks and a white form of energy are in correlation with the times I said things like, "I feel an energy in front of me," or "It's touching the side of my face." Also, at the click where Laura says, "It's all over me, I can smell it." That photo shows Laura's form being completely white, while everything around her is normal.

Not being able to interest Professor Paul Kurtz in the mysterious spirit voice or the photographs of bright lights moving about the bedroom, during the Laura and Bob case, I turned to Dr. Allan Canfield, because he, too, was a researcher with interests in parapsychology. His conclusion was that the white forms on the infrared film were due to its heat sensitivity, a finding similar to that of other scientists at the university with whom Dr. Allan Canfield conferred. The voice, however, was difficult to discern. Dr. Allan Canfield thought it might be a result of activity in the bedroom at the time, or outside voices bleeding through the walls of the house.

It disappointed me that the scientific community didn't show more interest in the paranormal activity that took place during that investigation. Disappointed, I filed the material and continued with my work, trying to gather the hard evidence that was required for the scientific community to take a serious interest in what I was doing.

My guest appearances on the radio and television programs, and the newspapers reporting of my activities must have piqued the interest of Mark Hamrick, a skeptical reporter, who at the time worked for WEBR News Radio and later became a business editor for the *Associated Press.*

Mark Hamrick came to my office unexpectedly and requested a taped interview.

[Broadcast February 23, 1983 as *Buffalo's Very Colorful People.*]

Mark began by telling the listeners that when I was a child I had what I termed unusual abilities. With that in mind, he followed up by asking me to do something I rarely do—which is a reading, and to focus on his past, since that was more tangible than his future.

I began by telling him that he had good family relationships. And, that his grandmothers had an influential role in his life. I then named one by nickname only his immediate family knew and asked about her health, because I felt she was ill. Mark told me she was fine. Later he learned from his father that she was not fine, she had been hospitalized recently. I went on to name his other grandmother by nickname not heard regularly since his grandfather was alive.

"I want to say for a prediction here, there is coming into your life, in three years, somebody very beneficial for you as a mate. This will be very good I do feel the relationship is good and there will be a marriage from this. I also get the name Judy with that. Now is Judy from the past or is Judy the one I'm referring to coming into the picture?" I asked.

"Ah, Judy is my mother's name." Mark answered. He ended the broadcast by saying, "I'm not from Western New York. No one within three hundred miles knows of these names. Nancy claims no special powers, and that anyone can develop psychic ability. If that is true and I don't pretend to know if it is, it appears Nancy has, if nothing else, certainly astounded me, a typical skeptic."

The reason I am including this interview by Mark Hamrick is to point out that even among skeptics there is a definite hunger for information about psychic ability, the sixth sense, higher sensory perception, or whatever one wishes to term it. We need only to look in bookstores to see this is true.

Following the interview with Mark Hamrick, various media continued to contact me. As I sat at my desk in my office on Main Street writing up a report on another case, the phone rang. "Psychic Awareness," I said, picking up the receiver.

"Nancy, its Mike Randall from WKBW-TV. Remember me? You did a television piece with me on the ghosts of Fort Niagara."

"Of course, I remember you. You're the famous Mark Twain and Charles Dickens impersonator, television personality and our weatherman. Who could forget you? What can I do for you, Mike?"

"I'm doing a television piece on haunted places in the Western New York area; do you have an interesting haunted house that I can add to the series?"

"I have a really scary case that I worked on in the town of Leroy but I don't think it would be wise to talk about that. I have one here on the west side of Buffalo, where a spirit voice is on the tape recording and I have photos of spirits. That would make an interesting story."

"Do you think the people would let us into their house for some live shots and agree to let us put the story on television?"

"I don't know Mike; I'll ask them and get back to you."

I made the phone call and had permission from Laura and Bob for Mike Randall to report the story on television. I contacted Dr. Allan Canfield and invited him to come along, hoping he would find validity in the mysterious spirit voice and spirit photographs.

Mike Randall, his photographer, Ed Riley, and Dr. Allan Canfield arrived at my house as scheduled. We settled ourselves in the living room, I sat on the sofa, Ed Riley turned on the video camera and Mike Randall began the interview.

Then, Mike stopped the interview and asked me to play the tape that was recorded during the session in Laura's bedroom. We all went into the kitchen where Dr. Canfield, Mike Randall and I sat at the table. Ed Riley turned on the video camera and recorded me playing my cassette tape with the spirit voice.

After we finished at my house, Mike Randall and Ed Riley followed as Dr. Allan Canfield drove me to the house on the West Side of the city. When we entered the house, Mike Randall, being a well-known entertainer and media personality was greeted warmly.

Following a short interview by Mike Randall, we went upstairs to the bedroom. Ed Riley turned on the video camera and recorded the bedroom—with the holy water spots still on the ceiling. It was late in the evening when Mike Randall finished his interview and Ed Riley finished his video recording. We thanked Laura and Bob and got ready to leave. Before we left, Laura told Mike, "Whatever it was, Nancy, the dear soul, got rid of it." Bob added, "I know this, there are ghosts—I know this for sure!"

The following morning, as I was putting the pot of water on the stove for a cup of tea, the phone rang. "Nancy, this is Mike Randall. Do you have some time? Can you come to the studio?"

"Why Mike? What's going on? You sound mysterious."

"The tape we used last night, was a new tape so there couldn't be any bleed-through, yet we have strange sounds and more voices on our video recording. I'd like you to listen to them and tell me what you think."

"Do you mind if I contact Dr. Canfield at the University and bring him along?"

"Sure, I'll tell security that I'm expecting you."

A few hours later, Dr Canfield and I arrived at the station. Mike Randall took us into the recording room, where we listened to the videotaping that Ed Riley made of me sitting at the kitchen table, playing my tape recording of the spirit voice. Immediately following the spirit voice, we heard more messages. The voice was the same high-pitched spirit voice saying, *"Help me ~ Where can I go?~ Help me!"* followed by more garbled sounds. Needless to say we were all surprised! The equipment and the tape that Ed Riley used was able pick up from my tape what our ears couldn't hear.

We went into the studio reception area, and Ed Riley made another video recording of Mike Randall interviewing Dr. Canfield and me regarding our opinion of what we heard.

From Mike Randall's interviews with Dr. Canfield, Laura, Bob, and me, and the video tapings that Ed Riley made, Mike Randall put together his story, aired on WKBW-TV in October 1983. To my surprise, many years later, Mike Randall also put the story on his You Tube as *GHOST SPECIAL PART#3.*"

Mike concluded his show by saying, "We didn't fake the voices, folks. Scouts honor! Now, I don't know what it is that we have here on tape. I'm not saying it's a spirit voice, but I'm not saying it isn't either!

CHAPTER ELEVEN
Family Forever

Love is all around us; all we have to do is close our eyes and open our hearts to see the goodness in others.

Trust takes time; it has to grow. As time passed, Dr. Allan Canfield and I got to know each other better; we played together, laughed together and experienced a wide range of feelings together. Dr. Canfield is a highly intelligent, scientifically minded person who analyzes nearly everything. Over the years, we often worked together. Like two sides of the same coin, our views may be different, but we agree that they are equally important.

On March 18, 1990, seven years from the day of our first kiss, dressed in a champagne-colored lace dress, I was married to Dr. Allan Canfield. It was a beautiful sunny day when I walked down the aisle of St. Paul's Episcopal Church on the arm of Joe Musca, the Vice Counselor of Italian affairs for the city of Buffalo. Following the wedding ceremony, a white limousine whisked us away to an elegant dinner reception where seventy-five of our closest friends celebrated in our joy, as strolling violinists serenaded us throughout the evening. Allan and I left the reception with a cheerful send-off. We flew to Puerto Vallarta, Mexico, for a honeymoon at a seaside resort. It was all so perfect!

A few years later, Allan and I bought a camp in the Adirondack Mountains. The camp is near the Fulton Chain of Lakes, providing us with sandy beaches for swimming, boating and fishing. Hiking the trails and golfing at the golf course across from our camp are some of the things we enjoy together. We have plenty of recreational activities to justify our relaxation at the nightly campfires.

While doing genealogical research, I discovered that my maternal ancestral roots reached back to John McClelland who came to these shores in 1774 and settled a town outside of Saratoga, New York, naming it after his birthplace of Galloway, Scotland. Every time I chop wood or help Allan take down a tree or watch the sun go down behind the tall white pines, I think of my ancestor and his struggles crossing the ocean and taking a hand in developing this great country of the United States of America.

On lazy days, dressed in my blue jeans and long-sleeve white shirt, I rest in the hammock that's strung between two tall maple trees and enjoy the fresh mountain air, while I listen to the chickadees flittering to and from the bird feeders. During one summer long ago, when I stayed a week at Aunt Loretta's house, I promised myself that someday I would have a hammock in beautiful surroundings, and now I do. Hopes and wishes can come true!

I no longer do fieldwork research. However, on occasion, I do assist in rescuing spirits from haunted houses. I am no longer teaching a class in the development of higher sensory perception. However, on occasion, I do meet people who ask for my advice on how to enhance their inner abilities. My higher sensory perception is not as strong as it once was. However, on occasion I am able to use my inner awareness to assist others in their life challenges.

My life may have been turbulent, but I'm grateful to have had the experiences that I had. They have taught me many of life's lessons. My life—happy, sad, funny, serious, and spirit-filled—has been richer, fuller and more exciting than I ever imagined it would be. As my big brother, Tom, had done, I now treat every day as an adventure, no matter how bad it may be. I look for the lesson and the good that will surely follow. If I make a mistake, I refuse to be discouraged. I keep after my dreams and never give up. Some things take longer than others, so I have learned to be patient and persistent.

We all have challenges in life. Although the challenges may be outside of our control, how we respond to them is within our control. As I was growing up, I wasn't given choices or allowed free will to express myself. Over the years, with the guidance of my inner wisdom, through the practice of meditation, I learned to express myself freely. My memoir is a result.

Putting my memories on paper has given me the opportunity to reflect upon the life I lived as a young girl and the lives that my siblings must have lived. Certainly my parents didn't realize that their drinking would have such a profound effect on their children. Despite their abuse of alcohol, I am pleased to say that my siblings and I have managed to live decent lives.

We are there for one another whenever the need arises. And, we have never forgotten that we are family forever.

The years have flown by. My father had not remarried in the twenty years since my mother's passing. He was quite independent and managed well with the help of my brother, Billy. At the ending of his life, it was heartbreaking for me to watch the man, who had always been so strong, fade away from the effects of Alzheimer's disease. He had become a mere shadow of the man he had once been. His clear, dark eyes that always held a smile were now growing dim. He stopped walking shortly after admission to the nursing home. He was no longer able to feed himself and his speech was usually garbled.

On August 25, 1995, as I walked into his hospital room, a nurse, standing at his bedside, looked at me and quietly said, "Your father has just expired." When the nurse left the room, I took my father's hand and kissed his forehead, a final goodbye. My father was laid to rest beside my mother in the cemetery on Genesee Street, not far from the housing project where we lived when I was a young girl.

Tom is gone now, too. He died of a heart attack on March 10, 2000. I remember when the phone call came, giving me the sad news. I took the next flight from Florida to Buffalo. Tom was cremated, so I didn't get to see him one last time. That really didn't matter, because whenever I think of Tom, I see him in my mind's eye, as he was in his younger years, with his big beautiful smile.

Billy, who married, but then divorced, lives alone now. He enjoys playing the lottery. That's probably because he has a gift of choosing the right numbers. Bobby, who married and divorced, is a good worker and father, staying in touch with his children.

Carol Jean, my beautiful sister, has become a country girl. She and her husband live outside the city where they grow most of their own vegetables. They're well known in their little village, where they are members of the Catholic Church. Jimmy and his wife have been happily married for over forty years.

Sometimes, when I visit the cemetery, I recall the day my father told me: "Remember whatever happens, your mother and I have tried our best to take care of all you children." In my heart, I know that my parents—in spite of their lack of coping skills—loved their children and each other. In my quiet moments of reflection, my memory takes me to the time in the hospital when my father brought... a rose for my mother!

APPENDIX A

The Hebrew sages say that the beginning of wisdom is silence; the second stage is listening.

WHEN I WAS A child, meditation was not something I knew about. Now, I do. It is a practice that allows our sensitivity to develop to a higher level. It is my belief that higher sensory perception comes from both natural ability and purposeful development. Also, one person may develop higher sensory perception to a greater degree than another, depending on the devotion to the meditation practices and willingness to follow their inner guidance.

The practice of quieting our mind is essential for learning how to listen to our soul awareness—our higher mind. It isn't easy to set aside our thoughts, our ego or our conscience, but it's possible and it's worth it. After practicing meditation over a period of time, we may enter into a state of higher awareness where we will experience total peace, love and oneness with and for everything; that is just one of the many benefits of meditating.

Renewing the body with vital energy and healing is another benefit. Studies of people meditating have shown a reduction in blood pressure, breathing rate and muscle tension. These are facts that prove that there is also a physical benefit in meditation. To reach the point of development in meditation that will allow us to successfully become in tune, without the least bit of effort, requires a great deal of practice. Ten, twenty or thirty minutes each day for several months is the general amount of time necessary to begin to develop a true flow of inner communication with our higher mind.

Relaxation, Cleansing and Meditation all require the same discipline and technique. The body posture with all of these exercises should be in a comfortable sitting position with feet flat on the floor, palms resting comfortably on your thighs or in your lap. This allows freedom of awareness in the flow of meditative thoughts.

You will find that after practicing the relaxation and cleansing exercises several times, you will have developed the ability to control the emotional you. Your body will follow the command of your own mind. Whenever you feel yourself becoming tense, take a few slow, even, deep breaths and tell yourself to relax.

I have taken the following exercises from the scripts of the recordings that I made available to my students in their daily practice in developing their higher sensory perception. I suggest that you read these exercises slowly, pausing where I have placed ellipses. If you choose to, you also can record the words of the following exercises and play them back, allowing you to be your own guide in the practice of developing your higher sensory perception. I will begin with the relaxation exercise.

Relaxation Exercise

Get very comfortable…as comfortable as you can and close your eyes…take a slow, even, deep, breath…and tell yourself to relax…know that the body follows the command of the mind…Take another slow, even, deep breath… and tell yourself to relax…know that a relaxed state of consciousness is an altered state of higher awareness.

Take another slow, even, deep, breath…and relax…know that you will always awaken from this and any altered state of consciousness…fully refreshed, fully relaxed and totally alert.

Let your mind travel to the area of your feet…fully and totally put your mind in your feet…tense up the muscles in your feet…tense up the muscles in your toes and feet…feel those muscles, tense and tight…hold that tension…and relax…totally relax…feel those muscles becoming loose and relaxed…feel the tension as it leaves your feet…becoming more loose and relaxed.

Now leave your feet loose and relaxed and move up to your calves… with your mind's awareness feel your calves…tense up the muscles in your calves…and relax…totally relax…feel those muscles becoming loose and relaxed…tell yourself…lovingly and gently, tell yourself to relax… relax a little bit more…deeper and deeper relaxed…totally and peacefully relaxed.

Move up to your thighs…with your mind's awareness feel your thighs…

tense up the muscles in your thighs...and relax...feel them becoming loose and relaxed...loose and relaxed...your feet, calves, and thighs feel very light...they are filled with awareness of relaxed peace...totally relaxed... loose and relaxed.

Move your mind into the area of your hips and lower back...feel your hips and lower back with your inner awareness...tense up the muscles of that area...and relax...feel them becoming loose and relaxed...relax a little bit more...loose and relaxed...deeper and deeper relaxed...know this feeling of relaxation...feel the peace of a relaxed body...loose and relaxed.

Move your mind into the area of your stomach and solar plexus... tense up these muscles...and relax...totally relax...feel the tension as it leaves your body...all the muscles are becoming loose and relaxed...all your intestines, muscles and organs are functioning properly and in perfect health...loose and relaxed.

Slowly...very slowly...take a slow, even, deep breath...and slowly... very slowly...exhale...and tell yourself to relax...feel yourself becoming deeper and deeper relaxed...loose and relaxed...another slow even deep breath...and slowly exhale...now relax...tell yourself to relax...relax a little bit more.

Tense up the muscles in your back...hunch up your shoulders...tense up the muscles in your chest...with your mind's awareness feel this tension... know this is the feeling of tension...now relax...loose and relaxed...know that the body follows the commands of the mind...tell yourself to relax... feel the tension as it leaves your body...your body is becoming loose and relaxed...fully alert...and totally relaxed...loose and relaxed.

Move into your upper arms...lower arms...and hands...tense up these muscles...make a tight clenched fist...feel that tension with your mind's awareness...and relax...open your fists and relax...relax the upper arms... lower arms, hands and fingers...feel them as all the tension leaves...feel them becoming loose and relaxed...totally and fully relaxed...loose and relaxed...to the very tips of your fingers...loose and relaxed.

Your neck...tense up the muscles in your neck...your scalp...the top of your head and forehead...tense up the muscles around your eyes...cheeks, jaw and tongue...make a tense, taut, tight face...hold that tension...and relax...tell yourself to relax...loose and relaxed...feel your neck...your scalp...the top of your head...your forehead...feel them becoming loose and relaxed...the area around your eyes...your cheeks...your jaw...your tongue...loose and relaxed...all the tension is gone...you are completely relaxed.

A slight smile comes to your face as you feel total peace...you are completely and fully relaxed...feel the lightness of your being...know that this is the feeling of a relaxed body…in your mind's awareness…see all the muscles completely relaxed…loose and relaxed…all the tension has left your body…feel the life energy that radiates from your body…feel yourself fully aware…fully alert…fully refreshed…and fully relaxed.

Know that anytime you desire this peaceful state of awareness you need only to sit quietly and tell yourself to relax. Your body will follow the command of your mind. You may open your eyes and you will remain completely relaxed, completely refreshed and fully alert with awareness of peace and love.

Cleansing Exercise

While in this very relaxed, receptive state of awareness and without opening your eyes, direct your attention to the crown of your head. Now, in your mind's eye, visualize a clear, bright white light…a vibrating and radiating beautiful, bright, white light above your head…welcome this radiating, clear, bright white light…it's the energy of love, protection and healing…the energy of God's love…see it as it settles upon the crown of your head…touching you with gentle love…feel this love and its energy… feel it as it flows into the top of your head, completely filling your head…feel the energy of the bright white light…flowing into you…cleansing you… bringing you love…healing…and protection.

Feel it pour down your neck and into your torso…completely filling you with its love…with its healing energy…with its protection…with its total goodness…the beautiful, bright white light flows into your arms…down to your very finger tips…cleansing and healing…loving and protecting.

Feel it as it flows down into your legs…your thighs…your calves and feet…into the very ends of your toes…completely filling your total being… feel the beautiful, vibrating energy of love…feel the force of healing…feel the comfort of complete peace and protection…feel the power of your being… as it its filled with God's love…the brilliant white light of cosmic energy.

In your mind's eye see it as it flows into your total being…into every cell of your body…the infinite flow abundantly fills you…see it overflowing into the area outside of and around your body…feel it as it flows down… over your head and face…over your neck and torso…flowing and cleansing the total area… outside of and around your body…feel the cleansing…the healing…the protective and loving energy…as it completely fills you and surrounds you.

Know that you are totally and completely enfolded in love, God's love. Your whole being is filled with health and peace. You are a beautiful being;

a complete and perfect being. Know that you may call upon this energy whenever you wish by just visualizing this pure energy, especially in times of trouble or uncertainty. Know that you will need only to desire, only to ask, and you will be instantly filled and surrounded with the energy force of the bright, white light protection of God's love.

Meditation Exercise

Visualizing colors and imagining the colors flowing into the body with each breathe and completely filling and surrounding the body will produce certain emotional and physical effects. Bright orange provides a sense of physical vitality. Green grass will render a restful, invigorating peace. Clear yellow enhances inspiration and illumination. Deep, dark blue will soothe and cool the emotions. Bright red has the effect of stimulating the life-energy force. Pink and violet will provide a sense of love and emotional comfort.

There are a variety of ways to structure meditation. There are no wrong ways to meditate. The following are the meditations that I have used many times over the years. Sit in a comfortable, upright position, feet flat on the floor. Give yourself a couple of slow, even, deep, breaths, and tell yourself to relax.

The Garden Meditation begins by mentally approaching your secret garden. Your garden is completely surrounded and protected by a wall made of large white stones. Entering the open gates, you stand within the walls for a moment and take in the total view of all the beautiful green plants and many colored flowers.

Slowly, walking along the tree-lined path, you pause to rest your back against the trunk of a strong oak tree. Feel the energy as the strength of the powerful oak tree enters into your body, recharging and refreshing you.

Moving along, you come upon a patch of red flowers in the garden. Stopping to study them, you choose one that is perfect in every way. Nothing can harm these flowers; they are forever flowers and they, too, enjoy the caress of a human touch. With the red flower resting upon your open hands, bring it closer into view. Looking deeply into it, breathing in the color red, absorb it into your being. Fully knowing and enjoying the pure, clear energy of the color red. When you have finished enjoying the color red, return the flower and move on to the next color.

After viewing and experiencing all of the colors in the garden: the red flowers, the orange flowers, the yellow flowers, the blue flowers, the green leaves, the purple flowers, and the white flowers, you arrive at a little pond of pure, clean, refreshing water.

Resting by the edge of the pond, you wet your lips with its crystal-clear, life-giving power. Looking into the reflection of the water, you see the presence of the one you know to be your creator, your God. As your creator stands beside you, feel your heart fill with the joy of knowing that He has been with you from your very beginning and shall remain by your side to the very end. Feel the love that radiates toward you. Sit quietly and enjoy a few moments as your creator communicates his love and guidance to you.

When you are filled with the awareness and presence of the spirit of goodness and love, simply retrace your path through the garden. Glance upon the many colored flowers, stop and take one that you especially feel a desire for—either red, orange, yellow, blue, violet, or green, whichever color that you desire to have with you for your journey today. With your flower in hand, you may now walk toward the white wall and pass through the gate.

Whenever you feel disturbed, you may enter your private garden and choose a blue flower; it will bring you emotional comfort. Whenever you feel a need for clarity of mind, select a yellow flower. In your walk through the garden, you will become aware of the benefits of the colors, and this will assist you in knowing which color will bring you the feeling that you are seeking.

Everyone could use a little guidance, not only in situations of difficulties, but also in the progression of spiritual growth. Insight makes everything easier to understand and accept. Through meditation we find that there is a purpose for everything, and how everything fits in relationship to other things.

Everyone who has a desire to improve his or her life should take the time to meditate. When meditation is done properly, it will lift us to the truth of inner awareness, bringing us in tune with the harmony and rhythm of our higher mind. It is a natural way to connect with loving energy. It is the feeling that we are never truly alone!

APPENDIX B

HIGHER SENSORY PERCEPTION MAY provide information that comes in the form of symbols, thoughts, feelings, or visual images. We have to learn to listen with our entire body—to listen without analyzing. Then, we have to learn how to recognize and interpret what the symbols, thoughts, feelings or visual images mean. Sometimes a flash of insight may come through with an inner knowing and a feeling that tells us the message is true. Sometimes messages are received in the form of quatrains as in the following examples.

BORN FREE

Boldly we cry with the sounds of protest
Only to find peace at our mother's breast
Rightfully choosing this moment of birth
New Life brings the soul down to earth

Forward we wander in search of reasons
Recalling the lessons in all the seasons
Ever gathering knowledge from peace and strife
Ensuring one a place in the eternal life.

LOVE LIFE

Look to this day with all its beauty
Observe nature in service and duty
Visit the woodlands, the meadows and seas
Enjoy each caress of the gentle breeze.

Listen and hear the sweet music of sound
Invite to your heart the peace newly found
Feel the oneness with all the earth
Echo vibrations; rejoice in your birth.

GOOD LUCK

Guess if you will, just hoping to win
Only to rely on luck is truly a sin
One day you'll awaken to the power within
Discovering it's not too late to begin.

List all the dreams you would have come true
Underline your wishes and keep them in view
Charge them with energy, a little prayer will do
Keep after your desires until they come to you.

BODY SKIN

Black or white, red or yellow
Outer color covers the fellow
Deep within there cries a voice
Yet to find peace and fully rejoice.

Silently praying, hoping to see
Kinship with all for eternity
Infinite wisdom provides the test
Never believe your color is best.

HOLD FAST

Heavy in sorrow, the heart does cry
"Oh," you ask, "Dear Lord, why?"
Let there be trust in the Father above
Didn't He create you in the light of love?

Feelings of sadness are yours to share
Ask for His guidance and he will be there
Sending you strength to accept the fate
Teaching the lessons of your immortal state.

FIND SELF

Friendships are necessary; they help you grow
Increasing your confidence when you feel low
No man is an island; that statement is true
Develop some friendships whatever you do.

Secure your contacts with pleasing sessions
Expand your awareness; there are many lessons
Love in friendship should be your signature
Faithfully strive as you become mature.

SOUL MATE

Searching you find the one who is right
Out from the heart comes the urge to unite
Universal love sparks the flames of desire
Longing to join souls to rise even higher.

Man finds love is the essence of life
Awareness of that, he chooses a wife
Trusting the heart has not acted in haste
Each partner will savor love's sweet taste.

SHOW LOVE

Scatter loving kindness in every direction
Harbor pure thoughts of noblest affection
Outwardly send this rebounding power
Warrant infinite love, every day, every hour.

Lavishly give what you are yearning for
Open the heavens from whence it shall pour
Victory in love is not difficult to attract
Everything you give will always come back.